Leading Educational Syst
Schools in Times of Disruption and
Exponential Change

Leading Educational Systems and Schools in Times of Disruption and Exponential Change: A Call for Courage, Commitment and Collaboration

PATRICK A. DUIGNAN
Australian Catholic University, Australia

United Kingdom – North America – Japan – India – Malaysia – China

Emerald Publishing Limited
Howard House, Wagon Lane, Bingley BD16 1WA, UK

First edition 2020

Reprints and permissions service
Contact: permissions@emeraldinsight.com

British Library Cataloguing in Publication Data
A catalogue record for this book is available from the British Library

ISBN: 978-1-83909-851-2 (Print)
ISBN: 978-1-83909-850-5 (Online)
ISBN: 978-1-83909-852-9 (Epub)
ISBN: 978-1-83909-853-6 (Paperback)

Printed and bound by CPI Group (UK) Ltd, Croydon, CR0 4YY

ISOQAR certified Management System, awarded to Emerald for adherence to Environmental standard ISO 14001:2004.

Certificate Number 1985
ISO 14001

INVESTOR IN PEOPLE

Contents

Their complicated Philosophy
= errors + deaths in a
morality we feel suits for
that the Police cant stop.

Support for this Book

Leading Educational Systems and Schools in Times of Disruption and Exponential Change offers deep insight into the complex, metrics-dominated and radically evolving contexts in which leaders are currently immersed. Professor Duignan cautions us about pursuing old solutions to new challenges and constructs a compelling case for how leaders might adopt radically *new* approaches to their work. While the scale of this challenge can seem overwhelming, Patrick Duignan reveals the breakthrough opportunities it presents. He draws on the wisdom of authentic leadership research to guide contemporary leaders towards human-centred and values-guided clarity, when their moral compass might otherwise be spinning wildly in these times of unparalleled change. Professor Duignan's insights apply to leadership generically but he applies them in depth to educational contexts. This is a ground-breaking work of hope, purpose, progress and inspiration for all educational leaders.

Dr Greg Morgan, *Allora Consulting* – Leadership and Coaching, West Launceston, Tasmania, Australia

In this book Patrick Duignan provides a comprehensively-researched account of the need for change in the way we approach educational leadership. His challenge is for us to act with urgency despite complexity and ambiguity, and to withstand the pull of gravity dragging us back to a safer, more orderly version of schooling. What education systems do, how they do it, and the way in which they are led, must change or else those education systems will become irrelevant. His firm belief in the role of ethics, human-centred learning, leadership that is authentic, and positive cultures provides the stability that will help us to navigate the unknown. Duignan provides an essential resource for educational leaders that is designed not to spook or preach but to stimulate and motivate.

Trent Moy, *Management Consulting*, Director of Halide Ethics and Leadership Consultancy, Sydney, Australia

Education has always been a dynamic enterprise within which the challenges of change have been a constant. However, in this deeply considered, thoroughly researched and finely nuanced work, Patrick Duignan applies considerable voltage to our understanding of the dynamism urging educational leaders to positively and urgently embrace the new narratives brought about by disruption and exponential change.

He describes a world of volatility, uncertainty, complexity, and ambiguity and poses questions about the relevance of a model of schooling in which flexibility, agility and adaptability struggle to find a place. More than ever educational leaders are called upon as reformers and people of authenticity to collectively and collaboratively inspire in others new ways of working and responding to the unknowns of the future. Such leadership involves all those engaged in the educational enterprise – teachers, principals, and system leaders and this book will challenge each. It is timely, comprehensive, provocative and essential reading as we each build up "the basket of goods" required in pursuing educational excellence. As an educational leader engaged in substantial reform initiatives in our system and schools, I recommend this book to other educators and educational leaders contemplating reform as collectively we strive to prepare our students for the future.

Pam Betts, Executive Director of Education,
Catholic Archdiocese of Brisbane

Patrick Duignan is renowned for his contribution to the field of authentic and ethical leadership. In this new book he takes a monumental leap, skilfully connecting the timeless character qualities of great leadership with the contemporary VUCA world of constant disruption and exponential change, including rapid technological advances in and into every sphere of life. Well researched across a wide range of areas, the book itself models the multi- and inter-disciplinary approach needed to lead contemporary schools, systems, and organisations. This leadership needs to be human-centred, authentic and values-based, agile and open to learning, 'ecologically' collaborative and connected, and future-focused. Models of schooling and approaches to learning also need to change radically and the book presents many examples of how this might be.

Participants in our leadership programs at the *Association of Independent Schools (AIS) Leadership Centre* are profoundly influenced by the concepts advanced in Duignan's earlier works. This new book will doubtless become a staple in our future programs.

Dr Leoni Degenhardt, Emeritus Dean, AIS Leadership Centre,
The Association of Independent Schools of New South Wales, Australia

In Leading Educational Systems and Schools in Times of Disruption and Exponential Change: A Call for Courage, Commitment and Collaboration, Patrick Duignan urges the reader to become a positive force in the transformation of education. As much as change may be a constant, there is no guarantee that schools and systems will cope, let alone transform and thrive in the future. With a sense of urgency and passion, as well as clarity and coherence, Duignan sets out valuable principles to help guide this transformation process. Drawing on a firm grasp of research in the field, he shows how leaders can integrate scholarship into reflective practice. It is a timely and relevant book offering signposts to educators navigating the tumultuous and frenetic environment in which they are expected to lead. Duignan's exploration of leadership and organisational structures beyond the educational sphere offers insight into 'successful disrupted organisations'. Through his extensive scholarship and lived experience, he spells out what it means for leaders to be fully aware and critically attuned to the nature and scale of changes in teaching and learning today. He exhorts educational leaders, including teachers, to be imaginative and courageous when adapting innovative technologies to support student learning. His clear-eyed approach instructs and inspires, challenging educators to live their values in authentic ways by fostering communication, connection and collaboration at all system levels. Duignan shows how it is an awareness of our shared humanity that provides the surest foundation for meaningful and enduring educational leadership.

> Barbara McMorrow, ground-breaking and transforming secondary principal and former Director of Education, *Peterborough Victoria Northumberland Clarington Catholic District School Board*, Ontario, Canada

If you are someone who likes leadership literature that is long on aspiration and short on evidence, this is not the book for you. If you want a simple solution to present challenges in education, this is not for you either. If you cannot be persuaded that there actually is a way forward for education in times of massive disruption, then don't waste your time on this book.

If, on the other hand, you are open to an exploration of education and leadership in what Duignan calls a "VUCA" (Volatility, Uncertainty, Complexity and Ambiguity) world – then start reading his latest book now. It is a deep, subtle and comprehensive exploration of the dynamics at play in a world stripped of stability and certainty. His response might well be captured in a slight variation on what Bill George (2017) called "VUCA 2.0". Duignan uses the breadth and depth of his scholarship and experience to explore responses through the lenses of Vision, Understanding, Collaboration and Adaptability – the fundamental requirements of one of his favourite themes – moral and authentic leadership. It is not a quick read, but it will amply repay the effort.

> Dr Michael Bezzina provides consultancy services focusing on leadership for learning. He has been Head of the School of Educational Leadership and the Director of the Centre for Creative and Authentic Leadership at *Australian Catholic University*, and Director of Teaching and Learning at *Sydney Catholic Schools*.

One cannot help but feel that this book is destined to become a seminal one in educational leadership. Timely, ambitious and wide-ranging, it draws on other key works from the educational and organisational literature to chart with the reader a way forward through a world of ever-increasing disruption and change. It is a book underpinned by hope; that the individual and collective moral and ethical compasses that we set for ourselves as a teaching profession will be the basis on which to navigate the shoals of often contradictory messages to which school leaders are called upon to respond. Patrick Duignan leads us gently to a deeper understanding of these messages, and of the polarities and tensions at play. It is a book that you will want to keep close by, especially for those times when you need to be challenged or inspired in finding your own way forward.

> Dr Norman McCulla FACE FACEL Educational Leadership and Organisational Development Program, *Macquarie University*, Sydney, Australia

Many education systems around the world are experiencing the consequences of political and socio-economic volatility, disruption and change and the actions and decisions of world leaders have never been more visible yet contested. Professor Duignan's call for 'courage, commitment and collaboration' in *Leading educational systems and schools in times of disruption and exponential change*' is therefore not just timely, but critical in providing educational leaders with a mandate to go beyond traditional approaches to schooling and school leadership. Duignan reminds us that 'Millennials are already taking up educational leadership positions and are emerging as a force for positive, courageous, and character-inspired change in the future.' Underpinned by extensive research and critique of current policy, this book will be essential reading for them, and all educational leaders, not only through its analysis of contemporary challenges, but in showing how reactive and adaptive responses to change and disruption are inadequate. To understand this better Duignan has reached beyond education to draw lessons from global organisations responding to change. In relation to education he rejects calls for a '*new narrative*' since, he argues, 'the proposed narrative is not new' but what is needed is a refocusing and rebalancing that emphasises the relational, moral and ethical dimensions of leadership. This book offers hope for a better future and courage for those who will help shape that and will be essential reading for all leaders in education and those involved in their preparation.

Margery. A McMahon, Professor of Educational Leadership, Head of
School of Education, *University of Glasgow*

Foreword

We are living in an age of disruption and exponential change, times that, argu-ably, the world has never seen or experienced before. These disruptions include big data, artificial intelligence, machine learning, blockchain, robots, digital auto-mation and an explosion in the speed of connectivity, all of which are emblem-atic of what has been termed, 'The Fourth Industrial Revolution'. According to Professor Klaus Schwab, Founder and Executive Chairman of the World Eco-nomic Forum, this revolution of skills and technology is disrupting almost every industry in the world (World Economic Forum, 2017). It extends from energy to education, mining to manufacturing, aviation to agriculture and it is pervasive and relentless.

In the context of education and schooling, the dynamics of the fourth indus-trial revolution bring with it a number of educational challenges, potential para-doxes and the need to re-imagine dominant assumptions, practices and beliefs about the ways in which we learn, teach and lead. These include the speed and duration of learning, the nature of knowledge boundaries, the role of the educa-tor and the educative process; the continual tension of addressing and balancing equity and excellence; and an ongoing commitment to the personal formation of the individual and the utilitarian value of the current models of schooling informed by the toolkits of a former industrial age. The French Nobel Prize (2014) winning economist, Jean Tirole, points out that we must anticipate the challenge that has come with the digital revolution so we can adapt to it, adjust and thrive rather than merely endure as we have with previous discernible revolu-tions (Tirole quoted in Frydenberg, 2019, p. 2).

A challenging question, therefore, arises: Are the education and schooling sec-tors prepared to embrace this fourth industrial revolution? In his book, *Leading Educational Systems and Schools in Times of Disruption and Exponential Change: A Call for Courage, Commitment and Collaboration*, Patrick Duignan provides a well-crafted narrative about the 'why', 'how' and 'what' of the fourth indus-trial revolution, especially the implications, opportunities and possibilities for the education and schooling sectors. Duignan issues a 'call to action' – a 'clarion call' for a distinctive form of system and school leadership to not only survive but to thrive in these disrupted and uncertain times; he concludes that educa-tional leaders at all levels will be required to act with *courage, commitment* and a willingness to *collaborate*. He uses this leadership frame to explore and analyse contemporary educational leadership practices, by providing commentary and analyses from a diverse range of sources, and makes a series of recommendations on ways in which educators and educational leaders can achieve transformations in the architectures of schools and schooling; pedagogy for rapidly changing educational environments; and technological connectivity and networking for a future that is presently unimaginable. He claims that educational leaders, including teachers, will need to change their leadership theories and practices if they wish to remain relevant and successful in a constantly disrupted future.

Duignan encourages leaders in education to be braver, to lead with new mindsets; rethink their assumptions; question the relevance of current customs and practices; and challenge the hegemonic notions of what is valued, measured and celebrated by policymakers, system leaders and broader communities of interests, that are currently an integral part of our education sectors. He recommends that educational leaders develop their ethical and moral guidance systems, inspired by core values, moral purpose and authentic processes and practices, in order to navigate shifting and dynamic pathways through environments of uncertainty and change. He also recommends that educational leaders at all levels need to act with curiosity in order to carefully examine and analyse the challenging, confronting and disruptive questions that are necessary for the 'flourishing' of school systems and schools now and into an uncertain future. Educators must according to Duignan lead the discourse and ask the important and 'right' questions for this age.

Leaders of schools and education systems will, he claims, need to be more courageous by issuing invitations to collaborate and be potentially vulnerable, to conjointly explore questions to which there is no immediate 'solution' and to be open to broader perspectives. In such circumstances he notes that educational leaders will require dispositions and capabilities to: collaborate across boundaries; create and leverage networks; embrace polarities, paradoxes and tensions; and leverage wisdom and advice from a diverse range of settings and sources. Duignan's book is a compelling read; one that challenges all educators to take action and clearly display a commitment to re-shaping the educational experiences and life chances for all current and future students. His discussions, analyses and recommendations will provide valuable insights for educational policymakers, leaders at system and school levels, leadership researchers and those responsible for leadership training programmes, including leadership professional development, in University settings around the world.

Dr Stephen Brown has a highly successful track record as an Educational Leader at system levels in different state systems in Australia. In 2010, he formed the *Queensland Educational Leadership Institute,* an innovative not-for-profit organisation committed to delivering excellence in leadership by supporting education leaders to establish a strong vision, improve student outcomes and lead change in their school context and wider school communities. In 2016, Dr Brown established the global professional services company, *The Brown Collective* – a company of international experts, specialising in providing customised responses to enhance individual, team and organisational performance. Today, the Collective has an extensive national and international client base and a deep understanding of the challenges that exist within the education and related sectors in their preparations for an unknown and uncertain future.

Acknowledgements

A tribute to a dear friend, colleague and educator *extraordinaire*
The late Dr Paul Brock

Dr Paul Brock was a popular, beloved and much celebrated educator who worked at the University of New England, New South Wales (NSW), Australia, and later for the Department of Education, NSW, before his untimely death due to motor neuron disease in 2016. He was a personal and professional friend. He was noted nationally and internationally for his scholarship and his mission to provide a better education for all young people everywhere, but, especially those disadvantaged and/or being treated unjustly. In the conclusion to his 2011 Australian Council for Educational Leaders' Monograph *Towards Schooling in the 21st Century: 'Back to the Basics' Or 'Forward to Fundamentals?'* he pleaded that future teachers of his two daughters, Sophie and Millie, to abide by three fundamental principles that should underpin teaching and learning in all schools. His passionately felt manifesto for educating young people, especially his two daughters, provides a heart-felt introduction to this book:

> First, nurture and challenge my daughters' intellectual and imaginative capacities way out to horizons unsullied by self-fulfilling minimalist expectations. Don't patronise them with lowest common denominator blancmange masquerading as knowledge and learning; nor crush their love for learning through boring pedagogy.
>
> Don't bludgeon them with mindless 'busy work' and limit the exploration of the world of evolving knowledge merely to the tyranny of repetitively churned-work-recycled worksheets. Ensure that there is legitimate progression of learning from one day, week, month, term and year to the next.
>
> Second, care for Sophie and Millie with humanity and sensitivity, as developing human beings worthy of being taught with genuine respect, enlightened discipline and imaginative flair.
>
> And third, please strive to maximise their potential for later schooling, post-school education training and employment, and for the quality of life itself so that they can contribute to and enjoy the fruits of living within an Australian society that is fair, just, tolerant, honourable, knowledgeable, prosperous and happy.

> When all is said and done, surely this is what every parent and every student should be able to expect of school education: not only as delivered within every public school in NSW, but within every school not only in Australia but throughout the entire world. (Brock, 2011, p. 24)

Thank you, Paul! Your wisdom from the soul constitutes a valued addendum to the arguments presented throughout this book, especially in the final chapter. Your credo represents a refreshing perspective on educational leadership and its possible positive influence on the quality of teaching, learning and learning outcomes, which will be more in tune with and better nuanced, for forming and reforming learning architectures and students' school experiences now and into the future. Throughout the research for and the writing of this book, I held Paul's pleas to educators on behalf of his own children constantly in my mind, and I am grateful to him for inspiring me to persist through the ups and downs of completing this treatise on reforming our educational systems and schools.

Chapter 1

Disruptive Environments with Leadership Challenges and Opportunities

This book focusses on the challenges and opportunities for organisational leaders in contexts of volatility, uncertainty, complexity and ambiguity – known as a VUCA world – and in conditions of exponential change and smart technologies; there is also an emphasis on potential responses by them to these challenges and opportunities. Currently, organisational environments are increasingly characterised by global disruptions and rapid changes that create unprecedented challenges for leaders of complex systems, such as businesses, hospitals and schools. Recent technological transformations have unleashed new disruptive forces that are presenting challenges for educational leaders, especially leaders and teachers in schools. We are living in the most technologically disruptive period ever and the potential for technological connectivity and networking in the future is presently unimaginable. It will be recommended in this book that we will need to change our mindsets and practices in life and in our organisations if we are to cope, never mind thrive, in this brave new world.

Kaplan, in an introduction to a ground-breaking book by Quick and Platt (2015), called *Disrupted: Strategy for Exponential Change,* suggested that:

> [...] new technologies relentlessly affect our lives, travelling around the planet at internet speed [and] social media enables people to self-organise and re-organise in ways that weren't possible during the 20th century. (p. 13)

Change and uncertainty, he claimed, surround us and influence us, making one thing crystal clear, '… relevancy is more fleeting than ever' (p. 13); this leaves leaders with the quandary of how to stay relevant in a VUCA world.

The good news for leaders is that the key to relevancy lies in the fact that these fast-changing challenges also contain the seeds for their responses. Leaders have access to the most powerful connectivity capabilities in history, which together with rapidly improving internet speeds and the miniaturisation of connective devices (e.g. smartphones and smart watches), provide them with capabilities they

Leading Educational Systems and Schools in Times of Disruption and Exponential Change: A Call for Courage, Commitment and Collaboration, 1–9
Copyright © 2020 by Patrick A. Duignan
Published under exclusive license
doi:10.1108/978-1-83909-850-520201002

once couldn't even imagine. Leaders, however, will need to change their leadership theories, mindsets and practices if they wish to remain relevant and successful in a constantly disrupted future.

All leaders, including those in educational systems, need to address the question of relevancy. To simply plan and act only on the basis of current and past conditions will be insufficient. Leadership of organisations in the future will not simply be a matter of: setting goals and objectives based on current conditions and experiences; assigning tasks or roles based on tried-and-true skills and processes; or generating five-year strategic plans and forecasts by focussing on extensions and projections of current and past plans. Instead, they must connect, collaborate and forge strong networks of relationships, within conditions disrupted by changes, risks, constraints and pressures; these conditions, however, are also full of potential and possibilities (Gurvich, 2018). A key argument in this book is that educational leaders in a disrupted future will need to establish clear indicators, even benchmarks, of what constitutes valued and worthwhile leadership approaches and educational practices and outcomes, while all around them the world and their organisations are changing.

Research evidence across a variety of industries (e.g. in business, health and education) and organisations (schools, hospitals and specific businesses), reported on and discussed in this book, indicates that leaders will need to develop their ethical and moral guidance systems inspired by core values, moral purpose and authentic processes and practices, in order to navigate shifting and dynamic pathways through environments of uncertainty and change. However, they will need to reconcile such degrees of clarity in their vision with a VUCA environment by collaborating with others to forge alternate pathways towards reaching the vision and have enough humility to allow for resetting their vision as circumstances dictate. It is important to facilitate and build a shared vision with others in a VUCA world, whereas in the past a single leader often imposed his/her vision on others under the guise of decisiveness and certainty. Caldwell (2019) stated that a vision is still necessary in a VUCA world; this vision, he claimed, should be '… developed collaboratively and embraced throughout the school's community. Vision should excite and unify, going beyond a statement of values and bundling of targets' (p. 14). He cautioned, however, that 'formulating a vision over time is difficult, such is the pace of change in each factor of the environment: physical, demographic, political, economic, technological, cultural [and] regulatory' (pp. 14–15). He concluded that visionary leadership requires '… strategic navigation … especially in times of turbulence and uncertainty' (p. 15).

Further, *visionary* leaders must interpret and action their ethical, moral and authentic ideals within the real world of pressure-filled environments (Cantwell, 2015). In the future, both public and private organisations will be encouraged to strive for higher standards of corporate citizenship and social responsibility and their leaders will be expected to lead using high ethical standards (Pompper, 2018; Stangis & Smith, 2017). In *The Executive's Guide to 21ˢᵗ Century Corporate Citizenship*, Stangis and Smith (2017) pointed out that many business companies have their reputation enhanced when their leaders activate strong corporate citizenship plans and processes, and when they '… see the opportunity to use the assets of business to solve some of our most pressing environmental, social, and policy processes' (p. xix). They claimed that change management is central to corporate citizenship, because leading change '… is about envisioning a different and better future for business and society' (p. xix). Based on their research, consultancies and executive training with selected leaders worldwide, they recommended that:

- *Leaders stake out a clear vision,* because without a vision people lurch in different directions or run in circles; visions focus minds, hearts and energy;
- *Leaders get the organisational architecture right* when they create structures and processes that provide the space for talent to soar. At a minimum, visionary leaders remove all the roadblocks that people must work around to be successful in their jobs; and
- *Influential leaders call for leadership from every seat* and make it clear that '… everyone should step up and find their spot as leaders, regardless of rank, title, or position'. (p. xxi, italics in original)

While Strangis and Smith are specifically targeting business organisations and their leaders, their advice applies, equally, to educational organisations and school leaders. It is argued throughout this book that school leaders must collectively strive to create authentic schools with clear moral purposes, driven by core values and a passionate commitment to a collective ethic of responsibility that places the wellbeing of all who work there, front and centre. Their schools' values and moral purposes:

[…] should guide and inspire everyone (all key stakeholders) and everything (policies, processes and practices) … to strive for the highest ethical standards in all planning processes and in all practices. (Duignan, 2012, p. 141)

A collective commitment to sharing leadership will not emerge simply from rhetoric or arguments that it is good for us all. Some much deeper motivating force is required and leaders need to nurture school cultures where every stakeholder feels a deep moral and ethical responsibility for the quality of the overall learning agenda and is willing to commit to a collective vision to achieve it. A collective and collaborative view of leadership is strongly promoted in the literature as well as by many influential educational policymakers and practitioners (e.g. Barber, 2011; Caldwell, 2006; Davies, 2006; Hargreaves & Fink, 2006; Sharratt & Fullan, 2009; Walker, 2011). Values and moral purpose in schools must constitute the benchmarks for collective efforts based on what is worthwhile and what is worth doing for students and their parents. Core values are key sources of meaning, purpose and inspiration for every school stakeholder, especially principals, their leadership teams, teachers, students, parents, as well as engaged community members. Such commitment to core values and moral purpose is both aspirational and inspirational.

While there are many challenges for leaders in disruptive environments, there are also numerous positive opportunities for agile leaders so long as they regard changes not just as disruptions but as '... potentially re-energising and re-organising opportunities' (Johansen, 2017, p. x). Agile, adaptive and flexible leaders are more likely to thrive during times of uncertainty and extreme disruption. Johansen (2017) advised leaders in a VUCA future to suspend, even discard, many of their hard fought-for-assumptions about the way things have been, the way things are and the way things should be, in favour of seeing people and change cycles as having great potential for new creative energies. Danita Bye (2017), in her insightful book *Millennials Matter*, stated that, as future leaders, Millennials will be very successful because: they tend to cultivate a character-driven and courageous core for their lives and their leadership; they are constructive change agents, willing to take responsible risks; and they communicate with confidence and act authentically with their teams. She concluded that a constructive '... balance of character and courage is foundational to their confidence' (p. 27). This is very positive news for education and for schools because Millennials are already taking up educational leadership positions and are emerging as a force for positive, courageous and character-inspired change in the future. In addition, they are not just digital natives; they are naturalised digitals and feel 'as-one' with a digital and artificial intelligence world.

Much is written in relevant leadership literature about ways in which emerging interactive, third-and fourth-wave technologies will impact education and educational leaders in the future. Case (2016), summarised his views on third-wave disruptions for organisations and concluded that the time has now arrived '... when the Internet transforms from something we interact with to something that interacts with everything around us' (p. 5). This will mean that almost everything we do will be enabled by an internet connection [and] '... this process will lead to the transformation of some of the industries that are vital to our daily lives' (pp. 187–188). He predicted that technological transformations will '... reimagine our healthcare system and retool our education system' (p. 5).

In Australia, our National Treasurer, The Hon Josh Frydenberg, in his August 2019 *Sir Zelman Cowan Oration*, suggested that we are living in the age of disruption and '... the world has seen nothing like it. Big data, artificial intelligence and the explosion in connectivity. It is the fourth industrial revolution' (p. 2). He claimed that this revolution is different in both nature and scope from previous ones, because it is:

> [...] developing exponentially rather than in a linear fashion. It is less about disseminating information to the wider public, as was the case with the invention of the printing press, but more about algorithms and data as new building blocks to fundamentally change the way we do things across every sector of the economy. (p. 2)

Today, he claimed, we are seeing:

> [...] the combined effects of:
> - a massive increase in digital data;
> - the growing force of computer power;
> - the ascent of new platforms;

- new organising principles of powerful algorithms;
- the development of advanced analytical tools and techniques; and
- unprecedented ease of connectivity between people. (pp. 3–4)

He stated that:

> [...] this perfect storm – decades in the making – has delivered what now seems like the overnight arrival of something that was previously inconceivable: artificial intelligence and machine learning. In simple language, machines are providing insights and recognising patterns by rapidly processing data which allows predictions, and in many cases decisions, to be made. (p. 11)

These developments will have far-reaching implications for all of us and, he concluded that, in an increasingly competitive, globalised and digitised economy:

> [...] we need to recognise the unprecedented scope and speed of technological change. It is creating both challenges and opportunities, as it changes every aspect of how we live and how we work. We cannot stop technological change nor should we try to. Rather we need to effectively adapt with a clear sense of what is important to us. (p. 11)

In education, we need to effectively adapt to our disruptions and have a clear sense of what is important. Hargreaves (2009) wrote about *The Fourth Way of Educational Reform* as characterised by '... renewed professionalism and active democracy [which] is defined by inspiration, innovation, social justice and sustainability' (p. 29). He summed up his major views on *The Fourth Way* of educational reform saying that it is resulting in:

> [...] less bureaucracy and more democracy; in collaboration more than competition; in innovation and inspiration more than data-driven intervention; in the fear factor giving way to the peer factor as the driver of school reform. (p. 32)

Emerging disruptions and technology-inspired changes and advances require educational leaders and reformers to see old educational landscapes with new eyes – Millennials already possess such visionary views and have growth mindsets to match. Carol Dweck (2016), Professor of Psychology at Stanford University, identified two general types of mindsets – a *fixed mindset* where people believe their personal characteristics and qualities are 'carved in stone' and a *growth mindset*, where they believe that '... the hand you're dealt is just the starting point for development' (p. 7). A growth mindset is based on '... the belief that your basic qualities are things you can cultivate through your efforts, your strategies, and help from others' (p. 7). It is central to any learning paradigm and, consequently, to positive educational change and reform.

There are still numerous obstacles to the reform and possible transformation of educational organisations, including leadership and pedagogical practices. In Gonski, Arcus, Boston, & Review Team Members 2.0 Report on education, *Through Growth to Achievement* (2018), they concluded that 'Australia still has an industrial model of school education that reflects ... a 20th century aspiration to deliver mass education to all children' (p. ix). While he was referring to the current state of education and schooling in Australia, it could equally apply in a number of other countries discussed in this book.

In her research into the progress of educational reform in the USA, Wilson (2018) came to a similar conclusion as Gonski, but offered a more positive perspective when she explained that while existing traditional industrial-era schools will be difficult to change they can be transformed into more '... flexible learning environment[s] that prepare our children for an unknown future' (p. 45). If education reform in schools is to respond positively to Wilson's view for the future then educational policymakers and leaders, including teachers, will need to find new and creative ways and means of encouraging the types of changes that will bring about changed mindsets – a paradigm shift – about the nature of learning, teaching as a process and a profession, the architecture of schools and schooling, as well as the nature of technologies that will complement and support all of these. Smart technologies and emerging educational innovations, including the physical and pedagogical architecture of schools, are changing educational systems and institutions and they will have considerable consequences for the nature and delivery of education in the future.

The good news is that over the past couple of decades, there is a growing movement to reinvent the architecture of education, especially at school level, to better reflect: changing views of learning environments; space and time configuration; the nature of pedagogical approaches and processes; and the dynamics for collective responsibility of quality learning and leadership in educational systems and schools. There are signs from a number of countries that the long-time emphasis on testing and accountability is being slowly modified by one that focusses more on students and the quality of their learning, teachers as leaders of curriculum and pedagogy and principals and leadership teams as leaders of learning (Bentley, 2008). In an important early contribution to this emerging perspective, an OECD (2008) report, titled *Innovating to learn, learning to innovate*, seemed to despair of the educational reform movements to that date and concluded that:

> [...] *reforms have ultimately come up against a wall, or rather a ceiling, beyond which further progress seems impossible, leading increasing numbers of school administrators and educators to wonder whether schools do not need to be reformed but to be reinvented.*
> (p. 22, italics in original)

A decade later, Schleicher (2018) pointed the way towards successful educational reinvention when he reported that:

> [...] schools now need to prepare students for more rapid change than ever before, to learn for jobs that have not yet been created,

to tackle societal challenges that we can't yet imagine, and to use technologies that have not yet been invented. (p. 29)

In schools, he claimed, the

[...] more interdependent the world becomes, the more we need great collaborators and orchestrators [who] need to become better at helping students learn to develop an awareness of the pluralism of modern life. (p. 31)

Wilson (2018) has hope for a brighter future for education as a result of her comprehensive research project on reform in schools across the USA. She observed teams of teachers, school leaders, students, parents and whole communities collaboratively and creatively attempting to transform educational learning environments and experiences for their students. Ironically, however, she reminded us that while '… the core of change is learning, … our institutions of learning are slow, some might even say immune, to change' (p. 1). She based her argument on the view that educational change is, essentially, a developmental task and, when we ask schools to change, we are asking human beings to change; '… this requires special tools and a human-centred approach' (p. 4). This human development approach, she claimed, requires that educational reformers '… rethink, reimagine, and redesign a school to unleash potential, spark curiosity, and invite learners to think for themselves and to take ownership of their learning' (p. 3). This view on human-centred education is central to arguments for transformational reform of education in this book, but it is acknowledged that we will require many well-intentioned, creative and energetic reformers '… to build new skills and an ongoing capacity for change and adaptation' (p. 5).

It is also recognised and accepted throughout this book that the data organisations currently have on performance outcomes provide opportunities to boost reform agendas and performance improvement. However, a downside to data-driven improvement processes is the potential devaluing of the qualitative judgments of teachers and professionals in educational systems and schools. Muller (2018), in *The Tyranny of Metrics*, cautioned about the possible consequences of a contemporary obsession with comprehensive assessment regimes, data use and metrics, generally. He stated that there are '… unintended negative consequences of trying to substitute standardised measures of performance for personal and professional judgment based on experience'. Drawing from his extensive research on the usefulness or otherwise of metrics for improving performance in organisations, he claimed that '… while they [metrics] are a potentially valuable tool, the virtues of accountability metrics have been oversold, and their costs are often not appreciated' (p. 6). His book is an important source of knowledge and insights for educators and educational leaders on how to achieve a more productive and rewarding balance between people-based (human character and qualities) and evidence-based (measurement and data) approaches to professional judgements and decision making in education.

Following his review of different countries' educational systems, Schleicher (2018), similarly, recommended a wise balance between the use of metrics and a greater reliance on the professional judgements of educators, especially teachers. He claimed that there is wide diversity in actual accountability processes and that '… approaches to accountability evolve as school systems themselves evolve – as rules become guidelines and good practice and, ultimately, as good practice becomes culture …'. This progression, he claimed, involves:…a shift in the balance between 'administrative accountability' and 'professional accountability' (p. 115) and concluded that this shift will be assisted by the use of smart technologies* and leaders who have a more expansive and broader views of reform drivers in education. (* For more on how technology will transform the work of human experts, see Susskind & Susskind, 2015).

Emerging leadership literature appears to conclude that educational leaders and reformers need to look beyond their own systems and schools to gain information and inspiration from a VUCA environment. The Gonski et al.'s 2.0 Report (2018) recommended that educational change leaders need to focus on and use forces outside their schools to assist in their reform initiatives. An OECD (2017) international report on innovation in schools concluded that too few innovations in education '… have looked at the broader context and the external relations of schools as drivers of innovation' (p. 3). The authors of the report argued that '… we need to see schools as networking institutions and part of encompassing ecosystems of learning and innovation' (p. 3). Teachers, they recommended, need to be partners in implementing this educational ecosystem because they should be '… participants, co-authors, co-designers, co-implementers and co-leaders of the process' (p. 116).

While smart technologies will greatly assist leaders in their reform initiatives, the authors of an OECD (2016) report on the use of technologies in education, cautioned that introducing digital technology into education for technology's sake '… does not materially improve results because educational reforms need to place teaching practice rather than technology in the driving seat' (p. 89). The authors claimed that many recent reform attempts have used the 'wrong drivers' of reform because, as Fullan (2011) concluded, '… they do not lead to culture change' (p. 5). The 'right drivers' to achieve educational reform, according to the OECD (2016) report, should focus on:

> […] the teaching-assessment nexus, social capital to build the profession, pedagogy matching technology, and developing system synergies [because these drivers] work directly on changing the culture of teaching and learning [and they] embed both ownership and engagement in reforms for students and teachers. (p. 90)

They pointed out that the real effectiveness of technology in teaching and learning environments comes from the effectiveness of the pedagogy that it supports.

A challenge for most educational reformers is to determine the ways and means to constructively drive educational change and reform in a VUCA world. The conclusions of Prince, Swanson, and King (2018) – authors of a 10-year forecast for education, called *KnowledgeWorks Forecast 5.0* – helped provide answers for this challenge. They concluded that while numerous drivers and changes have the potential to influence education over the course of the next decade, five '... identifiable drivers of change will strongly impact education and our lives, both positively and negatively' (p. 6). They identified the drivers as:

- *automating choices*: algorithms and artificial intelligence are increasingly embedded in and will influence our lives;
- *civic superpowers*: individuals, non-profits and volunteer organisations are flexing their civic muscles, encouraging all of us to be more socially responsible;
- *accelerating brains*: rapid advances in technology and neuroscience are combining to transform our cognitive abilities in intended and unintended ways;
- *toxic narratives*: these narratives and metrics of success and achievement will shape people's aspirations, choices and behaviours; some of these narratives can be destructive of people's lives
- *remaking geographies*: migration patterns, small-scale production and efforts to grow place-based and cultural assets are combining to reshape community landscapes in response to economic transition and climate volatility. (*Forecast 5.0*, p. 6)

These five narratives will influence educational landscapes in the future and educational leaders, especially teachers, should be prepared to respond constructively to them. If responded to intelligently and positively, these drivers can assist educational reformers to '... imagine new kinds of educational practices, programs, structures and roles that respond to the changing landscape' (p. 17). One of the key roles for reform identified by Anderson, Hinz, and Matus (2017), from their research-based and futures-oriented report in Australia, was the need to bring about a paradigm shift in schooling, which is better suited for the times, using students as '... creators and co-creators of their futures [and] active partners in the initiative' (p. 10). A focus on involving students in reform initiatives (Degenhardt & Duignan, 2010) will be discussed later in this book.

A key conclusion from this chapter is that, currently, educational leaders, as reformers, tend to respond and survive by adjusting through incremental changes but, as the frenetic pace of change increases, new leadership mindsets, processes and benchmarks for success will be essential; these are discussed throughout this book and summarised in the final chapter – Chapter 12. A key conclusion is that leaders can learn lessons from the current responses of successful disrupted organisations to help build well-developed and successful leadership frameworks, guidance systems and processes, in order to thrive in a topsy-turvy world. Leadership approaches, processes and practices are recommended that will assist educational leaders embrace and thrive in periods of disruption and constant change by making informed choices that generate long-term sustainable value and, above all, create human-centred schools with rich and engaging cultures, including educational-delivery processes that value people and help shape students to become future leaders and citizens of our precious world.

Chapter 2

Disruptive Environments Impact People's Lives and Work

Relentless technological changes are increasingly impacting both positively and negatively on our lives. Quick and Platt (2015) stated that:

> [...] new technology relentlessly hurtles into our lives. Ideas and practices travel around the world at Internet speed. Social media enables individuals to self-organise and re-organise in ways unimaginable in the 20th century. (p. 13)

In an increasingly disrupted world, changes may happen at warp speed and be scaled so quickly that organisational leaders will have to scramble to keep up. Quick and Platt (2015) paint a vivid picture of the confusing and often weird characteristics of our current and future topsy-turvy world context:

> Uber is the world's largest taxi company and they don't own any taxis. Airbnb is the world's largest hotelier and they don't own any accommodation. Skype is one of the world's largest phone companies and they don't own any telecommunications infrastructure. Netflix is the world's largest theatre company and they don't own any cinemas. Facebook is the world's most popular media channel and they don't create content. Apple and Google are the world's largest software vendors and they don't write apps. (p. 19)

We live in a confusing world and it will be a major challenge to accommodate these new and unfolding realities into our everyday lives; in fact, exponential change is so new to us that we do not really understand its emerging forms and its potential to impact on our lives. Historically, leaders developed stepping stones to comfortably navigate the challenges of incremental change but because of the magnitude and intensity of recent changes, our stepping-stone knowledge from the past will be grossly inadequate for us to cope, never mind flourish in VUCA times. Instead of attempting to reclaim a quickly vanishing past, it will be more

Leading Educational Systems and Schools in Times of Disruption and Exponential Change:
A Call for Courage, Commitment and Collaboration, 11–17
Copyright © 2020 by Patrick A. Duignan
Published under exclusive license
doi:10.1108/978-1-83909-850-520201003

prudent and productive for us to better understand the forces driving disruption and attempt to respond intelligently, creatively and effectively to them. After two decades of research into organisations that have been experiencing severe disruptions, Quick and Platt (2015) have identified five intrinsically linked factors driving disruptive changes that we must understand and appreciate (pp. 33–46, bold in original):

> ***Connectivity:*** Social media and other emerging high-speed networks enable us to connect, collaborate and plan together;
>
> ***Complexity:*** Newly connected people are enabled to increase the density and variety of their networks by, '… the speed at which they transact, and the interdependencies that form between them' (p. 37);
>
> ***Chaos:*** Chaos is characterised by discontinuous change and quantum leaps that are very difficult to foresee or predict; and
>
> ***Change cycles:*** Periods of rapid changes are characterised by '… systemic change cycles that continually trigger one another to create a compounded effect of system-wide and ever-accelerating exponential change.' (p. 43)

We can find examples of disruptions in the broader world of work, especially in some organisations, where people thrive, learn from them and apply these lessons to education and leadership. In his book, *Clean Disruption*, Tony Seba (2014) from Stanford University, warned that exciting new technological products and processes from places, such as Silicon Valley, '… will disrupt energy industries that have barely evolved over the past hundred years' (p. 4) – we often say similar things about education. Silicon Valley, he says, '… is about abundance, business-model innovation, participatory culture, and democratising power' (p. 4). He concluded that emerging energy architecture '… will be distributed, mobile, intelligent, and participatory [and it] will tend to transform the current energy structures and processes', which are '… centralised, command-and-control oriented, secretive, and extractive' (p. 3). He claimed that organisations that enable people to participate in the generation and distribution of information and content have already been very successful, for example, Facebook, Twitter and Linkedin.

His critique of energy systems can be, at least partially, applied to the future of educational systems and schools (see OECD Report, 2019a). In many current national and international educational reports, discussed in later chapters of this book, a consistent theme is emerging that contemporary educational mindsets, structures and processes are too heavily grounded in a conservative, centralised, command-and-control-oriented industrial model, characteristic of Seba's description of existing energy organisations and networks. The good news is that there can be positive outcomes for educational leaders and their organisations if they are alert to and knowledgeable about potential disruptions in other industries – they are then in a position to prepare and respond to the uncertainty and rapid changes in their own environments. Part of this preparation starts long before disruption hits us hard. Research evidence discussed in later chapters will support the view that in challenging and unstable conditions – in VUCA conditions – leaders are more successful when they stand for something of value, when they are authentic, because leadership authenticity matters in an uncertain and disrupted environment.

From his substantial research on the subject of leadership and disruption, Johansen (2012), reported that leaders faced with disruption and uncertainty need to be especially open and transparent in their engagements and relationships and this approach, he concluded '... allows followers to see in their leaders not only a bit of themselves but also that which makes them aspire to more' (p. 128). He noted the prestigious USA's *Centre for Creative Leadership's* deep commitment to authentic leadership, to be open, trustworthy, firm but empathetic, attending to what really matters. From their research into the nature of workplaces in contemporary organisations, Goffee and Jones (2016), also found that the most motivational, inspiring and ideal work places are constantly striving for and trying to live up to the ideal of authenticity and '... their efforts at building authentic organisations are often inspirational' (p. 11). Leaders, they say, need to create working environments where others can follow their own 'authentic obsession' and leadership must be '... as much about an authenticity of task or place as it is about the person leading ...' (p. 11). They urged leaders to constantly ask themselves the question: '*Why should anyone work here?*' (pp. 2–3, italics in original). They noted that while many organisations are thriving in the midst of exponential change, some who continue to do what has made them successful over a number of years, fail. A key question is, why?

Gans (2017), in his book *The Disruption Dilemma*, posed the question: Why do very successful companies, continuing to do what made them successful, end up falling to the point of failure? Despite its great success over decades, the very prestigious *Encyclopedia Britannica* fell to strong disruptive forces coming from newer companies, such as, Microsoft, Wikipedia and Apple. Other famous companies also collapsed, including Kodak and Blockbuster Video, because of emerging powerful disruptors, for example, digitised cameras and Netflix. *Matson Navigation Company*, however, a company established in 1882, not only survived the containerisation revolution in shipping, but thrived by embracing it. It was not simply a matter of making and using more and more containers, it was much more complicated than that:

> ... ships had to be redesigned so that the container could sit on the top deck rather than down below for easy loading and unloading. Ports needed to be redesigned with large cranes to handle container traffic and load containers onto truck and rail transport. Finally, the entire logistics, information flow, and contracting space had to be reengineered. (Gans, 2017, p. 5)

Matson Navigation Company cleverly chose a new architecture specifically optimised for its customers and thrived as a result. Drawing on the scholarship of Henderson whose research focussed on the difficulties incumbent firms, like Blockbuster Video, had in responding to new competing entrants into the marketplace (e.g. Netflix), Gans (2017) concluded that existing firms could deal with large changes to their context so long as they impacted only specific components of their technology, but they were still confused and stymied by the fact that new start-ups were presenting them with 'architectural innovations' (p. 22). Based on Henderson's research conclusions, Gans pointed out that with quantum, disruptive jumps, involving new architectures, new technologies, new logistical approaches, companies such as *Blockbuster Videos* and *BlackBerry phones* required substantial, even wholesale reorganisation of their business models and modus operandi.

Netflix's great advantage over Blockbuster Video was that it could, at first '... efficiently deliver DVDs directly to people's homes' (Gans, 2017, p. 23). This involved the capacity to sort and deliver DVDs to post offices and process them again when they were returned. This eventually led to the development of a revolutionary business model '... based on subscriptions' (p. 23). Meanwhile, Blockbuster's business model required customers to physically walk into their stores to select and later return videos. Blockbuster, therefore, had to maintain large and costly stores within and across many countries, while Netflix was on a business trajectory that allowed them '... to provide products of superior value to customers relative to the costs of producing them on existing technological paths' (p. 24). Netflix's new approach did not at first create new technology – they continued to use videos – but they generated an architectural disruption for Blockbuster that changed the rules and processes of the game. When Netflix adopted online-technology, they did not have '... to worry about presenting inventory in a shopping-friendly way' (p. 27) and they could offer customers a much greater and richer variety of videos; as well, late fees, hated by customers, were now much lower and electronically generated. Eventually, Netflix transitioned to another new disruptive technology – internet streaming – which delivered on-demand videos and films.

The introduction of containerisation caused a similar architectural disruption for the shipping industry; many companies couldn't cope and failed but *Matson Navigation* proved to be very creative and agile. Malcolm McLean, a former trucking magnate, sold his business and moved into container shipping in the 1950s by starting to load the container bodies of trucks onto customised ships. To be successful, he had to struggle with '... the prevailing architectural characteristics of shipping', which included the '... shape and size of ships, the structural features of docklands, the loading and unloading methods and machinery, as well as union employment challenges and investment procurement' (Gans, 2017, p. 6). McLean persisted, succeeded and the rest is history.

The concept of architectural disruption applies to a wide variety of organisations and its key tenets will be applied to educational disruptions in a later chapter. For now, the leadership challenges presented by the ossification of people, ideas, thought processes, habits and peoples' behaviours in a range and variety of organisations, due to the existence within them of silo-mentalities and structures, will be discussed. Community, connectivity and collaboration can be seriously disrupted by the influence of silos within organisations. Tett (2015) argued that many bankers prior to the 2008 global financial crisis did not appreciate the risks they were taking because they lived in a banking world where different teams of financial traders '… did not know what each other was doing, even inside the same (supposedly integrated) institution' (p. x). She concluded:

> Indeed, almost everywhere I looked in the financial crisis it seemed that tunnel vision and tribalism had contributed to the disaster. People were trapped inside their little specialist departments, social groups, teams, or pockets of knowledge. Or it might be said, inside their silos (p. x) …. The paradox of the modern age, I realised, is that we live in a world that is closely integrated in some ways, but fragmented on others. Shocks [or disruptions] are increasingly contagious. But we continue to behave and think in tiny silos. (Tett, 2015, p. xi)

A weakness in many organisations, despite our increasingly interconnected world, is that they tend to be '… divided, and then subdivided into numerous different departments, which often fail to talk to each other – let alone collaborate' (p. 16). People, she stated, often live in '… separate mental and social "ghettos" talking and coexisting only with people like us' (p. 16). Such ghettos or silos, she claimed, '… breed tribalism [and] tunnel vision' (p. 17) [or create] '… mental blindness, which causes people to do stupid things' (p. 18).

Silos can create substantial obstacles and disincentives to change initiatives. Howard Stringer, the British CEO of Sony Corporation in Japan (appointed in 2005), recognised that a major contributing factor to Sony's then decline was the widespread presence of silos within the company, exacerbated by the fact that their employees stayed with the company for life. Stringer explained to Sony's Japanese staff through an internal newsletter that: 'The silo metaphor in business is really a description of the subcultures within an organisation that have become islands and don't communicate horizontally or even vertically within their own organisations' (quoted in Tett, 2015, p. 87). Silos can often constitute powerful sub-culture groupings that are very difficult to challenge and change – in reality, they constitute sheltered spaces with tunnel vision, characterised by negative attitudes that resist change and improvement. Stringer put a great deal of effort into changing the behaviours within and between the silos at Sony. He reasoned that if '… he couldn't kill the silos, he could at least try to make them cooperate. After all, the company's motto was "Sony United"' (Tett, 2015, p. 93). He, ultimately, failed and left the company.

Tett (2015) also used the example of Facebook as a company that was well aware from the beginning of the negative effects of silos. She reported that the Facebook platform:

> […] enabled communication to occur in a horizontal way, instead of via a rigid hierarchy. When somebody made a post, everyone

could access that piece of information. This was a contrast to the usual communication pattern of many big companies via email, where information tended to get passed up, or down hierarchies, creating potential bottlenecks and logjams [and Facebook] provided a way for the staff to build deeper connections with each other, on multiple different levels. (p. 226)

Based on Facebook's success at silo-busting in a large company, Google and Apple achieved similar successes but the *Cleveland Clinic* in the USA is an example of a very large organisation that was able to remove silos from a traditionally hierarchical and segregated set of structures. Toby Cosgrove, a world-famous cardiothoracic surgeon, proved that even a large and world-famous health conglomerate, *Cleveland Clinic*, could change its structure and approach to care giving. He became CEO in 2004 and soon announced that he was going to implement '… two big revolutions' (Tett, 2015, p. 252). He announced that it was time for the hospital's 43,000 staff to:

[…] rip up their existing taxonomy for defining a 'doctor' or a 'nurse'. Instead of simply defining this in purely medical terms, all the staff would now be considered 'caregivers' responsible for not just treating the physical ailments but the spirit and emotions as well; he set about changing how the hospital was organised. (Tett, 2015, pp. 252–253)

Instead of the traditional internal silos organised around departments and doctors' specialties, he defined them around '… the patients and their illnesses'. He, in fact, created new 'multidisciplinary institutes' and thus '… forced surgeons, physicians, and others to work together in treating patients' (p. 253). While the backlash from self-interested health professionals was huge, Cosgrave persisted and, seemingly against all odds, on 1 January 2008, 'Clevland [clinic] announced its Big-Bang revolution: twenty-seven new "institutes" were created' (p. 258) clustered around such broad labels as, 'Digestive Diseases Institute', 'Head and Neck Institute', 'Heart and Vascular Institute' and 'Cancer Institute'. While Cosgrove and his supporters continued to be subjected to harsh criticisms for their revolutionary ideas from more traditional silo-generated mentalities and mindsets, they received very strong support in 2013 from a survey of patient satisfaction, which stated' … as measured by *U.S. News and World Report*, … *Cleveland Clinic* was the top-ranked hospital in America in terms of patient satisfaction' (p. 264). In a speech on American Health care, President Obama lauded the Cleveland Clinic as a place '… where patients' care is the number-one concern, not bureaucracy' (Tett, 2015, p. 265).

Perhaps we should regard schools as places where students' care is the number-one concern and reorganise the architecture for learning accordingly – more on this idea is presented in a later chapter. The impact of silos on the structures and caregiving at the Cleveland Clinic has been reported at some length here because, in many ways, large health-care systems, especially hospitals, have similar structures and leadership challenges to education systems and schools. As a Trustee for 13 years of a large health-care system in Australia and New Zealand with 15 hospitals and a variety of care services, the author of this book developed an appreciation of the similarities between these two service oriented and care-based entities – hospitals and schools – and I came to understand that we can learn a great deal about silos and how to reform them from successful examples in other organisations. In fact, Tett (2015) pointed out that '… our schools and universities put students into boxes at a young age, and academic departments are fragmented' (p. 314). She argued that one key message that can be derived from organisations that have effectively transformed their silos '… is that our world does not function effectively if it is always rigidly streamlined'. She claimed that:

> [...] living in specialised silos might make life seem more efficient in the short term, but a world that is always divided into a fragmented and specialist pattern is a place of missed opportunities and if we become blind creatures of habit … our lives are poorer as a result. (Tett, 2015, p. 315)

Under the leadership of Malcolm McLean, *Matson, Navigation Company* broke down the silos within and re-configured them, and Toby Cosgrave had similar results at Cleveland Clinic. Educators and educational leaders wishing to break-down silos and transform educational architectures – especially the organisational structures and pedagogical delivery processes – can learn many practical leadership lessons from these company examples.

As with the Cleveland clinic, is it time for schools to rip up their existing taxonomy for defining a principal or a teacher? Instead, could all school staff be considered educational 'caregivers' responsible for treating – educating – the whole person, the intellectual dimensions as well as the spiritual and emotional ones as well. Instead of the traditional internal silos in secondary schools, organised around subjects and departments, why couldn't they be organised around students' learning needs and developmental stages. Could secondary schools be organised as multidisciplinary institutes and thus require leadership teams, teachers and other educational assistants to work together in educating students. These possibilities will be examined later in this book, with special attention to secondary schools.

Chapter 3

Traditional Leadership Approaches Can Be a Liability in Times of Disruption

The learnings of leaders from observation or from past experiences can be found wanting when they are faced with dynamic disruptions and constant changes. Taleb (2010), in his book *The Black Swan*, pointed out the possible flaws in leadership learnings based on prior experience when he claimed that '… before the discovery of Australia, people in the Old World were convinced that *all* swans were white, an unassailable belief as it seemed completely confirmed by empirical evidence' (p. xxi). The sighting of the first black swan in Australia, however, exposed the potential inadequacy of prior experiences of swans. He pointed out that '… one single observation [first black swan sighted] can invalidate a general statement derived from millennia of confirmatory sightings of millions of white swans' (p. xxi). According to Taleb (2010), a Black Swan event has three attributes:

1. First it is an *outlier*, as it lies outside the realm of regular expectations, because nothing in the past can convincingly point to its possibility; (italics in original)
2. Second, it carries an extreme impact; and
3. Third, in spite of its outlier status, human nature makes us concoct explanations for its occurrence *after* the fact, making it explainable and predictable. (p. xxii, italics in original)

Taleb provided evidence to support his rather large claim that,

> […] a small number of black swans explain almost everything in our world, from the success of ideas and religions, to the dynamics of historical events, to elements of our own personal lives. (p. xxii)

He argued this case very convincingly using hundreds of real-life examples. He especially claimed that social scientists, including in education, have, for

Leading Educational Systems and Schools in Times of Disruption and Exponential Change: A Call for Courage, Commitment and Collaboration, 19–32
Copyright © 2020 by Patrick A. Duignan
Published under exclusive license
doi:10.1108/978-1-83909-850-520201004

over a century, '... operated under the false belief that their tools could measure uncertainty' (p. xxii). He suggested that if we ask our financial investment advisors about possible risks in the marketplace, odds are they will supply you with:

> [...] a *measure* that *excludes* the possibility of the Black Swan – hence one that has no better predictive value for assessing the total risks than astrology, [and] this problem is endemic in social matters. (p. xxiii, italics in original)

He also pointed out that if we examine the progress and paths taken in our own personal lives, few happenings have unfolded according to our plans for the future. Having written my own memoirs, I can attest to fact that most of what has eventuated in my life story did not unfold neatly, according to a carefully constructed plan. In my numerous leadership development workshops with large numbers of leaders, I explore Taleb's contention with them and find that very few (if any) of them have lived according to a pre-ordained plan for their lives.

Taleb criticised professionals who behave as if they have predictive powers with regard to the future in their area of expertise but, unfortunately, many seem to act as if they do. He elaborated on this point:

> [...] certain professionals, while believing they are experts, are in fact not. Based on their empirical record, they do not know more about their subject matter than the general population, but they are much better at narrating – or worse, at smoking you with complicated mathematical models. (p. xxv)

He stated that there are two possible ways to approach and understand phenomena in our world (pp. xxviii–xxix):

1. The first is to rule out the extraordinary and focus on the 'normal' i.e., leave aside 'outliers' and study ordinary cases.
2. The second approach is to consider that in order to understand a phenomenon, one needs first to consider the extremes – particularly if, like the Black Swan, they carry an extraordinary cumulative effect.

The crux of Taleb's thesis is that:

> [...] almost everything in social life is produced by rare but consequential shocks and jumps; all the while almost everything studied about social life focuses on the 'normal', particularly with 'bell curve' methods of inference that tell you close to nothing. Why? Because the bell curve ignores large deviations, cannot handle them, yet makes us confident that we have tamed uncertainty. (Taleb, 2010, p. xxix)

Taleb is well aware that he is proposing an alternative to what he calls, 'naïve empiricism' and 'self-deceiving statistics', when measuring social and economic events and when theorising about our world. Instead, he argued that:

> [...] our world is dominated by the extreme, the unknown, and the very improbable (improbable according to our current knowledge) – and all the while we spend our time ... focusing on the known, and the repeated. (Taleb, 2010, p. xxxii)

He paraphrased Daniel Kahneman (discussed below) to show how we tend to achieve psychological comfort when faced with daunting challenges: '... for psychological comfort some people would rather use a map of the Pyrénées while lost in the Alps than use nothing at all' (Taleb, 2010, p. 367).

Kahneman (2011) was familiar with the work of Taleb when writing his book, *Thinking, Fast and Slow,* and used some of Taleb's arguments to support his own views on why so many people seem to commit errors of judgement and biases of intuition, especially when making decisions. Kahneman's aim is to '... improve the ability to identify and understand errors of judgment and choice, in others and eventually ourselves, by providing a richer and more precise language to discuss them' (p. 4). Working with a colleague researcher, Amos Tversky, they concluded, based on their own robust statistical analysis methods, that:

> in spite of years of teaching and using statistics, we had not developed an intuitive sense of the reliability of statistical results observed in small samples, e.g., at a classroom level. (p. 5)

In addition, he pointed out that our subjective judgments are often biased because we are far too willing '... to believe research findings based on inadequate evidence and prone to collect too few observations in our research' (Kahneman, 2011, p. 5). These are somewhat alarming conclusions for those in educational contexts who, on a daily basis, make life-changing decisions for their students based on an intuitive sense of the reliability of statistical results, often observed in small samples within classrooms. To test their argument, Kahneman and Tversky decided to compare their research conclusions against those of a number of 'expert colleagues' (p. 5) and found that '... our expert colleagues, like us, greatly exaggerated the likelihood that the original result of an experiment would be successfully replicated even with a small sample'. They discovered that they also gave '... very poor advice to a fictitious graduate student about the number of observations she needed to collect. Even statisticians, they concluded, were not good intuitive statisticians' (p. 5). From their longer-term study in this area, they concluded that part of the research problem is that, too frequently, we '... think associatively, we think metaphorically, we think causally, but statistics requires thinking about many things at once' (Kahneman, 2011, p. 13). He concluded that most researchers and practitioners are not good at thinking about the many!

They concluded that we are prone to overestimate how much we understand about the world and to underestimate the role of chance in events. Kahneman, especially, urged us to '… intelligently explore the lessons that can be learned from the past while resisting the lure of hindsight and the illusion of certainty' (pp. 13–14). His view on the importance of understanding the nature of uncertainty, our ignorance of the role of chance, and the illusion that hindsight will assist us to prepare for a disruptive future, is very similar to Johansen's (2017) idea of '… looking backward from the future' (p. 15), which helps us see '… long-term patterns of change ten years ahead, beyond the noise of the present' (p. 15); such a perspective, he stated, '… makes better decisions in the present more likely' (p. 15).

Shapiro (2013) claimed that '… taking risks does not have to be reckless or random; it involves exploring options, assessing likelihoods, and making rational decisions' (p. 53). Above all, it means actively seeking feedback, listening with focus and attention, and '… weighing the consequences of any decision *before* pulling the trigger' (p. 53, italics in original). He also assured us that when making decisions in times of uncertainty, honesty is the best policy because:

> […] even if it's painful, you can never go wrong with honesty. Honesty is moral, ethical and, of course, always the right thing to do. If you are honest, you don't have to remember who knows what and worry about the truth coming out. (p. 209)

Normore and Brooks (2017, p. 142) argued that trust goes hand-in-hand with truth and honesty and that a '… breach of trust goes hand-in-hand with *deception*: "telling the truth establishes trust, and lying destroys it" (quote from Solomon & Flores, 2001, italics in original). They go on to say that when leaders deceive intentionally, their '… falsehood is deliberate and so this implies the deliberate undermining, damaging, or distorting of others' plans and their capacity to act' (pp. 142–143).

For educational leaders and reformers, these messages seem to urge them to deal respectfully and honestly with all those involved with them in their reform agenda if they wish to ensure that they will positively engage with the innovation. They need to be careful in interpreting and communicating much of the research evidence based on narrow statistical analysis, as it can differ from their professional judgements and intuition based on their own experiences of what works for their students in their school context. Also, they must guard against seeing patterns in data too early, which can prevent them from thinking associatively, metaphorically or causally because, as discussed above, statisticians, for the most part, are not good intuitive statisticians.

Part of the difficulty for educators in achieving educational reform is that many of the education policies and practices related to proposed changes are driven by politicians and educational bureaucrats who seem convinced that education must be, primarily, a force for economic and industrial development. They often proclaim that employers want school graduates to have very specific skills that are best developed by concentrating on a narrow range of subjects (the basics) and then testing to see how well students have mastered basic skills in these subjects. When asked directly, however, most employers say they want '… creative thinkers, problem solvers, potential innovators and entrepreneurs, team players, and graduates who are adaptable and self-confident' (Robinson, 2011, p. 69).

Some claim that a central obstacle to education transformation is that it is overly focussed on preserving a dying paradigm and protecting the *status quo*. They claim, for example, that too many state schools in Britain and elsewhere have become 'factories', when they should be 'places of engagement, excitement and delight' (Seldon, 2010, p. 1). Seldon pointed out that while the results of test scores on paper in England may seem to indicate improved results, this achievement comes at a great cost:

> [...] reluctant students are processed through a system which is closely controlled and monitored by the state. No area of public life is more important than education to prepare people to live meaningful, productive and valuable lives. Yet our schools turn out young people who are often incapable of living full and autonomous lives. (p. 1)

His subtitle, *An Education Manifesto 2010–2020*, despite its many insights and merits, has largely been ignored by politicians, educational policymakers and even by leaders of educational change initiatives. It would appear, in fact, that educators, especially at school level, are often confused and torn between the demands of national curricula, standards for teachers and students, national testing and accountability regimes, and yet, as professionals, they are expected to create caring cultures, authentic relationships, and enhance the personal efficacy and wellbeing of all their students. What are they to think and do? These questions and challenges are also applicable to a number of education systems in a variety of countries.

Size does matter! In his OECD Report (2018), *World class education: How to build a 21st-century school system*, Schleicher concluded that a major reason for the difficulty in reforming education '… is simply the scale and reach of the sector' (p. 204). He claimed that the regulations, structures and institutions on which policymakers tend to focus when reforming education are just like the small, visible tip of an iceberg; the reason why it is so hard to reform education systems is that there is a much larger, invisible part under the waterline. This invisible part is composed of the interests, beliefs, motivations and fears of the people involved. In addition, many countries have responded to new demands for what students should learn by layering more and more content on top of their curriculum, with the result that '… curricula have often become a mile wide but just an inch deep' (Schleicher, OECD Report, 2018, p. 249). Some countries have looked to broaden the learning experiences of students by integrating new subjects, topics and themes into traditional curriculum areas, '… often under the flag of an interdisciplinary approach' (p. 249). Schleicher advises change leaders to think '… more systematically about what [they] want to achieve from the design of curricula, rather than continuing to add more "stuff" to what is being taught' (p. 249).

A negative result of this increasing pressure is that many teachers have become sceptical, even questioning, over '… incoherent reforms that disrupt rather than improve education practice because they prioritise variable political interests over the needs of learners and educators' (Schleicher, OECD Report, 2018, p. 206). Instead, Schleicher proposed that twenty-first-century curricula need to be characterised by:

> [...] *rigour*, i.e., building what is being taught on a high level of cognitive demand; *focus* – aiming at conceptual understanding by prioritising depth over breadth of content; and by *coherence* – sequencing instruction based on a scientific understanding of learning progressions and human development. (pp. 249–250, italics by this author for effect)

In summary, Schleicher claimed that top-down governance based on political preferences and agendas, which works through layers of administrative structures, is no longer useful in educational settings. The challenge is to build on the passion and expertise of '... the hundreds of thousands of teachers and tens of thousands of school leaders and to enlist them in the design of superior policies and practices' (p. 207). Wilson (2018) echoed this viewpoint when she recommended that leaders of change need to be part:

> [...] of not just a rising consensus of what needs to change, but also a rising army of hundreds of thousands of people doing something about it – with humility, with heart, and with faith. (p. 107)

Educational reformers need to be aware of what world-renowned researcher, scholar and writer, Pavan Sukhdev (2012) warned about the negative forces operating in *Corporation 1920* – a current organisational form stuck in an older environmentally destructive paradigm. Instead much literature on educational reform discussed in this book would seem to suggest that there are important lessons to be learnt from new organisational forms, like Sukhdev's *Corporation 2020* – he recommended this type of organisation to educational change leaders and reformers. It is argued throughout this book that education systems and schools should have a similar DNA to *Corporation 2020*, nuanced to fit with the special purposes of educational organisations in our societies; they need to be fit-for-purpose. Interestingly for educators, Sukhdev also urged the 2020 Corporation to become '... a modern-day community, tied by a shared culture created by its values, mission, goals, objectives, and governance' (p. 201). Above all else, he stated it needs to be a community '... of networks of relationships instead of a rigid hierarchical ... army of production units making goods to sell' (p. 201). This modern-day community will be, he claimed:

> [...] tied by a shared culture created by its values, mission, goals, objectives, and governance [and] it can re-create the sense of belonging that has been lost to the forces of modernisation and globalisation (p. 200)

This business-inspired DNA can provide educational organisations, especially schools, with a dynamic framework for reform and also mouthpieces for our societies and civilisations.

Another problem in educational reform attempts is the unequal information different groups in reform transactions possess and this can impede change and reform in schools. There is need for what Taleb (2018) refers to '... as more skin in the game'. He explained that this condition is a prerequisite for fairness, commercial efficiency, risk management and all actors in the game, he advised, must bear a cost when they fail the public but, if they have no skin in the game, it can lead to many negative consequences for others. Many leaders of corporations during the global financial crisis (e.g. especially banks and other financial organisations) had insufficient skin in the game, which led them to take unreasonable and irresponsible risks with their customers' investments, leading to disaster for those investors, without, in many cases, any negative consequences for themselves.

Taleb argued that '... asymmetry [is] the core concept behind skin in the game. The question becomes: to what extent can people in a transaction have an informational differential between them?' (p. 55). He claimed:

> [...] simply, as the aim is for both parties in a transaction to have the same uncertainty facing random outcomes, an asymmetry becomes equivalent to theft. *Things designed by people without skin in the game tend to grow in complication (before their final collapse)*. (Taleb, 2018, p. 29, italics in original)

Much of the analyses on the failings of educational reform, reported throughout this book, accepts the complaints by many who are expected to implement proposed reforms that their views are too often ignored or that they are deliberately excluded from key information, so do not feel they have skin in the game. Also, policymakers and reform leaders are often not held to account for poorly planned and failed reform initiatives, so they too have no skin in the game.

Perhaps teachers, students and their parents have more skin in the game than anyone else in education; certainly, they have a lot to lose if educational initiatives and reform agendas fail them. Leaders, too, have skin in the game and they need to be sensitive to the needs and feelings of others and be able to adjust to changing circumstances and organisational realities. They must be informed, adaptable, agile and, above all, authentic.

Adaptive and Agile Leaders Do Best in Times of Disruption

Johansen (2017), a distinguished fellow at the *Institute for the Future* in Silicon Valley, predicted that in a disrupted and uncertain future '... leadership will be much less centralised and more distributed' (p. x). Hierarchical and bureaucratic organisations and structures, he claimed, '... will give way to shape-shifting organisational forms that function like organisms' (p. x). Enduring leadership qualities like authenticity, humility and trust will still be foundational, but the future requires new strengths for leading. Johansen gives advice for current and future leaders who will have to provide leadership during periods of extreme disruption and change; he singled out two areas of focus as being especially useful for leaders in different types of organisations, including education:

1. *Learn to look backward from the future:* 'The future will reward clarity but punish uncertainty', so a leader must be '… a student of the future and learn about rapidly unfolding trends that are likely disrupters for their organisation' (p. x). He claimed that the best leaders will '… work backward from the future …' to better prepare them for that future (p. 23).
2. *Embrace shape-shifting organisations*: New organisational forms are becoming increasingly possible by creating '… networks that have no centre, grow from the edges, and cannot be controlled, where hierarchies come and go' (p. 61). These conditions will require leaders to loosen up their structures, processes and practices in order to be successful.

Learning to look backward from the future is more traditionally known as backward mapping, which involves '… dilemma flipping' – the ability to turn dilemmas, problems and challenges into 'advantages and opportunities' (p. 25). Shape-shifting organisations, Johansen stated, will have advantages in an uncertain and rapidly changing future and they '… will win consistently over centralised hierarchies' (p. x). Leaders of such organisations will need to be adept at leading in contexts where distributed networks don't require '… centralised management' (p. 62). Excitingly, work environments, thanks to this distributed capability, will have the capacity to manage '… *liquid data*, which means that data created in one place can flow easily to other places' (p. 69, italics in original). These data flows will enable 'liquid leadership', meaning that leadership '… created in one place can flow to another across boundaries' (p. 69). This is ideal leadership for shape-shifting organisations and IBM, a formerly centralised organisation according to Johansen, is becoming '… increasingly shape-shifting' (p. 69).

It is important to realise that currently cloud networks connect millions, even billions of devices on the Internet of Things and so shape-shifting organisations are not fanciful ideas for the future. Johansen claimed they are becoming increasingly common and diverse and '… what they share in common is the ability to distribute authority and move beyond traditional centralised ways of organising' (p. 75). While educational leaders currently are not generally familiar with this new leadership language or the on-the-ground operation of shape-shifting structures and forms, there is emerging evidence from a large number of educational reform initiatives in many countries, discussed in a number of chapters in this book, that these are the innovative paths educators have begun to explore, even if they don't yet have the language to describe what is actually happening – Silicon Valley can help provide them with this language.

In Johansen's (2012) book, *Leaders Make the Future*, he predicted that cloud-served supercomputing will provide a new infrastructure for innovation, informed risking-taking and global connectivity that will enable and amplify '… the biggest innovation opportunity in history, namely, *reciprocity-based innovation*' (p. 12, italics by this author for emphasis). This innovation involves non-linear thinking and acting by giving '… things away in intelligent ways, in the faith of getting even more in return' (p. 12). Johansen (2012) stated that the '… currency of the cloud will be reciprocity' (p. 171), which involves '… creating a digitally-connected "commons" through which assets are shared for the benefit of all involved' (p. 170). Inherently, a reciprocal-commons provides a leader's motivation '… to promote not only business profit but social profit as well' (Johansen, 2012, p. 172).

It also requires a shared, socially responsible approach to leadership, grounded in ethics and moral concerns and the capacity to lead events, where countries' education systems and schools are enabled to share socially responsible educational leadership approaches, grounded in ethics and moral standards with the enabling capacity to lead events, instead of being led by them (Bezzina & Tuana, 2011). This capacity to help shape the future socially, morally, intellectually, even creatively has always been the dream of educational leaders, especially teachers, and it would appear that they now have access to the understanding, knowledge and know-how (super-connected reciprocal technologies) to help achieve their dreams. While educational leaders may initially find this language and these leadership concepts far-fetched, even questionable, they need to consider that even now, and especially in the (near) future, reciprocity-based innovation is real, as evidenced by the knowledge that more and more educational innovators and reformers are sharing their reform ideas and processes in many worldwide reports on the future of education (see extracts from Schleichel's comprehensive OECD Report, 2018, in Chapter 5). Such reports will help educational leaders to, as Johansen (2017) advised, learn to look backwards from the future and better prepare themselves and others for such a future.

To lead reciprocity-based innovation will require inspired leadership but, as Stein (2018) cautioned, this will require them to be more visionary and proactive than they currently are. In 2015, he reported that the IESE Business school in Madrid, Spain – where Stein is a professor – carried out a survey among 22,000 managers throughout the world which focussed on the leadership styles of their bosses. He summarised the results:

> The respondents replied that two-thirds of their bosses were reactive when undertaking change and that it was mainly due to fear of failure, comfort, lack of perspective, and the rigidity of their approaches; the message is clear, one should overtake events prudently and skillfully in order to govern them instead of being governed by them. (p. 351)

From these research results, Stein concluded that too many leaders lack moral fibre, thereby providing a negative leadership model; he concluded that many leaders have '… moral anorexia …' (p. 352). While the challenges of moral and authentic leadership are discussed elsewhere in this book, it is important to note that Johansen ends his 2017 book, *The New Leadership Literacies*, on a challenging but positive note, when he claimed that in this coming decade:

> Leaders *will* be distributed, whether they like it or not. Centralised organisations and authoritarian personalities constrained by

> certainty will not succeed in a world twisting toward distributed everything. It will be up to leaders – and there will be lots of them in a shape-shifting world – to make a hopeful future. (p. 148)

In fact, much of the literature about leaders and leadership in an uncertain future tends to be positive, claiming that there will be many opportunities for them in times of constant change. To be successful, leaders of change and reform in the future will need to engage with emerging technologies to assist organisational members '... make sense of and derive benefit from our rapidly changing world' and they will also need the '... tools of the mind that will help [them] keep up with these accelerating change cycles' (Quick & Platt, 2015, pp. 45–46). Successful leaders of change will need to craft approaches specifically designed for disruptive environments and cycles of change, learn how to anticipate the future and '... change ahead of change' (p. 48). By learning to change the way they perceive and understand change cycles – not just as disruptions but as potentially re-energising and re-organising opportunities – and anticipate, prepare and plan well for unpredictable events, they can manage them and add positive value to their lives and relationships.

Words of caution, however, are also clearly evident throughout the literature on educational reform reported in this book. There seems to be a consensus that traditional strategic planning policies and strategies are unlikely to prove effective during rapid change cycles. Traditional policies often run on linear, 5-year cycles, which may cause them to lag behind unfolding events; they may be overrun by events even before the plans are executed – a common experience for educational planners. Quick and Platt are clear that, '... in a fast-changing world, planning actions for the future based on an expectation that conditions will remain stable and predictable is a recipe for certain discontinuity' (p. 200). In such conditions, they concluded, decisive action is called for: 'dithering is not your best bet in a time of exponential surges ... timing is everything, missing a beat can be disastrous' (p. 208). What leaders will require are dynamic, cyclical planning processes, informed by risk-management assessments, which are in tune with emerging conditions and sensitive to risks and possibilities in real-time. Collaborative planning using a diverse group of educators and educational leaders is also recommended, because there is strength, insight and wisdom in diversity (Surowiecki, 2005).

A key concern for leaders of change in many organisations, including educational ones, is that the dynamics and relationships between risk management and strategic planning departments are often conflicted and confrontational due to the existence of hierarchical silos that separate the two organisational processes. Quick and Platt (2015) explained this silo mindset and perspective:

> strategy people and risk management people tend to occupy strict silos, tucked away in their separate departments. The strategy-people create plans meant to drive the organisation forward but pay little heed to the inherent risks in the plan. (p. 126)

If the plan does not deliver on planned outcomes, the time lag for this realisation is often too long before the risk becomes apparent. They cautioned that linear, strategic planning processes will be found lacking in a complex and interconnected world where collaborative relationships and networks are a necessity for sustainable planning and successful change to occur.

Leaders will not only have to adjust and adapt to these new realities, they will require a transformation in their thinking and practices. Bye (2017), in her insightful book, *Millennials Matter: Proven Strategies for Building Your Next-Gen Leaders*, is confident that the generation we refer to as, *Millennials*, will be ideally prepared and suited to this new, fast moving and disrupted world. From her extensive research on this group, she claimed that help and insight is on hand, in the form of a new tech-smart and super-connected generation, many of whom will become system and organisational leaders in the near future; indeed, some are already behind the leader's desk. She predicted that Millennials are potential winners in times of disruption and change.

Based on this research, she argued that leaders in times of great change need to cultivate a character-driven and courageous core for their lives and their leadership and that:

> [...] when leaders are healthy on the inside [i.e., have a character core] and operate with both high character and high courage, they have a positive influence and are constructive change agents.

Millennials, as leaders, are willing '... to take responsible risks and communicate authentically with their teams. This balance of character and courage is foundational to their confidence' (Bye, 2017, p. 27). Drawing on her Finnish ancestry, Bye (2017) used the word *sisu* to describe her own deeply embedded character core, which is about her '... internal strength, unapologetic perseverance, unwavering determination, and relentless courage to be proactive. It's beyond mental toughness' (p. 140). She quoted from the work of Emilia Lahti who is completing her PhD on the importance of the word *sisu,* especially its practice in people's lives:

> At its core is the idea that there is more strength to us than what often meets the eye. *Sisu* means to exceed yourself, take action against slim odds, and transform barriers into frontiers. It is the action mind-set of eating small nuisances for breakfast and diving into the storm even when there is no silver lining in sight. (Bye, 2017, p. 140)

Millennials, she claimed, have large reserves of *Sisu*, which is ideal for a future of great uncertainty and rapid change. They have the capacity to lean inwards '... in order to stretch their comfort zone' (p. 141) and thereby take courageous action in a topsy-turvy world. Bye claims that they already seem to have this core strength in some measure and it certainly fits with their world view. She pointed to the fact that Millennials will be the new star performers in our organisations in the near future, especially in launching innovative products and services but, she advised they will need strong mentoring and support because '... the world is undergoing a rapid shift, and millions of young adults struggle to find their footing' (p. 6).

Based on her research on this exciting group of young people with so much potential and promise, Bye identified three key leadership imperatives, which they have in abundance:

1. **Strengthen your character**: She claimed that '... character and virtue are at the core of who we are and guide all our decision making ... character development is [or must be] the highest priority for every leader';
2. **Lead with confidence**: Some leaders claim that Millennials are confident enough and that we don't need to address this topic with them but Bye believes otherwise and urges contemporary leaders to encourage and support them to develop their confidence in a safe environment; and
3. **Engage in collaboration**: She stated that while many may think Millennials are particularly strong in collaboration and teamwork, they will still have to grow and develop within cultures of diversity and disruption and leaders should model the way for them. (pp. 11–12, bold in original)

As leaders, Bye (2017) cautioned us to be careful about believing superficial generalisations about Millennials, which often ignore: '... the promising leadership potential that many possess' (p. 16). She claims that they're eager to build authentic relationships and they know the importance of really listening and valuing others. These young people, she concluded '... give me great hope for future generations' (p. 16). By the early 2020s, Millennials are going to '... drive our economy, and they will continue to do so for thirty years' (p. 17). They have a key characteristic that will serve them well in a global environment of uncertainty, rapid change and smart, high-speed, interactive technologies:

> They are digital natives and know how to leverage technology; they do not feel intimidated by breakthrough technologies, and they have strong digital connectivity for the global world, which has incubated them. (p. 17)

Sarros, Cooper, Hartican and Barker (2006) presented a similar leadership argument, based on their research on successful managers in Australia, when they advised that despite ever-changing technology and the rapid pace of globalisation:

> [...] the character attributes of exemplary leadership are timeless ... This becomes clear when you understand that leaders need to wear their character on their sleeves, and that the best character attributes are transparent, visible and actionable. (p. 11)

They concluded that leaders who exhibit strong character best serve their organisations, their wider community and themselves. A character trait of Millennials is that when faced with challenges and choices they usually choose to do the right thing.

Espinoza and Uklega (2016), in their book on *Managing Millennials*, concluded that their traits are generally shared across their generation and they are more alike than any other generation before them, due in large part to rapid advances in connective technologies that facilitate them in sharing more experiences together. They recommended that leaders now and into the future need to actively attract and retain these high-performing workers with very different values and expectations from previous generations. In an article on Millennials in the *NHRD Network Journal* (October 2011), Espinosa stated that because of their high-level technology skills, they can be regarded as *glocal*, meaning '… what happens globally is local for them' (p. 4, italics by this author for emphasis). They tend to do things differently and current leaders, therefore, need to suspend the biases of their own experience. Espinoza and Uklega pointed out that successful managers of Millennials have particular characteristics that fall within three behavioural categories: 'adapting; communicating; and envisioning' (p. 6):

> *Adapting* is the willingness to accept that a Millennial employee does not have the same experiences, values, or frame of reference that you had when you were the same age;

> *Communicating* refers to their ability to make a connection at a relational level … it is about staying engaged even when both parties are frustrated; and

> *Envisioning* is about lifting the horizons among the unmotivated and myopic. In practice, envisioning entails connecting employees' personal goals and aspirations with the organisation's objectives.

This is valuable advice for educational leaders who have increasing numbers of Millennials on their staff. They need to understand that Millennials are not merely responders to situations and circumstances; they are proactive, step-up *trans-formers* of circumstances and situations. A step-up transformer receives a low voltage and converts it into a higher voltage; in organisational settings, they are people who add value to the circumstances in which they find themselves. They inspire others to higher levels of aspiration, motivation and performance. They are creative, spontaneous improvisers who learn to 'dance' through times of uncertainty and rapid change, just as jazz players learn to improvise, and free-form dance companies learn to dance with no planned steps or moves. Millennials tend to see positive patterns and opportunities in challenging situations while others may see them as extremely problematic and confusing.

A refreshing understanding of leadership in complex organisations is emerging suggesting that Millennials, and teens in general, know and appreciate its subtleties, complexity and opportunities, and they will dance gracefully with it; their dance will be spontaneous, creative and involve step-up transformations. Millennials and the generations following them will have the creative foresight and interpersonal skills to achieve what many of us in this and previous generations have failed to accomplish – reducing complexity to simplicity (Bodell, 2017; Fullan,

2008), thereby helping create a future full of potential, promise and extraordinary performances.

A word of caution, however, is worth noting. Leaders and mentors will need to be careful that their advice and guidance to upcoming generations, especially Millennials, is not seen as patronising, because '… millennials don't want to feel like projects for the previous generation to fix, in part because [they] often feel like the previous generation is the one that needs fixing' (quotation from a Millennial respondent in Bye's research, 2017, p. 20). Bye advised that, 'millennials want to be with honest, authentic leaders, favour trusting and transparent relationships with their superiors [but] they don't like this latter term' (p. 20). She advised leaders to '… open your eyes, ears, and heart to see who are the up-and-coming leaders in your sphere of influence who might be open to a relationship with you' (p. 21). To be successful, contemporary educators and educational leaders need to be sensitive to the emerging realities of Millennials and other upcoming generations and learn quickly how to get the best from them, because they are not going away. They are here to stay and they will be around much longer than we will. Millennials' emphasis on character strength, ethics, morality, respect and honesty in relationships, seem to be reflected in societal expectations for leaders in our contemporary society, especially as a result of recent leadership failings in many countries. We will discuss these expectations in the following chapter.

Chapter 4

Societal Support for Ethical, Moral and Authentic Leadership

Our leaders are increasingly expected to commit to and demonstrate ethical and moral standards in their practices and relationships but a problem is that they do not always embody and live up to these standards; this can lead to feelings of cynicism from colleagues, stakeholders and the general public. Too many leaders present the rhetoric of ethical and authentic practices but the reality, as perceived by many in their organisations and outside of them, is that when the pressure is on they tend to lose their way. There appears to be a general scepticism in the community about the sincerity and credibility of leaders in some of our private and public organisations and in public life generally. Many of them have come under the ethical microscope in recent decades and politicians, generally, are on 'the nose' as are CEOs and managers of many companies that are household names. The ethical turmoil during the global financial crisis (GFC) focussed criticism on many contemporary leaders.

The ethical, moral and legal failings of many industries and organisations before, during and after the GFC are well known and documented publicly. For example, Ireland, for years known as *The Celtic Tiger*, suffered disastrously from the greedy and morally bankrupt behaviours of many financial institutions, including major banks and other lending institutions. The unethical consumer deception policies and practices that triggered the collapse of *The Celtic Tiger* destroyed corporations and ruined the lives of hundreds of thousands of people. Similar trends occurred in a number of other countries. The collapse of large corporations, including banks and other financial institutions, such as, Anglo Irish Bank; Royal Bank of Scotland; HIH in Australia; Enron in the USA and others are also well documented and known to many people through print and the media.

A general consensus from these financial disasters was that cultures of greed, reckless practices in pursuit of quick financial returns, and the payment of astronomical bonuses to bank executives who gave very large unsecured loans to borrowers with no apparent means of paying them back, were at the root of the financial collapse for both financial institutions and individuals who borrowed

Leading Educational Systems and Schools in Times of Disruption and Exponential Change:
A Call for Courage, Commitment and Collaboration, 33–41
Copyright © 2020 by Patrick A. Duignan
Published under exclusive license
doi:10.1108/978-1-83909-850-520201005

more than they should have. All around, there was a lack of integrity and a failure to meet ethical and moral standards in transactions and relationships.

What did we learn from the GFC failings? The 2019 findings of the Final Report of the *Hayne Royal Commission into Misconduct in the Banking, Super-annuation and Financial Services Industry* in Australia seem to indicate that the answer to this question is: We didn't learn much at all. Headlines from *The Australian* Newspaper (5, 8–10 February 2019) indicated continuing ethical problems with banks, insurance companies and most financial services in Australia. Anna Bligh, Australian Banking Association Chief Executive, stated: 'This commission has put the entire banking sector under the microscope and this final report lays bare how banks have failed their customers and let down the Australian public' (*The Australian* Newspaper, 5 February 2019). The Hayne (2019) Report clearly suggested that lessons from the past (e.g. GFC) have not been taken seriously in Australia and, too often, ethical standards and leadership character were ignored.

It takes courage to develop and nurture strong leadership character and to support its emergence in others. Gail Kelly (2017), the first female CEO of one of Australia's largest banks, Westpac, was listed by Forbes in 2010 as among one of the most powerful women in the world. In her memoirs, *Live Lead Learn*, Kelly (2017) shared her wisdom on life and leadership, which included commentary on how she developed confidence and conquered her fears of leading a large international bank:

> Fear of failure, fear of being embarrassed, fear of being found wanting, of being socially awkward, of being thought to be stupid, of looking like you don't belong – these are paralysing fears. I have faced them and I have got better at staring them down. I have learned to ask for help and to willingly accept it. I have learned to be less perfectionist and less defensive. I have become more comfortable with my own judgements [but] it takes courage to back yourself. (p. 41)

Kelly's philosophy on courage in leadership provides us all with the wisdom we require, not alone for success in leadership but for a successful life. She claimed that:

> [...] as a leader, one has the responsibility to help others find meaning and fulfilment in their work. For me, this starts with being very clear on not just what the company is about and needs to achieve, but why it matters – in other words, the company's purpose. (p. 61)

A clear vision and purpose, she claimed, become beacons for others if one can '... bring them to life with stories and examples. [her motto is] Be authentic. Be transparent. Keep listening and learning' (p. 62).

Authentic leadership, she stated, requires purpose, courage and commitment and these requirements can be challenging in today's organisational context of uncertainty and rapid change where '... leaders are confronted with increasingly complex and interconnected issues'. Leading with courage is her catchword, and she encouraged all leaders to '... persevere when the pressure is on, to stand firm under fire from the naysayers, and to persist in what you believe is right' (pp. 91–92). She highlighted a number of lessons she learned from her journey as the CEO of a large international bank:

1. *Short-termism is a damaging drug*: She warned leaders to, '... beware of the insidious pressures that mount to deliver short-term results whatever the cost; they represent the slippery slope and are anathema to a culture focused on customers' (p. 105).
2. *Inculcate a 'both/and' philosophy*: Things that on the surface appear to be at opposite ends can, in reality, sit comfortably alongside each other and even reinforce each other (pp. 105–106).
3. *Resource allocation*: Always remember that the list of potential opportunities is always much longer than the list of initiatives that can be successfully delivered to conclusion (p. 110).
4. *One Team*: A 'One-Team' approach is different from teamwork. It involves everyone in the organisation thinking and acting as One Team – across silos, across hierarchies, people all pulling together to serve customers; they will never stand back and say, 'That's not my role' or 'That's not my fault' (p. 112).
5. *Relentless focus*: Leaders who are passionate about delivering results are never complacent. They bring a relentless focus to what they do. Day-in, day-out, they pay attention to the detail, celebrate the small wins and pivot quickly to where problems exist (p. 115, all italics by this author for emphasis).

Kelly reflected on her career and claimed that she has frequently met very successful leaders who would describe themselves as generous-spirited and kind. She regards kindness in leadership as a virtue and stated:

> [...] we need a lot more of this in the political sphere, across communities and in our day-to-day lives. It starts with a deep respect for others, and holding ourselves to a higher standard of behavior. (p. 127)

Quick and Platt (2015) provided similarly wise advice to leaders in times of disruption and change. Using research evidence from a variety of international organisations and industries, they indicated that values-inspired, virtuous organisations and their authentic leaders perform better than their counterparts who seek to win or achieve at all costs. Warren Bennis, the late great American leadership scholar, organisational consultant and author, widely regarded as a pioneer of the contemporary field of leadership studies, suggested in 2005 that the image of an effective leader as, 'Charlton Heston atop the mountain, a grand figure who dwarfs others' is a myth (quoted in Parks, 2005, p. x). He urged leaders to discover their authenticity and integrity in order to hear the '... underlying meanings and voices of others' (Parks, p. 115).

In a five-year study of corporate leaders and leadership, Jim Collins and his research team selected 11 'good-to-great companies' – those who had been good but became great – and contrasted them with comparison companies – good but not great – and they were '… surprised, shocked really, to discover that the leaders who turned a good company into a great one [were] self-effacing, quiet, reserved, even shy'. They concluded that they were not '… high-profile leaders with big personalities who make headlines and become celebrities', as was the case in many of the comparison companies' (Collins, 2001, p. 12).

Bill George (2003), former CEO of the very successful Medtronic Company and author of a ground-breaking book, *Authentic Leadership: Rediscovering the Secrets to Creating Lasting Value*, studied the quality of leadership in a large number of highly successful companies and concluded that an authentic, mission-driven approach to leadership '… works for all companies' (p. 68) and that '… authentic leaders know that only by pursuing their missions with passion and commitment can they create sustainable value for their customers, their employees, and their shareholders' (p. 70).

Successful leaders, according to Cain (2012), do not have to be dominating, hard-nosed extroverts. Based on her comprehensive research on introverts in life and work, including in leadership, she reported that Peter Drucker's conclusion – a management consultant, educator and author, whose writings contributed to the philosophical and practical foundations of the modern business corporation – that the most effective leaders had '… little or no charisma and little use either for the term or what it signifies' (p. 53). She reported that Agle (2006), based on a research study of 128 major companies in the USA, found that '… those considered charismatic by their top executives had bigger salaries but not better corporate performance …' (quoted in Cain, p. 53).

Cain concluded that '… contrary to the Harvard Business School model of hard-nosed leadership, the ranks of effective CEOs turn out to be filled by introverts' (p. 53). Research-based evidence from positive psychology also clearly indicates that positive authentic leaders inspire greater performances among all key stakeholders in their systems and organisations. It appears that authentic leadership approaches emphasise what '… elevates individuals and organisations, what goes right in organisations, what is life-giving, what is experienced as good, what is extraordinary, and what is inspiring' (Cameron, 2008, p. 3). All these researchers and authors are describing real, authentic behaviours and the good news for leaders appears to be that '… the majority of people follow a moral path, which orients them when no one is watching' (OECD, 2018b, p. 12).

Research evidence, therefore, supports the view that societal expectations support ethical, moral and authentic leadership values and approaches. In the next section, consideration is given to leadership philosophies and practices that can help shape ethical leadership within what is referred to as virtuous organisations.

Nurturing Ethical Leaders and Leadership within Virtuous Organisations

While leadership has been a major topic of research in traditional psychology for almost a century, the field of positive psychology, by contrast, while relatively young has a lot to offer the long-established field of leadership. Martin Seligman (2003) is credited with formally launching the science of Positive Psychology in his book, *Authentic Happiness*. He claimed that traditional practises of leaders tended to be problem-oriented, correctional and deficit-based (see Cooperrider & Whitney, 2005; Wooten & Cameron, 2010), but positive psychology has a different orientation in that it encourages and facilitates organisational members and leaders to maximise their interpersonal relationships and optimise organisational performance by creating the conditions that allow employees to thrive and flourish.

Within a positive psychology approach, a leader's role includes discovering the positive core in each employee in order to promote and support employee development. This approach encourages leaders to create workplaces that provide meaning and transcendence to their own lives, the lives of their employees and the lives of the broader community (Cameron, 2013). In this approach, the leader's role becomes one of creating '… enabling institutions' (Peterson, 2006, p. 275). Cameron, Bright, and Caza (2004) explored the nature of such enabling organisations when they focussed on defining and measuring '… the concept of organisational virtuousness and exploring its relationship to the performance of organisations' (p. 766). They claimed that:

> […] virtuousness is associated with what individuals and organisations aspire to be when they at their very best [and it produces] … moral muscle, willpower, or stamina in the face of challenges. (p. 767)

They concluded that:

> […] virtuousness in organisations … refers to transcendent behaviour of organisational members and such virtuousness … refers to features of the organisation that engender virtuousness on the part of all members.

A general definition of virtuousness includes individuals' actions, collective activities, cultural attributes and '… processes that enable dissemination and perpetuation of virtuousness in the organisation' (p. 768).

They identify three key dimensional attributes of virtuousness (italics in original):

1. *Moral Goodness*, which represents what is good, right, and worthy of cultivation. It is similar to Aristotle's idea of '… that which is good in itself and is to be chosen for its own sake' (p. 769).
2. *Human Impact* is associated with … human beings' individual flourishing and moral character, with human strength, self-control and resilience, and with meaningful purpose and transcendent principles' (p. 769).
3. *Social Betterment,* which extends beyond mere self-interested benefits; '… great organisations contribute to social betterment and they strive hard to be ethical in intent, processes, and outcomes. They foster the moral good not just redressing the bad or harmful' (p. 769).

The relationship between virtuousness and performance in organisations is a focus of much recent research. Cameron et al. (2004) concluded from their research on the subject that the association between virtuousness and performance is explained by two key attributes of virtuousness: (1) '... *amplifying* qualities, which can foster escalating positive consequences' and (2) '*buffering* qualities, which can protect against negative encroachments [because] virtuousness becomes self-reinforcing and it fosters resiliency against negative and challenging obstacles' (p. 770, italics in original). Based on their research in 52 organisations in the USA, Cameron et al. (2004) concluded that, '... when virtuous behaviour is displayed by organisational members and enabled by organisational systems and processes, the organisation achieves higher levels of desired outcomes' (p. 783).

Another important conclusion from their research was that a key characteristic of leaders in virtuous organisations is that they are authentic in intent, behaviours, actions, relationships and in their ethical choices. Authenticity in leadership is based on personal integrity, credibility, trusting relationship and a commitment to ethical and moral conduct (Duignan, 2012). Authentic educational leaders earn allegiance through authentic actions and interactions in trusting relationships and through the shaping of organisational structures, processes and practices that enshrine values in everyday practices and encourage collective action on the development of quality learning and teaching. Over two decades ago, Selznick (1992), in his ground-breaking book, *The Moral Commonwealth*, stated that authenticity '... is the experience of continuity and wholeness in thought, feeling, and moral choice' (p. 65) and it is derived from moral experience which forms the '... crucible within which enduring values are established and institutional learning takes place' (p. 37).

Authentic educational leaders are centrally concerned with ethics and morality and with deciding what is significant, what is right and what is worthwhile. (Branson & Gross, 2014; Duignan, 2012, 2014) Authenticity, however, is not about behaving like saints, or pious, self-righteous people, it is about ordinary everyday people who are credible, earthly, practical and, despite their human frailties, strive to be ethical, caring and conscience-driven in the real world. They don't always get it right but they try to live their values to the best of their ability; they make mistakes but they learn from them. They also enable the emergence of authentic and virtuous organisations where all members feel engaged and valued, within a sense of community.

Goffee and Jones (2015) focussed on the expectations of organisational members for their leaders and concluded that their key expectations for them were '... authenticity, significance, excitement, and community' (p. 191). They highlighted four key expectations:

1. *First and, above all, followers demand authenticity*. Followers want their leaders '... to show us who they are – to reveal some of their real human differences [and they] know inauthenticity when we see it' (p. 192, italics in original).
2. *Second, followers need to feel significant*. 'In simple terms, they need recognition for their contribution' (p. 192, italics in original).

3. *Third, followers need a sense of excitement.* 'At root, leadership involves exciting others to higher levels of effort and performance' (p. 194, italics in original).
4. *Fourth, followers want to feel part of a community.* 'Human beings are hard-wired for sociability – and desire solidarity. They have a deep-rooted desire to belong, to feel part of something bigger, to relate to others, not just the leader' (p. 195, italics in original).

Salicru (2017) emphasised that '... leadership is fundamentally relational ... it's a social process that emerges from the relational dynamics in organisations' (p. xxxix). In every organisation, he claimed, '... there is extraordinary capacity and untapped potential beyond what is immediately visible and obvious' (p. 4) [and] '... healthy and trusting relationships are critical to achieving extraordinary performance' (p. 11). Because leadership is essentially relational, a social process, that emanates from the dynamics of organisational life, effective leadership is, essentially, an influencing process and/or an influence relationship. Rost (1991) made a seminal contribution to this perspective on leadership when, in a major review and critique of definitions of leadership, suggested: 'if there are few other unifying elements to our collective thought about leadership, the notion of leadership as influence is one that clearly stands out' (p. 79).

Maxwell (2005) also concluded that 'the true measure of leadership is influence – nothing more and nothing less' (p. 4) and '... in leadership – no matter where you are in an organisation – the bottom line is always influence' (p. 13). Nixon and Sinclair (2017) claimed that for effective leadership to emerge:

> [...] influencing is pivotal [but] they also want to focus on enabling others [that is] ... encouraging and giving confidence to others to try new things, whether they are more junior, a peer or superior, or an external stakeholder or ally. (p. 86)

They concluded that '... great ideas and reforms fail because people don't know how to use subtle processes of encouragement and persuasion' (p. 86).

In recent years, the *Ethisphere Institute* has established itself as a global leader in '... defining and advancing the standards of ethical business practices that fuel corporate character, marketplace trust and business success'. In its Mission Statement, it states that '... integrity and transparency impact the public trust and the bottom line of any organisation' (*Ethisphere* mission Statement, 2018). Annually, it recognises publicly and in its international magazine, *Ethisphere*, the World's Most Ethical (WME) industry professionals who are committed to influencing business leaders and advancing business ethics as an essential element of business culture and performance. In the Quarter 2, 2017 edition of its magazine, it featured *the 2017 World's Most Ethical Companies* and introduced them by claiming that they '... outperform their peers when it comes to promoting ethical business standards and practices both internally and externally'.

In October 2015, this author attended the *Global Integrity Summit* (2015) at Griffith University, Brisbane, Australia. The focus of the summit was to provide participants with the opportunity to consider the role of integrity in relation to some of the most significant and pressing global challenges of this time. Representatives from business, government, academia, education, the media and community, attended and actively participated in lively debates on these challenges and their possible solutions. Professor Paul Mazerolle, Pro Vic-Chancellor of Griffith University, chaired the event and in setting the tone, focus and agenda for the summit participants, stated: 'The *Global Integrity Summit* provides a unique platform for engaging with inspiring speakers on topics with local relevance and global significance'.

The most insightful and provocative set of challenges for both leaders and their organisations came from Pavan Sukhdev in his keynote presentation. He is an environmental economist whose field of studies includes the green economy and international finance; the focus of his talk was on contemporary and future corporations. Pavan's specialist consulting firm helps governments and corporations discover, measure, value and manage their impacts on natural and human capital. Sukhdev (2012) presented a number of points from his book, *Corporation 2020: Transforming Business for Tomorrow's World*, in which he claimed that while there is an emerging consensus that all is not well with many of today's corporations, there are signs of hope and he laid out a new vision for tomorrow's corporations: one that will increase social equity, decrease environmental risks, while still generating profit. He devotes many chapters in his book to describing what future business corporations will look like and ways in which current ones can transform themselves and still be profitable. In the final words of his book, he stated:

> The time has come to end all this waste and capital misallocation, and invest in a real future. We have to rebuild today's economy and transform it into a green economy, a sustaining economy which takes the poor out of poverty and delivers well-being to all, an economy of permanence. To do so, we urgently need to transform today's dominant Corporation 1920 model of business into *Corporation 2020*. (p. 235)

Bill George (2015), professor of management practice at Harvard Business School, in his research-based book *True North: Discover Your Authentic Leadership*, based on interviews with 172 leaders in the USA, argued that leadership is a journey that requires a special compass if it is to be authentic. To follow your true north, he says, means leading and inspiring others by mastering and sharing what is special and unique inside you and others. Educational leaders, for example, need to recognise that schools are living, complex and interconnected organisations that are required to forge a dynamic balance with their constantly changing environments. For example, some contemporary educators and educational leaders use the language of 'schools as communities of learning' but, too frequently, they think and act in hierarchical and bureaucratic ways, which does not facilitate the building of relationships, community and networks.

In addition, linear, hierarchical and bureaucratic leadership language and processes are likely to be found wanting when leading education systems and schools in times of disruption and rapid change. Leaders and educators also have to live and work with the increasing speed and impact of smart technologies within constantly changing organisational environments. This latter challenge is a focus in the next chapter.

Chapter 5

Successful Leadership within Technologically Smart Environments

The increasing pace and impact of smart technological changes will create disturbed and disturbing environments for many leaders, including educational leaders. Case (2016), *Co-Founder of America Online* (AOL), identified three waves of technology and internet development that transform our work and our lives. The First Wave of the Internet, he claimed, was all about '… building the infrastructure and foundation for an online world' (p. 2). It was enabled by companies such as Cisco Systems, HP, Sun Microsystems, Microsoft, Apple, IBM and AOL '… who built the hardware, software, and networks that were the on-ramps to the information superhighway' (p. 2). Search engines like Google made it easier to access and explore huge volumes of information on the web, while Amazon and eBay became one-stop shops for a variety of goods and services.

At about this same time, Case reminded us, Second Wave developments emerged as social networking took off, quickly attracting over a billion users – Apple introduced the iPhone, Google the Android and '… a mobile movement was born' (p. 3). There was a huge surge in Internet usage because of the rapid adoption of smartphones, social media rapidly accelerated and a thriving 'app' economy developed. Successful companies, such as Snapchat and Twitter, became '… overnight sensations, requiring none of the partnerships and perseverance that had come to define the previous era' (Case, 2016, p. 43).

The Third Wave of the Internet, Case expects, will be defined not by the *Internet of Things* but by the *Internet of Everything*, and he suggested:

> We are entering a new phase of technological evolution, a phase where the Internet will be fully integrated into every part of our lives – how we learn, how we heal, how we manage our finances, how we get around, how we work, even what we eat. As the Third Wave gains momentum, every industry leader in every economic sector is at risk of being disrupted – that's the Third Wave – and it's not just coming, it's here. (p. 43)

Leading Educational Systems and Schools in Times of Disruption and Exponential Change: A Call for Courage, Commitment and Collaboration, 43–58
Copyright © 2020 by Patrick A. Duignan
Published under exclusive license
doi:10.1108/978-1-83909-850-520201006

In summarising his views on Third Wave disruptions, Case concluded that the time has now arrived:

> [...] when the Internet transforms from something we interact with to something that interacts with everything around us [this will mean that] everything we do will be enabled by an Internet connection [and] this process will lead to the transformation of some of the industries that are vital to our daily lives. (pp. 187–188)

He predicted that The Third Wave will '... reimagine our healthcare system and retool our education system' (p. 5).

He presented a number of possible implications of Third Wave disruptions for education. Emerging educational innovations, he stated, will:

> [...] harness the power of the Internet to expand access to learning. Emerging edtech startups have the potential to democratise learning, personalise it for each student, and offer more teaching, with greater convenience at lower cost. That isn't untethered futurism; it's happening now, in a growing number of schools, and we need to take the best approaches and scale them nationally. (p. 190)

These technological effects, when taken together, constitute what Gans (2017) called *Architectural Changes*, and he concluded that existing organisations can deal with rapid technological changes so long as they impact only specific components of their technology. He reported that when quantum jumps occurred in the business world, involving new architectures, new technologies and new logistical approaches, a need arose for substantial re-organisation of business models and modus operandi. It is likely, therefore, that emerging political, cultural, economic, contextual, architectural, technological, pedagogical and performance-oriented pressures on and in education will require substantial re-organisation, even transformation, of educational architectures, including structures, processes and, especially, pedagogies.

In recent decades, there have been substantial changes in the expectations placed on schools by politicians, policymakers, communities, education bureaucracies, and by discerning parents. At this point in time, many system and school leaders are struggling to respond positively and creatively to these challenges, partly because adaptation involves new learning and the development of capacities that prepare us for unfamiliar circumstances and environments. Unfortunately, more traditional leadership responses, based on experience of what was successful in the past, tend to be hardwired into both individuals and their organisations in order to maintain some sense of equilibrium, but this is not, necessarily, an effective response in a rapidly changing environment.

Drawing inspiration from the influential leadership work of Ronald Heifitz of Harvard University, Parks (2005) referred to leadership in a turbulent, uncertain and rapidly changing world as '... a call to adaptive work' (p. 1). She concluded that a critical challenge for today's leaders is to be capable off responding '... adaptively to the depth, scope, and pace of *change* that combined with complexity creates unprecedented conditions' (p. 2, italics in original). Central to this change and complexity are a number of emerging characteristics of educational contexts that will have considerable impact on policies and practices in educational systems and schools. These include:

1. increasing use of interactive technologies that enable connectivity of people and institutions like never before;
2. pressures for a pedagogical paradigm shift, including mindset changes, to respond to these new technological capabilities, as well as the changing learning needs of contemporary and future students;
3. an increasing evidence base for the positive power and efficacy of collective professional commitment and action in our schools; and
4. evidence of emerging architectural disruptions in education will require structural and pedagogical reform in system and school policies and practices, including leadership responses.

The nature of leadership required to encourage and support these architectural changes will also change; emerging, evidence-based models, as well as expert observation of highly effective leaders, indicate in such circumstances that values-inspired and socially-responsible leaders are more successful than those driven by hierarchical, bureaucratic and performance standards and outcomes (e.g. Goffee & Jones, 2015, 2016; Johansen, 2012; Kelly, 2017; Quick & Platt, 2015; Salicru, 2017; Stein, 2018; Sukhdev, 2012). During periods of disruption and great changes, a leader's life, according to Quick and Platt, represents '... a change cycle among change cycles' because disruptions accelerate, but it is possible for educators to keep up with disruption and '... even better – to generate *life* in the middle of it' (p. 235, italics in original).

It will be a major challenge for educational leaders, not just to have a life (balanced or otherwise) but to generate a meaningful life when their lives become '... an expression of flux' (p. 235). In order to survive, and preferably flourish, in a context of exponential change, Goffee and Jones (2016) recommended that organisations '... rediscover their moral purpose', and their *raison d'être* (p. 5). Drawing on a global survey of employee engagement by *The Hay Group* (2012), they claimed that the best organisations create environments where all stakeholders are connected and engaged and, as a result, they '... outperform firms with the most disengaged – by 54 percent in employee retention, by 89 percent in customer satisfaction, and by fourfold in revenue growth' (Goffee & Jones, 2016, p. 11). In a world-wide research project conducted by Goffee and Jones (2016), in which they asked organisational workers what their ideal organisation would look like, respondents highlighted a number of workplace imperatives:

Difference: They stated: 'I want to work in a place where I can be myself, where I can express the ways in which I'm different and how I see things differently' (p. 12). If leaders get this right, they found that the reward is '... higher levels of commitment, innovation, and creativity' (p. 14).

Radical honesty: Respondents clearly indicated that: 'I want to know what is really going on …' (p. 12) but I feel many professional communications '… remain stubbornly connected to an old-world mind-set in which information is power and spin is their skill … their imperative should be to tell the truth before someone else does' (p. 15). They recommended a culture of trust and honesty that '… fosters loyalty, pride, and trust among employees' (p. 52). They reported: '… the organisations we most admire, don't do "spin"' (p. 54) [because] 'spin backfires' (p. 55).

Extra value: Respondents claimed: 'I want to work in an organisation that magnifies my strengths and adds value for me and my personal development' (p. 12). Goffee and Jones (2016) concluded: '… our research shows that high performance arises when individuals all over the organisation feel that they can grow through their work – adding value as the organisation adds value to them' (p. 15).

Authenticity: The respondents stated: 'I want to work in an organisation I'm proud of, one that truly stands for something' (p. 12).

Meaning: Respondents wanted their day-to-day work to be meaningful (p. 12).

Simple rules: Respondents said they didn't want to be hindered by 'stupid rules' or 'rules that apply to some people but not others' (p. 12).

Goffee and Jones (2015) concluded that ideal organisations '… stand for something real' and emphasise the centrality of '… respect, integrity, communication and excellence' (p. 101). They summarised their research findings:

> What the respondents in our research have asked for are organisations where they can be themselves, know the truth, grow, believe in the purpose, and be given the freedom to pursue it. (p. 198)

In another inspiring book on leadership, *Why Should Anyone Be Led by You: What It Takes to Be an Authentic Leader*, Goffee and Jones (2015) reported that in an organisational context '… authenticity manifests itself in context and in relationships with others. It is never solely an attribute of individuals' (p. x). They claimed that '… throughout, the focus of our research has been on leaders who excel at inspiring people – leaders who succeed in capturing hearts, minds, and souls' (p. 2). They stated that a key foundation of leadership is that it is relational and influential leaders are '… actively and reciprocally involved in a complex series of relationships that require cultivation and nurture' (Goffee & Jones, 2015, pp. 14–15). A key conclusion from this research is that organisational workers, above all, '… look for leaders who are authentic [and] without it, there can be no significant investment of trust on either side' (p. 15). As well, their research indicated: '… our central contention [is] that leadership is *situational, nonhierarchical, and relational* … what's required of leaders will inevitably be shaped by context and relationships' (p. 204).

In his book on leadership, *Leaders Make the Future*, Johansen (2012) emphasised that leaders, especially in times of disruption and rapid change, need to be open and transparent in their engagements and relationships. Transparency, he stated, involves authenticity and trust and '... it also allows followers to see in their leaders not only a bit of themselves but also that which makes them aspire to be more' (p. 128). He noted the prestigious *Centre for Creative Leadership's* (in USA) belief that '... more than ever before, successful leadership hinges on learning agility and the experience necessary to navigate and lead others through complex situations' (p. 128). In such circumstances, leaders need to be open, trustworthy, firm but empathetic, attending to what really matters and '... leading the way' (p. 128).

From their research into the nature of workplaces in contemporary organisations, Goffee and Jones (2016) concluded that the most motivational, inspiring and ideal work places are '... constantly striving for and trying to live up to the ideal, and their efforts at building authentic organisations are often inspirational' (p. 11). They claimed that leaders in organisations today '... confront a world of complexity and diversity, where old certainties are shaken to their core [and] old assumptions about employment and careers no longer hold' (Goffee & Jones, 2016, pp. 5–6). Established assumptions, 'facts' and received wisdom, will have to be challenged, critiqued and revised depending on unfolding events and circumstances.

Leaders in an accelerating world of change need to question the relevance of their received wisdom and their taken-for-granted assumptions. An internationally renowned geneticist, Arney (2016), in her scholarly book, *Herding Hemingway's Cats: Understanding How Our Genes Work*, cautioned readers and leaders about the dangers of accepting some received wisdom. She wrote that, according to legend, Ernest Hemingway was once given a six-toed cat – known as Hemingway's cat – by an old sea captain and her unusual descendants roam around the writer's Florida estate to this day. She reported that while attending a scientific conference at the Royal Society in London, a lecturer pointed at a large cat on the screen behind him and said:

> This is Hemingway's cat ... They have six toes – they're polydactyl. Ernest Hemingway was said to be fond of them, and they still live on his estate in Florida today. And here – he poked at the computer, changing the slide to one covered with photos of misshapen human hands – are polydactyl children with extra digits. It's the same genetic mistake that causes them. (p. 9)

Arney claimed that '... looking at a six-toed cat or six-fingered human, a natural assumption might be that it's due to a fault in a gene. But it's not'. During her explorative journey into the oft expressed phenomenon of Hemingway's six-toed cat, she wrote:

> [...] I've certainly felt like I've been herding cats – grasping after slippery ideas and trying to pin down concepts that wriggle and shift as new data come to light. Things that I thought were solid fact have been exposed as dogma and scientific hearsay, based on

little evidence but repeated enough times by researchers, textbooks and journalists until they feel real. Ironically, even the story of Hemingway cats seems to have been an invention, told time and again by tour guides at the writer's home until it became the truth. (p. 259)

She reported that a Hemingway scholar, James Nagel, claimed the writer didn't have cats when he lived at his estate in Florida, as his wife preferred peacocks instead. She emphasised that what has been accepted as fact seems to have turned into a conundrum!

In education, we have our preferred assumptions and beliefs about the nature of teaching and learning and many have become solidified as unquestionable facts after many years of repetition in our professional conversations and practices. Perhaps we need to revisit many of our accepted assumptions about learning, teaching, educational leadership and place them under closer scrutiny. The architecture of schooling, originating in the industrial age, which has lasted for over 150 years, needs careful interrogation and analysis with a view to its transformation. There is much accepted wisdom on the nature of teaching and learning that requires similar attention. I have done so throughout this book but, especially, in the final two chapters.

In an attempt to avoid relying too heavily on received wisdom and taken-for-granted assumptions based on our experiences of a world that is fast disappearing, an argument based on finding antidotes to disruption and change is presented in the next section. The gist of this argument is that assumptions and ideologies are simply ideas, often disguised as science or philosophy, that purport to explain the complexity of the world and offer remedies that will improve, even perfect it. Ideologues, according to Peterson (2018), are people who pretend they know how to make the world a better place before they've taken care of their own chaos within.

Finding Antidotes to Disruption in Our Lives and Work

In 2018, the Canadian international scholar, clinical psychologist and best-selling author, Jordan B. Peterson published a an influential book, *12 Rules for Life: An Antidote to Chaos*. This is a book on the human condition to answer his own question: 'What are the most valuable things everyone should know?' (p. xxvi). In his earlier book, *Maps of Meaning: The Architecture of Belief* (1999), he posited the view that deeper meanings of life for us as a human species tend to be moral in their intent and mostly people-oriented. While Peterson's books are controversial, his insights on personal, interpersonal, and collective, group or community change, are especially useful for educational leaders and teachers involved in change to better understand and deal with the disruptive and chaotic nature of the contemporary world.

He claimed that in a time of uncertainty and rapid change, educators must understand: '… how human beings and the human brain deals with the archetypal situation that arises whenever we, in our daily lives, must face something we do not understand' (Norman Doidge in the *Foreword* to Peterson's (2018) book, p. xiii). Peterson believes that:

> [...] no matter how different our genes of life experiences may be, or how differently our plastic brains are wired by our experience, we all have to deal with the unknown, and we all attempt to move from chaos to order. (Doidge, in *Foreword* to Peterson's (2018) book, p. xiv)

Doidge emphasised that Peterson is careful to warn the unwary to be cognisant of the ideology underpinning '... most plans or approaches to change our and others' behaviours' (Doidge, in *Foreword* to Peterson's (2018) book, p. xiv). As educators and educational change leaders we can benefit from Peterson's cautioning words.

In his predictions about *The Fourth Way of Educational Reform* (2009), Hargreaves paralleled Peterson's views on how human beings should act in times of uncertainty and change when faced with challenges they do not fully understand. He suggested that this *Fourth Way of Reform* is '... strategically driven not by markets and bureaucracy but by renewed professionalism and active democracy [and it] is defined by inspiration, innovation, social justice and sustainability' (p. 29). He enumerated a number of implications and likely directions for this approach that are instructive for educational leaders, reformers and teachers:

- Policymakers will have to concede that innovation and creativity require different, more flexible conditions of teaching, learning and leadership than those that have prevailed in the era of test-driven and data-obsessed educational reform (pp. 29–30).
- Educators will need to learn once more how to spread innovation through networks, relationships and interaction (p. 30).
- Teachers will gain key insights and learn more by going outside their own classrooms and connecting with other teachers and schools (p. 30).
- Millennial generation leaders with their characteristic '... more swift, assertive, direct, team-based, task-centred and technologically savvy leadership styles, will bring about the classroom and organisational transformations necessary for 21st century schools' (p. 31).

In the concluding paragraph to his Monograph, Hargreaves summed up his major views on educational reform:

> The inspiring future of Fourth Way reform lies in less bureaucracy and more democracy; in collaboration more than competition; in innovation and inspiration, more than data-driven intervention; in the fear factor giving way to the peer factor as the driver of school reform ... Our better future lies in a hopeful vision of a more just world that we can create together, rather than a swift

and superficial one that will distract us, or a greedy and fearful one that will control and eventually destroy us. This is our fragile world. This can be its future. Now is our moment of choice. (p. 32)

Throughout the literature on educational change there is a perceptible emphasis on the need for leaders to focus more on the people involved in the change processes than on the change itself. Wilson (2018), in *The Human Side of Changing Education*, reminded educational leaders and reformers that it takes considerable time to achieve real changes, advising that it '… is generational work' (p. 106). An emphasis on people – character, authenticity, relationships and interrelationships – instead of on systems, strategies, plans, data and logically ordered change processes, are identified and recommended as keys to effective, long-term reform in organisations.

The contributions of Peterson, Hargreaves and Wilson have just been summarised, but many more researchers and experts on leadership discussed throughout this book reinforce this perspective, including, among others, Quick and Platt (2015), Johansen (2017, 2012), Salicru (2017), Goffee and Jones (2015, 2016) and Fullan (2011).

Based on the depth and spread of research literature on the characteristics of educational reform and transformation, including that of Schleicher's comprehensive OECD Report (2018) on countries that have had considerable success in achieving such transformations, success is usually credited to the people involved – those leading it and those who are to be transformed. While this seems obvious, too frequently, this crucial point is forgotten by educational policymakers and change leaders because they focus too much on the nature, processes and mechanics of change itself. It is important to remember that even technology change is really people change. While we may talk of the potential for interactive and connected technologies to change education – and they do provide us with the capacity to interact and connect – it is real people who connect and interact. There is no interactive technology without connected and interactive people.

If we wish to reform and transform education, we must start with the people who will reform and be reformed by understanding their needs, desires and what is likely to inspire and drive them. We must ask 'Why' questions: Why do they want to change others? Who do they want to reform? Why would those being reformed agree to be reformed? How will we know when they are reformed? Simply put, reform is all about people, first, second and always! Any attempts to reform school systems, schools, teachers or students must start with a consideration of these key questions and a willingness by policymakers and reform leaders to question themselves about their own leadership paradigms, beliefs, especially their mindsets, and reform them if necessary.

One of the most important researchers, scholars and writers on the topic of mindset change is the world-renowned Stanford University psychologist, Carol Dweck (2016) in her book, *Mindset, The New Psychology of Success: How We Can Learn to Fulfil Our Potential*. She provided valuable insights into the nature of personal and collective change; she also provided advice that is essential for those attempting to lead educational change at any level. She explained in her introduction that '… changing people's beliefs – even the simplest beliefs – can have profound effects [and] guides a large part of your life' (p. 1). She stated that '… *the view you adopt for yourself* profoundly affects the way you live your life' (p. 6, italics in original) – this concept she calls mindset. She identified two general types of mindsets – a fixed mindset where people believe their personal characteristics and qualities are 'carved in stone' (a *fixed mindset*) and a *growth mindset*, where they believe that '… the hand you're dealt is just the starting point for development' (p. 7). This latter view '… is based on the belief that your basic qualities are things you can cultivate through your efforts, your strategies, and help from others' (p. 7). A growth mindset is necessary for learning improvement for students, teachers and leaders in education. Dweck's key point in her argument, which is central to our discussions and conclusions in this book, is that '… although people may differ in every which way – in their initial talents and aptitudes, interests, or temperaments – everyone can change and grow through application and experience' (p. 7).

Leaders and practitioners of educational change should be aware of and understand the implications and applications of Dweck's two mindsets because those with fixed mindsets tend to be more negative in their views of both the present and the future and are, usually, not optimistic that things will change for the better. They also tend to have negative views of themselves – their potential and capacity to influence and change others. Many people with fixed mindsets populate a variety of our systems and organisations, including educational ones. They are a challenge to change leaders as they, frequently, dig in their heels and show distinct preferences for the maintenance of the *status quo*.

On the other hand, leaders of educational reform will be more likely to succeed if a majority of their organisational members have a growth mindset (or are open to it) because they have strong beliefs in their personal and interpersonal capabilities, as well as in their ability to change themselves, others and, indeed, the world. The good news for us all from Dweck's conclusions is: 'You can change your mindset' (p. 14) and become a re-formed person. Leaders, themselves, in times of uncertainty and instability are advised to look at the world with new eyes, an open mind and develop the capability to think outside the current triangles and squares of leadership. In fact, Fullan (2013) and Perkins (2000) claim that leadership in such conditions requires the capacity to lead at and from the edge, which can require a mindset transplant for most leaders.

Fullan (2008) draws on Mintzberg's (2005) book, *Managers not MBAs*, to highlight the human dimensions of leadership:

> Leadership … is about energising other people to make good decisions and do other things. In other words, it is about helping release the positive energy that exists naturally within people. Effective leadership inspires more than empowers; it connects more than it controls; it demonstrates more than it decides. It does all of this by *engaging* – itself above all and consequently others. (Mintzberg, 2005, p. 143 in Fullan, 2008, p. 128)

Mintzberg's perspective on leadership helps simplify what is often treated as complex in leadership and, as Fullan (2013) claimed, '… when people learn from each other, everyone can gain without taking away from others' (p. 128). He states that educational leadership is, essentially, people leadership and he got down to its essence, its nitty-gritty, by referring to it as 'skinny leadership' (p. vi). He explained it this way:

> What's the skinny? It means give me the essence of something, the inside dope, not some convoluted or contrived explanation. You need the skinny when something is complex. The skinny is about rendering the complex actionable. (p. vi)

He used the concept of *simplexity* to describe his skinny leadership approach:

> As I use it *simplexity* means that there are a small number of key things you need to know and be good at (simple part) and then be able to create the chemistry and coherence with large numbers of people that make for effective outcomes (the complex part). (p. vi, italics by this author for emphasis)

Skinny leaders, he stated:

> […] maximise clarity of action in the face of complex situations while … never being totally sure that they got it right. But never mind, they are learners and get it right more times than not. (p. vii)

In the light of Fullan's skinny view of leadership, it could be argued that too many leaders in educational systems are stymied by and find it overwhelming to cope with 'the complex part' of leadership, and respond by justifying the *status quo*, use of lengthy approval processes, and too many rules (Bodell, 2017).

In examples of educational systems that have failed to realise the promises of their reform agendas, Fullan suggested that in recent decades:

> […] most of the administration's political energy has focused on structural reforms and accountability measures. What's missing – the complex part – is capacity building for all teachers and school leaders and ownership of the reform strategy. (p. 2)

From his research analysis and comprehensive knowledge of successful educational reforms across a number of countries – described in his 2013 book identified above – Fullan is in an informed position to provide advice to leaders on how to be 'skinny' and, thereby, maximise the outcomes of their reform initiatives. He advised that:

> […] the key to effective whole-system reform is the action of leaders – motion leaders who by definition mobilise the leadership of

others and end up being part of a system that is palpably on the move. (p. 9)

In a summary of key learnings from successful educational systems, schools and leaders, Fullan claimed that all the highly successful leaders he identified '... immersed themselves in the real excitement of accomplishment, always building capacity, avoiding complex plans, using data to pinpoint next moves, and mobilising the group to change the group' (p. 107). Their motto was, 'be proud of your wisdom and humble about what you might not know' (p. 108). In advice to would-be change leaders he stated:

> In the 21st century, to survive, it is getting to the point where *everyone* needs to think of themselves as a leader of their own destiny, and as we have made it clear [earlier] you better hitch your destiny to others in a collective effort to make things better for yourself and others ... leaders within education have a special, timely responsibility. The current system is just about bankrupt, with increased boredom of students and alienation of teachers.' (p. 109, italics in original)

While Fullan has been engaged in educational reform and the leadership of change in educational systems and schools in a variety of countries for at least four decades, with noteworthy success, he is very conscious of the fact that there is still a long way to go to achieve the type of transformation he wishes to see. This author has championed forms of leadership that encourage growth mindsets among teachers and students (e.g. from Dweck, 2016); human development perspectives focusing on the minds, hearts and souls of people in change (from Wilson, 2018); building personal and interpersonal capacity (from Fullan, 2013), as well as the ideas of numerous other change researchers, scholars and successful practitioners. The simplexity advice for educational leaders emerging from such sources is: constantly grow yourself – cultivate a growth mindset; collaborate with others; build collective capacity; and mobilise the group to change the group. Above all, educators need to constantly learn and grow to be the best and most accomplished persons and leaders they can be. They need to draw deeply on their own talents and those of others in their organisations and creatively envision and re-envision new and exciting ways to change the architecture of learning and to improve the creative skills of teachers and students in these times of uncertainty and rapid change.

Fullan's concept of motion leaders is reinforced in Wiseman's (2017) book, *Multipliers: How the Best Leaders Make Everyone Smarter*. She discussed 'the multiplier effect' (p. 10) of highly successful leaders and claimed that they:

> [...] invoke each person's unique intelligence and create an atmosphere of genius – innovation, productive effort, and collective intelligence [and] at the most fundamental level, they get dramatically different results from their people ... because they are

leaders who look beyond their own genius and focus their energy on extracting and extending the genius of others. (p. 10)

In the early 2000s, in an educational leadership workshop focusing on why so many hierarchical and bureaucratic organisations, including schools, have resisted change initiatives, a participant advised this author to read Gordon Mackenzie's (1996), *Orbiting the Giant Hairball*. Mackenzie's book intrigued me and gave me new insights and understandings of the multiplicity of ways in which the existing rules, norms, structures, expected behaviours, even extant values in many organisations, including schools, seemed to stifle creativity and initiative. He provided insights into ways leaders create cultures that promote and support unique intelligence and an atmosphere of genius, innovation and productive collective efforts. He likened most bureaucratic and pyramid models of organisation to giant hairballs and argued that while organisations require creativity to grow, learn and succeed, too often, even the most innovative systems and organisations, including schools, quickly become 'giant hairballs'. He described the organisation hairball as a tangled, impenetrable mass of rules, traditions, structures, processes and systems, all based on what worked in the past but which are now killing initiative and creativity.

For 30 Years, Mackenzie was a creative force in *Hallmark Cards Inc.*, an organisation which their customers believed was artistic and creative; on the contrary, Mackenzie used a description of Hallmark, given by George Parker Head of the Creative Division, as a 'giant hairball' (p. 29), a tangled web, even a mess, of 'hairs' that suffocated each individual strand. He explained that Hallmark's creative forces – they employed many creative artists and designers – were crippled because of '… a Gordian knot of Corporate Normalcy, i.e. conformity with the *"accepted model, pattern or standard"* of the corporate mindset' (p. 30, italics in original). Mackenzie concluded that the hairball of normalcy grows and grows in most organisations because:

> […] hairs are never taken away, only added. Even frequent reorganisations have failed to remove hairs, people sometimes; hairs, never. Quite the contrary, each reorganisation seems to add *a whole new layer* of hairs. The Hairball grows enormous. (p. 31, italics in original)

The trouble with corporate normalcy, he claimed, is that it:

> […] is dedicated to past realities and past successes. There is no room in the Hairball for original thinking or primary creativity. Re-synthesising *past* successes is the habit of the Hairball. (p. 31, italics in original)

All is not lost, he stated, for creative corporate individuals who live within or slightly beyond – in orbit around – the Hairball. He claimed that with a number of creative colleagues he avoided '… being sucked into the Hairball of Hallmark', a feat he accomplished by *Orbiting* (p. 32, italics in original). He defined orbiting as:

> [...] responsible creativity: vigorously exploring and operating beyond the Hairball of the corporate mindset, beyond *"accepted models, patterns, or standards"* – all the while connected to the spirit of the corporate mission. (p. 33, italics in original)

In such an orbit you should be able to '... benefit from the physical, intellectual and philosophical resources of the organisation without becoming entombed in the bureaucracy of the organisation' (p. 33). In this heady space, he claimed, he was able to discover his own uniqueness, while still establishing a dynamic relationship with many others in Hallmark. He explained further: 'Hairball is policy, procedure, conformity, compliance, rigidity and submission to *status quo*, while Orbiting is originality, rules-breaking, non-conformity, experimentation, and innovation' (p. 39). His book constitutes a critique of Corporate Hairballs and suggests creative and inspiring ways of finding your orbit around them.

While Mackenzie is playfully parodying corporate organisations in general, and Hallmark Inc. in particular, he also focused his analysis and recommendations on educational institutions, especially schools. He provided commentaries on his work with a large number and variety of schools across the USA and provided advice to school leaders, teachers and students on how to achieve orbit around those schools that qualify for the label 'Hairball'. In his conclusions, he encouraged all of us living in Hairballs to make every effort to discover our own uniqueness and support others to do the same. The journey into orbit, he says, begins with you:

> You have a masterpiece within you, you know. One unlike any that has ever been created, or ever will be. If you go to your grave without painting your masterpiece, it will not get painted. No one else can paint it. Only you. (Mackenzie, 1996, p. 224)

Another perceptive analysis on the leadership of reform – its success and failures – was presented by Perkins in his book, *Leading at the Edge* (2000). He provided a creative and perceptive analysis of leadership, drawn from the experiences of Shackleton's and Scott's exploits in Antarctica. Prior to a recent cruise to Antarctica (Christmas and New Year 2018–2019), the author of this book became more aware and appreciative of the exploits of key explorers to the sub-continent of Antarctica in the early years of the 20th century, especially those by Ernest Henry Shackleton and Robert Falcon Scott. A school principal friend recommended that I read the book because it covered similar leadership territory to what I am exploring throughout this book. Perkins, began his interest in 'leading at the edge' when he attended the United States Naval Academy as a member of the Marine Corps and from his experiences as a platoon leader in Vietnam. From his study of leaders and their teams facing life and death challenges in circumstances close to the '... physical limits of human endurance' in polar exploration, mountain-climbing expeditions, airplane crashes and shipwrecks, he identified '... ten leadership principles ... as critical factors that distinguish groups that triumph from those that fail' (p. xiv). Throughout his book, he discussed each principle against the leadership of Shackleton, who successfully saved himself and his crew when their ship, *Endurance*, was crushed in the ice, and Scott whose autocratic, indecisive and ill-planned decisions led to catastrophic failure and death for himself and his crew on his return journey from the South Pole. While Perkins' conclusions may be somewhat unfair to Scott and overly fair to Shackleton, his ideas are worthy of consideration as he describes in some detail the distinctions, in terms of advantages and disadvantages, of two different, even opposing views of leadership.

He claimed that Scott, in the tradition of a British Navy trained officer at that time, was impatient, not a team player and had '... severe deficiencies in his personal style and leadership abilities' (p. 87). For Shackleton, *leading at the edge* meant:

> [...] seizing every opportunity for decisive action and refusing to be discouraged when some efforts proved unsuccessful. The very act of doing something concrete creates a sense of momentum, and a series of small victories will lay the foundation for eventual success. (pp. 18–19)

Perkins claimed that leaders at:

> [...] *The Edge* need to be comfortable with the discomfort of risk. Unnecessary risks should be avoided, but there are also times for bold moves and it is necessary to understand the risks and evaluate them carefully. (p. 137)

It is crucial, he claimed, to balance risk and return, and have the courage to '... step up to those calculated risks that are worth taking' (p. 137). He goes on to say that:

> [...] the spirit of reaching for *The Edge* is one of exploration – of breaking new ground and pressing the limits. This process of exploration carries with it the inherent risk that your original mission [e.g., reach and return safely from the South Pole] will fail, or that it may have to be changed as a result of new discoveries [or challenges]. (p. 228)

There is much educational leaders and reformers can learn from the ideas and conclusions in Perkins' book.

Fullan (2008), an admirer of the creative leadership skills of Shackleton, quotes from Morrell and Capparell's (2001) book, *Shackleton's Way*, when comparing and contrasting the leadership styles of Scott and Shackleton:

> Scott ... was rigid and formal. For him the prize was paramount and his military training would have dictated that some loss of

life was inevitable ... Scott was dour, bullying and controlling; Shackleton was warm, humorous and egalitarian ... Scott tried to orchestrate every movement of his men; Shackleton gave his men responsibility and some measure of independence. Scott was secretive and untrusting; Shackleton talked openly and frankly with the men about all aspects of the work. Scott put his team at risk to achieve his goals; Shackleton valued his men's lives above all else ... Scott's men died. All of Shackleton's men survived the wreck of the ship, *The Endurance*, in crushing Antarctic ice, stranded twelve thousand miles from civilisation with no means of communication. (Morrell & Capparell, 2001, p. 36, in Fullan, 2008, p. 132)

As discussed in an earlier chapter, Bye (2017) – based on her research on the leadership potential of Millennials – claimed that they are constructive change agents, '... willing to take responsible risks and communicate and act authentically with their teams' (p. 27). She used the Finish word *sisu* to describe the key characteristics of Millennials, which comprise '... internal strength, unapologetic perseverance, unwavering determination, and relentless courage to be proactive' (p. 140). These are very similar leadership characteristics to what Fullan and Perkins recommend for *Skinny Leadership* and for *Leading at the Edge*. This appears to be what Shackleton actually did in life-threatening circumstances for both himself and his crew.

Bye's claims on the approaches of Millennials to leadership are similar to Fullan's and she predicts they will be star performers at all levels in their organisations; they will be at ease leading at the edge. They will attempt to change current negative or toxic cultures in schools and reform them by emphasising people's positive strengths (Morris & Garrett, 2010), as well as creating authentic interpersonal relationships and greater shared responsibility for the quality of learning and learning outcomes. They will not be confused or restrained by their organisational hairballs and will, without fear or favour, demonstrate perseverance, determination, courage and the capacity for taking action in difficult circumstances. They will transform barriers into frontiers and recreate structures and processes where needed, just as Shackleton did. Perhaps Bye is overly fulsome on the positive potential of Millennials in the future but it seems obvious that educational leaders in an uncertain and disturbed future will need to be leading at the edge.

In summary, reform leaders will need to ensure that they enhance the capacity for all teachers to embrace and accept ownership of the reform strategy and the processes to achieve it. They need to immerse themselves in the real excitement of building capacity by avoiding complex planning and mobilising the group to change the group. In the 21st century, it is getting to the point where all engaged in reform processes should think of themselves as leaders of their own destiny, and hitch themselves to others in a collective effort to make things better for themselves and others. As Fullan warned, the current system is just about bankrupt, with the increasing boredom of students and the alienation of teachers. Above all, leaders will need to constantly learn and grow to be the best and most accomplished leaders they can be.

We know that successful educational leaders in schools already create cultures that promote and support unique intelligence and an atmosphere of genius, innovation and collective efforts. While many bureaucratic and pyramid models of organisation may be giant hairballs, schools, as learning communities, require vision and creativity to grow, learn and succeed. This latter viewpoint is the focus in the next chapter.

Chapter 6

Schools as Vibrant Communities of Learning

> [...] Australia needs to review and change its model for school education. Like many countries, Australia still has an industrial model of school education that reflects a 20th century aspiration to deliver mass education to all children. This model is focused on trying to ensure that millions of students attain specified learning outcomes for their grade and age before moving them in lock-step to the next year of schooling. It is not designed to differentiate learning or stretch all students to ensure they achieve maximum learning growth every year, nor does it incentivise schools to innovate and continuously improve. (Gonski et al., 2018, p. ix)

This quote from Gonski et al.'s (2018) Report on *The review to achieve educational excellence in Australian schools* refers to the current state of education and schooling in Australia but, most likely, it applies to education in a number of other countries identified in this book. Gonski et al. stated that weaknesses in the current conditions for learning in Australia include '... inflexibility in curriculum delivery, reporting and assessment regimes and tools focused on periodic judgements of performance, rather than continuous diagnosis of a student's learning needs and progress' (p. ix). They claimed that progress on these challenges is thwarted by:

> [...] a lack of research-based evidence on what works best in education, the absence of classroom applications readily available for use by teachers ... multiple calls on the time of teachers and school leaders, and a lack of support for school principals to develop their professional autonomy and prioritise instructional leadership. (p. ix)

Earlier in this book, an evidence-based case was presented to support the view that in the future '... leadership will be much less centralised, more distributed'

Leading Educational Systems and Schools in Times of Disruption and Exponential Change: A Call for Courage, Commitment and Collaboration, 59–71
Copyright © 2020 by Patrick A. Duignan
Published under exclusive license
doi:10.1108/978-1-83909-850-520201007

(Johansen, 2017, p. x), and hierarchical and bureaucratic organisations will give way to shape-shifting organisational forms. Johansen advised that current and future leaders providing leadership during periods of extreme disruption will be required to embrace new organisational forms characterised by '… entangled networks that have no centre, grow from the edges, cannot be controlled [and] where hierarchies come and go' (p. 61). Changes in organisational forms, structures and capacity for connectivity is being revolutionised by the new digitally, super-connected, seriously disruptive force, called 'blockchain', a form of '… distributed computing that can track the status of autonomous objects and provide security *without centralised authority* … it is a tool for both efficient coordination and disruption' (p. 82, italics in original). Johansen concluded that 'distributed computing infrastructures similar to blockchain will [also] empower diversity' (p. 83), including '… diverse perspectives, diverse heuristics, and diverse predictive models' (p. 84).

These evolving organisational forms '… represent a digitally-connected 'commons' through which assets are shared for the benefit of all involved' (Johansen, 2012, p. 170). He claimed that this commons will require mutual trust and a greater shared, socially responsible approach to leadership, grounded in ethics and moral concerns. There are many positives for leaders within this distributed world so long as they regard change not just as disruptive but as presenting potentially renewing opportunities. Leaders will need to develop inquiring and inquisitive minds about ways in which taken-for-granted assumptions and received wisdom can be challenged and critiqued in their shape-shifting organisations. Currently, organisational cultures are, partly, built around received certainties and assumptions about people, relationships and roles, but these may no longer be relevant in an increasingly uncertain and turbulent environment. In such circumstances, educational leaders and their colleagues may need to suspend, even discard, many of their hard-fought-for assumptions about the way things have been in the past, even if successful, in favour of seeing people and change cycles as having potential for new creative energies.

Christine Nixon, Chief Commissioner of Victoria Police in Australia from 2001 to 2009 and leader of the Victorian Bushfire Reconstruction and Recovery Authority after the horrendous Black Friday bushfires of 2009, cautioned that it is especially risky to form fixed assumptions about people and to take for granted that you know what people want:

> […] one day soon after the fire emergency had passed, I came across an old woman wandering near the crowded chaos at the emergency relief centre. She looked shocked and bedraggled and her feet were bare and filthy with ash. 'We'll get you some shoes,' I told her in my most reassuring tones, dropping a comforting hand on her shoulder. 'Why?' she said, looking at me quizzically. I haven't worn shoes for twenty years.' Here was my lesson. Never assume you know what people want, or need. (Nixon & Sinclair, 2017, p. 67)

On the basis of the potential shortcomings of taken-for-granted assumptions and received wisdom, we can ask: Will the knowledge we possess about change and reform in an industrial model of education today be useful in a future of disruptions and exponential changes?

Wilson (2018) claimed that evolving from a traditional model of schooling, requires a cultural shift away from a narrow management model to one of '... self-efficacy and partnership' (p. 26). An acid test in school settings is:

> Do your students feel empowered to identify and solve their own problems or is there a culture of waiting for the teacher to both define and solve the problem? Do teachers and administrators feel empowered to define and solve their own problems or is there a culture of waiting for leadership to both define and solve the problem? (p. 26)

If leaders wish to support '... more creativity, collaboration, and appetite for risk in schools, then the organisational structures, systems, and processes must change, and change significantly' (Wilson, p. 32). She cautioned educational leaders, especially teachers, that if they wish students to be '... collaborative, creative, and self-directed learners, the system [or organisation] in which this work happens must reflect a collaborative, creative, autonomous culture' (p. 32). She emphasised that existing traditional industrial-era schools will be difficult to change and will require deep culture change if they are to be transformed into more '... flexible learning environment[s] that prepare our children for an unknown future' (p. 45). A key part of this transformation in organisational structures, systems and processes will be in the use of time and space to deliver quality teaching and learning, because:

> the industrial model has dictated the physical set-up of classrooms and the school schedule and, for many schools, the use of space and time has not changed much in the last one hundred years. (Wilson, p. 54)

Once substantial pedagogical reform starts, however, '... the constraints of the schedule and the space of the traditional classroom quickly become apparent as obstacles to deeper change' (p. 54).

While it is fair to say that many educators in a number of countries have changed and enlarged their learning spaces by introducing team teaching and personalised learning spaces in recent years, the overall traditional pedagogical mindsets of school leaders and teachers appear to have changed little, especially in secondary education. We continue to have: subject departments, too often operating competitively as silos; students still changing classrooms, frequently stopping at their lockers in hallways; and loud bells ringing periodically. A control model of teaching and learning is still evident in many schools. Despite intelligent attempts by well-intentioned leaders and teachers in many systems, schools and countries to reform the architecture of learning, it is still, for the most part, too piecemeal, disjointed and confusing. As Wilson (2018) stated so eloquently: 'there is no single model to follow when it comes to redesigning space and the schedule' (p. 54). She advised that 'it is important to start with the curricular and pedagogical priorities first, before rethinking and redesigning the use of time and space' (p. 54). In planning for such changes, she reminded school and system leaders that time use and schedules, as well as intelligent uses of pedagogical technologies which have parental and community implications, must have their support.

She directly addressed the role of technology in schools and queried the degree to which it is a disrupter for driving pedagogical change. Based on her substantial research on the use and impact of technology in schools conducted in 2015 for the *Woodrow Wilson Foundation* in the USA, she concluded that:

> [...] there is the semblance of schools moving into the 21st century with iPads and apps and big data. But scratch under the surface and a significant percentage of this 'innovation' is simply technologising the traditional system. (p. 91)

She queried the real impact of contemporary technology innovations on creative reform of teaching and learning, and suggested that:

> [...] any technology that helps facilitate the processes and procedures existing in the current system is a much easier sell than something that will disrupt the status quo and support a more creative – and risky – approach. (p. 91)

She advised that if educational reformers do not stop and think:

> [...] about the overarching outcomes [they] seek, then the default path is one of consumption, increasing isolation of the student, and reduced risk taking – aided and made more efficient by technology. (pp. 91–92)

She also warned that:

> [...] the overall pace of change is too slow and that too many innovations, in particular technology innovations, are not actually that innovative. A deeper change is needed and technology (alone) is not our saviour. (p. 92)

She recognised that:

> a new learning ecosystem is taking form and shape [but] the default of that shape, could become a technologised version of the industrial model because our [current] collective narrative of what 'school' looks like is so strong. (Wilson, p. 92)

Innovators, therefore, need to ask themselves, 'what needs to end?' because, in education we tend to add more and more to teachers' workloads without considering what their innovations should supplant or what should become redundant as a result of these innovations. She cautioned educational change leaders and reformers to be very aware of the magnitude of the task before them as it will be a major challenge '... to change a century-plus-old bureaucracy' (p. 92) and, she advised, we should not judge our progress '... based on quarterly results' (p. 106).

It is becoming increasingly clear to leaders of educational change that they must engage energetically with significant others to achieve creative educational reform in their innovative enterprises. Duignan and Cannon (2011) concluded from their research on building sustainable collective leadership in schools that '... sustainable leadership has a number of inbuilt principles that support collaborative and distributed leadership in schools' (p. 23). A key principle, they stated, is that sustainable leadership spreads; it sustains as well as depends on the leadership of others and they urged leaders of educational reform to use '... the power of many' (the title of their book). In his book, *Educational Leadership: Together Creating Ethical Learning Environments*, Duignan (2012) claimed:

> Leaders cannot do it all by themselves. They have to work with and through others to achieve their organisation's vision and goals. There is simply not enough time in the workday for one person to provide the scope and depth of leadership required in contemporary school communities. A principal encapsulated it when s/he said that, 'You have got to be a strong communicator and relationship builder. You have got to have the capacity to build relationships, to make connections, to build partnerships, to build strong alliances with others. (pp. 54–55)

When teachers, principals and system personnel engage together in collective improvement projects, they can create learning cultures that engage, inspire and nurture deep, rich student learning. Levin and Datnow's (2012) research findings emphasised the importance of simultaneous, collective and co-constructive engagement in order to amplify the influence of all those involved in pedagogical-improvement projects. They concluded that decisions made and actions taken in such projects must be '... appreciative of the complex, dynamic and connected world of schools as communities of learning' (Duignan, 2012, p. 192). Collaboratively inspired leaders create and nurture professional and collective processes when leading change for learning improvement and they achieve this by generating and facilitating school cultures energised by collective action and an ethic of collective responsibility.

From this perspective, educational leaders can encourage all key stakeholders, especially teachers, to embrace collective responsibility for the learning and well-being of all students in their fields of care. They can commit to collective and collaborative processes and actions that tap deeply into the core professional belief that teaching is, essentially, a vocation and a collegial one as well (Duignan, 2014). The research of Cameron (2008, 2013), Avolio and Gardner (2005) and

Walumbwa, Avolio, Gardner, Wernsing, and Peterson (2008) have enhanced our understandings of how leaders can create organisational cultures that promote and improve the well-being of all key stakeholders as well as the performance of individuals, groups and organisations. In educational leadership, there has been a focus, for some time, on creating a collective professional desire for school cultures that value collaboration and a committed collective sense of responsibility for the quality of learning and teaching, in order to make the most of change efforts that aim to transform the lives of young people in schools. (e.g. Bridges, 2009; Starratt, 2011).

It has become obvious in recent years that principals cannot be the only or primary driving force in such transformational reform initiatives. The increased complexity and multi-dimensionality of the principal's role, as well as its increasing responsibilities and accountabilities for learning outcomes, create the need for sharing and distribution of leadership, both within schools and across schools. An important OECD report, *Innovating to Learn, Learning to Innovate* (2008), focussed on how educators can build deep, rich, active and engaging learning environments, and its conclusions have many implications for school leaders and school leadership, now and into the future. The report claimed that an innovation's success is, for the most part, '… determined by the social interaction of group members through the successive stages of the change, especially its adoption and implementation' (p. 17). It is nowadays well recognised in relevant literature that school leadership practices should be distributed among a number of key individuals and groups. Harris (2002, 2006, 2009) emphasised that:

> while principals are undoubtedly an important source of leadership in schools there are compelling reasons to investigate other forms and sources of leadership [and] there is growing evidence to associate distributed forms of leadership with certain organisational benefits and student outcomes … (2002, p. 38)

While initiating collaborative leadership processes and practices in schools is a necessary innovation, it may be insufficient because sustaining it over time is a big challenge. Hargreaves and Shirley (2009) promoted the need to generate '… sustainable leadership that can build innovative professional communities [and] dynamic communities of distributed leadership' (p. 29), Scaffolded, sustainable and collaborative-leadership, they claimed, is further strengthened by deliberately building greater *depth*, *breadth* and *diversity* of leadership in a school. Having depth in leadership means, according to Davies (2006), that '… sustainable strategic change must affect the deep and underlying principles of the school's moral purpose and its learning imperative' (pp. 144–145). Having breadth in leadership, he explained:

> […] means not only spreading new ideas across the staff and students within the school [but also] extending the strategic vision, direction and understanding of strategic change across the wider school community of parents and those in the local community. (p. 145)

Such breadth of involvement increases the diversity of opinions and perspectives and leads to more informed, robust and greater-quality decision making. Greater involvement by a variety of stakeholders will lead to increased commitment to and ownership of reform decisions (Spillane, 2006). It has been long recognised in research and literature on educational change that it is wise to engage those affected by a decision or a change in its formulation, because those engaged in making key decisions about a change or development are more likely to be committed to its implementation.

Achieving sustainable collective leadership capacity in complex systems and schools, involves a re-visioning of the educational architectures of schools – that is, the structures, processes, time and space – for delivering education to students in an uncertain and rapidly changing world. School leaders are increasingly being held accountable for their own performance and that of the teachers and students under their care, and they are expected to comply with the highest ethical and moral standards in their relationships, practices and decision making. In recent years, their wise professional response is to work more collegially with key colleagues and stakeholders and use their gifts and talents to promote, support and sustain collective approaches to improving the teaching and learning landscapes in their schools.

A key question emerging from research findings reported throughout this book is: 'What approaches to leadership will best promote, support and sustain high quality learning environments and student outcomes in our schools?' Based on a widespread review of recent national and international reports on educational improvement for an uncertain future, there appears to be a view that we need to fundamentally rethink and redesign school leadership to be more inclusive, collaborative and distributed, especially if the desire is to build world-class communities of leaning. Fullan (2010) addressed this issue when he claimed that, currently, the missing link for system and school leadership is the:

> [...] powerhouse force of collective capacity building and efficacy [and] there is no force so durable and potent as a social force ... gale-force commitment occurs because peers commit to peers and hierarchies become flatlined in their interactions. (p. 71)

He concluded that 'collective capacity generates the emotional commitment and the technical expertise that no amount of individual capacity working alone can come close to matching' (p. xiii) and that collective capacity building in schools should have a specific educational-improvement focus. According to Sharratt and Fullan (2009), capacity building should be viewed '... as investment in the development of the knowledge, skills and competencies of individuals and groups to focus on assessment literacy and instructional effectiveness that leads to school improvement' (p. 8). In their description of systemic leadership capacity building in York Region District School Board, in Ontario, Canada, they highlighted four enduring understandings for systemic capacity building:

1. commitment to a shared vision and staying the course with a single priority – for example, numeracy or literacy;

2. knowledge of and resources for focused assessment linked to instruction at all levels;
3. strategic leadership emanating simultaneously and consistently from the centre and the field; and
4. meaningful engagement of parents and community. (pp. 9–10)

Educational leaders and reformers must take seriously this latter notion that schools are communities of learners and learning and put the leadership of learning improvement up front and centre. All stakeholders within a community of learning, including parents, should be able to participate in agreed and specified ways in leading that learning initiative, because when we tap into the multiple talents and potential of key organisational members, depth, breadth and diversity of leadership grows and flourishes. The challenges involved in building schools as communities of learners include the re-culturing of existing school cultures – a daunting challenge, especially considering the current power of industry models of leaning, hierarchical and bureaucratic paradigms of leading, teaching, learning and assessment.

Re-culturing is the most effective way to bring about lasting change in schools, because no permanent change will be embedded in a school until it becomes part of that school's culture (Degenhardt & Duignan, 2010). The heart and soul of a school's culture is its paradigm of learning and teaching. That is, what people believe, the assumptions they make about how schools work, and what they consider to be true and real. At the heart of every school culture is a belief system, a theory or paradigm and a learning paradigm that act as drivers of change. The history of change in education systems and schools is littered with improvement attempts that have stalled or been subverted because, too frequently, changes have been imposed from the top downwards, resulting in many people resisting them. Greater involvement by a variety of stakeholders in key decisions on curriculum improvement, as well as pedagogical and assessment reform can lead to the development of greater collective commitment and a deeper sense of ownership of these decisions.

The involvement and engagement of professional colleagues based on their ethical sense of professional responsibility is more likely to build a positive culture of trust where people feel valued, motivated and passionate about serving their students' needs. It also helps create energies and synergies that raise group members, especially teachers, up to higher levels of aspiration, inspiration, morality and performance. It involves an appeal to them to re-appraise their vocation, their calling, if they are falling short or avoiding their professional responsibilities. Educational leaders, including teachers, must always remember that parents entrust their precious children to their care so that they can help transform them as learners and as human beings. This is an awesome privilege but with such a great privilege goes important personal and professional responsibilities. Their vocation requires them to share their gifts, talents and expertise in the interests of their students and for the common good.

Building Collective Cultures of Responsibility in Schools

Within collegial learning environments, it is not sufficient for individual teachers to suggest that they take responsibility only for their own students, that is, those in their classroom(s); they must share responsibility for the quality of their school's learning and learning outcomes. An important question is: How can leaders help create and nurture school cultures that value collective responsibility for quality learning and enhance the collective efficacy of teachers? Changing structures, roles, processes, or simply distributing leadership tasks and responsibilities among key stakeholders are desirable, but it will not ensure that a collective sense of responsibility for quality learning and learning outcomes follows; motivating forces much deeper than these are required. A collective culture of responsibility emerges and flourishes when educators interrogate the very reasons they became teachers in the first place. Teaching has long been regarded as a vocation, a calling to serve students under their care; it is this sense of vocation that should fire their enthusiasm and make them passionate about being the best teachers they can possibly be. Teachers, need to constantly remind themselves that they are members of a very special and highly influential profession; their responsibility is to ensure that collegially they provide stimulating and inspiring learning opportunities and environments for all their students.

As discussed earlier in this chapter, schools are frequently described as learning communities and it is widely recognised in relevant literature that educational leaders, including principals, leadership teams and teachers, more effectively influence the quality of learning environments and learning outcomes when they work closely together in teams as connected communities of learning (Darling-Hammond, 2010; Dinham, 2009; Duignan, 2012; Fullan, 2011; Robinson, 2008). There are many educational processes that educational leaders engage in to positively impact the quality of teaching, learning environments and learning outcomes and it is important that they understand the ways in which this influence occurs and can be enhanced. As far back as 1992, Senge pointed out that leadership involves:

> [...] seeing circles of influence rather than straight lines [where] ... every circle tells a story. By tracing the flows of influence, you can see patterns that repeat themselves, time after time ... From any element in a situation [e.g., teacher feedback or direct instruction], you can trace arrows [e.g., relationships] that represent influence on another element [e.g., learning environment or student outcomes]. (p. 75)

If we treat schools as self-generating and fluctuating networks of communications within dynamic learning communities, then we need to '... break with simple cause-and-effect models, linear predictability and a dissection approach to understanding phenomena, replacing them with organic, non-linear and holistic approaches' (Morrison, 2002, p. 8). Fullan (1999) claimed that in educational systems and schools:

> [...] the link between cause and effect is difficult to trace, that change (planned and otherwise) unfolds in non-linear ways, that paradoxes and contradictions abound and creative solutions arise

out of interaction under conditions of uncertainty, diversity and instability. (p. 4)

An important implication of Fullan's perspective is that leaders in educational systems and schools need to think, plan and act in non-linear as well as in traditional linear ways when building their feedback loops on improvement processes for students' learning and achievement. In numerous successful examples of learning communities from Canada and the USA, he concluded that their leaders '... employ the collaborative', and use '... the power of collective capacity' (Fullan, 2011, p. 9). He stated:

> The collaborative, sometimes known as professional learning communities, gets these [excellent] results because not only are leaders being influential, but peers are supporting and pressuring each other to do better. (p. 9)

In their ground-breaking book, *Breakthrough*, Fullan, Hill, and Crévolla (2006) argued that when leading educational reform, the leadership challenge '... is not simply a job of alignment, but rather one of establishing dynamic connectivity among the core elements' (p. 15).

In his book on leadership, *The Power Paradox*, Keltner (2016) provided a creative example of Charles Darwin's ways of working as an example of the power of collective influence. He argued that '... an individual's capacity for influence – power – is found in ordinary actions tailored to specific contexts that advance the group's interests' (p. 35). He stated that Charles Darwin collaborated with a wide variety of people, through his letters, when developing his revolutionary theories on evolution and explained that:

> Darwin's writings are an expression of many people's ideas from all walks of life. What appears to be an influential act of an individual typically will prove to be a collaboration of many minds, the action of a social network (Keltner, p. 36) [and] our everyday actions within social networks can be catalysts of influence and social change. (p. 39)

Successful collaboration, Keltner claimed, largely depends on '... your ability to empower others [and] on their willingness to be influenced by you' (p. 43). He advised that the key to enduring influence is to:

> *stay focused on other people. Prioritise other's interests as much as your own. Bring the good in others to completion, and do not bring the bad in others to completion. Take delight in the delights of others, as they make a difference in the world.* (p. 71, original in italics)

Corporate-managerialist approaches to educational leadership, often evident in many schools, mostly fail to transform educational environments and the quality of teaching and learning outcomes, mainly because educators and educational leaders '... have a very different set of values from those who focus on corporate life' (Gross & Shapiro, 2005, p. 2). In educational systems and organisations, leaders are accountable, not to shareholders but to stakeholders who are, essentially, students, their families and their communities. Gross and Shapiro stated that '... *while business is transactional* ... [educators'] *work is transformational*' (p. 2, italics in original). The efforts of many influential educational leaders are transformational insofar as they promote and support positive and enlightened cultures of teaching and learning and they bring their deepest principles, beliefs, values and convictions to their work. These principles and beliefs point the way towards more co-responsible form of relationships and actions, which encourage leaders to act with the good of others, for example, students, teachers and parents, as a primary reference point.

Educational leaders would be advised to respond to Starratt's (2004) challenge of transforming students each day into something special and something that enables their human spirits to soar, so that their actions are so inspiring and uplifting that their schools become flourishing places for students, parents, teachers and all key stakeholders. Seligman (2011) suggested that:

> [...] happiness, flow, meaning, love, gratitude, accomplishment, growth, and better relationships constitute human flourishing [and that] learning that you can have more of these things is life changing. Glimpsing the vision of a flourishing human future is life changing. (p. 2)

In his terms, educational leaders, especially teachers, have the potential and capacity to create flourishing schools that are life changing!

Salicru (2017), an Australian business psychologist and international management consultant, focussed much of his research and leadership advice on enabling organisations to build the leadership capability and learning agility required to achieve their strategic goals by creating cultures of high engagement, collaboration, innovation and high performance. In his recent book, *Leadership Results*, Salicru (2017) pointed out that leadership is, essentially, a relational, collective activity using integrity-driven engagement to encourage extraordinary performances to achieve breakthrough results. Based on his comprehensive research on how to create adaptive leaders and high-performing organisations for an uncertain world, he concluded: '... the most valuable thing my 25 years' experience has taught me is that relationships and integrity used in coordinated collective action have a unique power to achieve the extraordinary' (p. xxxi). He claimed that trust is critical to establishing communal cultures, it is central to the degree of confidence team members have in you: '... trust involves team members' willingness to make themselves vulnerable and be open, and confidence that you will consider their interests in their absence' (p. 93). He stated that a key characteristic of effective collective leadership is that it is relational, enabling '... everyone to be active in leadership roles as it flattens hierarchical workplace structures' (p. 189); such empowered leaders are '... motivated, believe in their ability to perform successfully, and are also more creative' (p. 191). Salicru claimed that collective leadership, when implemented properly, '... benefits everyone, allows for more innovation, allows organisations to adapt to change quickly, and delivers outstanding performance and results' (p. 201).

Educational leaders whose aim is to create collective professional cultures that nurture and celebrate outstanding performance and results can gain useful insights from Salicru's work. From his extensive research in a number of large international business organisations, Salicru identified key benefits of collective leadership which can apply, equally, to educational systems and schools. These include:

1. It helps break down silos.
2. It increases social capital and knowledge sharing.
3. It dissolves power structures and bureaucracies that obstruct change.
4. It promotes collective responsibility and mutual accountability.
5. It creates higher levels of commitment and engagement.
6. It produces unprecedented levels of performance and business or community results. (p. 197)

These are substantial claims but he has supported them using research results and actual examples from real-world organisations – he uses the example of the New Zealand All-Blacks Rugby Team – as an organisation that is totally committed to collective leadership or, as he calls it, '... leading from the back seat of the bus' (p. 199). He explained that the All Blacks' culture, including their leadership paradigm, is largely responsible for '... an extraordinary 75 percent test match winning record over a 100-year period' (p. 198). The key to their continuing success, he claims, is the '... presence of strong senior collective leadership in the team' (p. 199). This collective model of leadership has:

> [...] instilled a commitment to honesty, team evaluation, and reflection ... the bottom line was that in the All Blacks' organisation, at any time, there was somebody ready and willing to step up for the collective benefit of the club. (p. 199)

Importantly in today's performance-driven times, Salicru pointed out that collective leadership, implemented properly, '... benefits everyone, allows for more innovation, allows organisations to adapt to change quickly, and delivers outstanding performance and results' (p. 201). This would seem to be the aspiration of a majority of educational leaders at all levels.

In his book on the extraordinary vision and success of Elon Musk of Tesla Motors and SpaceX fame, Ashlee Vance (2015), championed contextual and collective leadership approaches and processes for leaders in uncertain times. He concluded that '... leadership does not take place in a vacuum: you must be yourself in context. Great leaders are able to read the context and respond accordingly' (p. 20). In responding to uncertainty '... they practice and hone their context-reading skills and realistically appraise their ability to rewrite that context' (p. 83). They '… work with their followers to socially construct an alternative reality' (Vance, 2015, p. 89). Referring to the power of groups, he reminded leaders that relationships represent '… the square of the number of the group – and thus the complex social structure of the group itself' (p. 99). He concluded that:

> [...] *communal cultures* are high on both sociability and solidarity. On the face of it, these have the best of both worlds. Their appeal has certainly been celebrated in accounts of innovative high-performance businesses – think of Apple [and] Microsoft. (pp. 117–118)

Many very successful organisations identified in the leadership research literature in this book, reported that they promote and support positive and collective approaches to leadership and in promoting productive relationships. Examples of organisations that create enabling and generative contexts were identified above (e.g. Salicru, 2017; Vance, 2015) and lessons for leaders were derived and discussed. While many of the examples were from the business world, the lessons learned apply to leaders of different types of organisations, including educational systems and schools who operate in challenging contexts of uncertainty and disruption. The implications for school leaders, especially teachers, who lead in disruptive contexts will be more fully discussed in the following chapter.

Chapter 7

Shaping the Future of Education

> There is no more important issue facing education, or human-
> ity at large, than the fast approaching revolution of Artificial
> Intelligence, or AI. This book is a call to educators everywhere,
> in primary, secondary, further and higher education (HE), in all
> countries, to open their eyes to what is coming toward us. If we
> do so, then the future will be shaped by us in the interests of all.
> If not, others, the large tech companies, governments and even
> the bad guys will decide, and we will only have ourselves to blame.
> (Seldon & Abidoye, 2018, p. 1)

Seldon and Abidoye (2018) presented an insightful account of the likely future
impact of Artificial Intelligence (AI) on schools but claimed that schools, generally, are not well prepared to use it intelligently; they warn that schools are not
even clear about the future for which they have to prepare. However, they cautioned that:

> [...] doing nothing is not an option. Hard though it may be to peer
> into the future, and unsettling though some scenarios may be, not
> to prepare is to court serious risk. (p. 175)

These authors charge educators with the responsibility for ensuring that AI
becomes the servant not the controller of education in the future and they
concluded:

> Nothing but nothing is more important than education in ensur-
> ing that AI works in the interests of all humanity. We need to reim-
> agine our schools from the ground up to teach our young to be
> more fully human and ... not be content any longer with giving
> them just factory-era skills. (p. 312)

For readers who wish to delve more deeply into a future of education,
informed and driven by AI, Seldon and Abidoye's book is a rich source of

Leading Educational Systems and Schools in Times of Disruption and Exponential Change:
A Call for Courage, Commitment and Collaboration, 73–84
Copyright © 2020 by Patrick A. Duignan
Published under exclusive license
doi:10.1108/978-1-83909-850-520201008

information, advice and inspiration; examples are provided of current case-study schools that have started on the AI journey. While AI and other smart technologies will, no doubt, require educators and educational leaders to change the way in which education is designed and delivered to future generations of students, there will need to be a transformation in within-school architectures to facilitate it, including: the design of learning spaces; times and timing of teaching and learning delivery systems; building creative and enabling processes within learning environments; and creating inspiring pedagogical approaches and practices. In the final chapter of this book – Chapter 12 – it is, however, pointed out that many recent education reform attempts, characterised by increasing access to a variety of interactive technologies in the classroom have, by and large, not delivered on their promises.

The essence of Seldon and Abidoye's (2018) concerns about the general lack of preparation of educators and schools for a technological future, and the need to reimagine our schools from the ground up is the focus of discussions later in this chapter and also in Chapter 12 of this book. Their plea is that educators need to open their eyes to what is coming at great speed and respond so that the future will be shaped by them in the interests of all because educators need to equip their students with the skills necessary to thrive in such a challenging and uncertain world. Wagner (2014) is cautious, however, and pointed out that even our best schools don't teach the new survival skills our children need for rapidly-changing environments.

If education reform initiatives in schools are to respond positively to the curricular and pedagogical practices children need for the future, then the metaphor of schools as communities of learning, discussed elsewhere in this book, needs to be front and centre. When educators focus, primarily, on the separate functions of the system parts or on individual human behaviour – e.g. the functioning of math or science departments, individual classroom teachers, or data-driven assessment of students' results – they can miss out on the rich complexity of connections and patterns of relationships, as well as on '... new possibilities that emerge when humans interconnect, collaborate and engage with each other in morally purposeful and mutually influential relationships' (Walker, 2011). An important implication for educators and educational leaders who believe in the metaphor of learning community is that they shouldn't attempt within their school to solve large and complex challenges on their own but should reach outwards for assistance. Weber (2010) in, *Waiting for Superman: How We Can Save America's Failing Public Schools*, cautioned that the '... era of schools and educators talking only to themselves must come to an end' (p. 7). He suggested that no education system, no matter how innovative:

> [...] will survive in the modern world by closing itself off to good ideas from a wide array of sources. Failed schools fail in part due to their inability, or unwillingness to seek help on behalf of their students, while successful schools are constantly looking and reaching out. (p. 79)

Caldwell (2006) urged schools to join in learning networks to '... support the lateral transfer of knowledge', and transform themselves into dynamic learning hubs. This development will be facilitated, he suggested, by:

> [...] tailoring to the needs of the school an advanced capacity for knowledge management, building a powerful learning community to ensure that staff are at the forefront of knowledge [and] participating in and sharing the leadership of networked learning communities .... (p. 193)

He concluded that students, teachers and others at the coal-face can be empowered by what he called a '... new enterprise logic' (p. 80), which is based on the promise of responding '... to the needs of ... students and parents by radically changing pedagogies for learning' (p. 81). Key characteristics of such new 'radical pedagogies' (Degenhardt & Duignan, 2010), include a capacity in schools to '... work in teams ... operate in networks to share knowledge, address problems ... share resources [and develop] a sense of community and the building of strong social capital' (Caldwell, 2006, p. 81). While it will take time for this new enterprise logic to become embedded in the educational profession and in schools, the effort will be both a '... challenging adventure [and an] exhilarating journey', which will require a '... readiness to engage in daring action' (p. 116).

In her research on the leadership roles and influence of middle leaders in improving the nature and quality of learning, Gasston-Holmes (2019) claimed that leaders can positively contribute to '... building capacity for quality teaching and leadership for learning' (*Abstract*, p. 15). She emphasised that leading learning from the middle can drive reform improvements, '... thus building the capacity of both teachers and middle-level leaders within a school' (*Abstract*, p. 15). The role of middle leaders in schools and ways in which they influence the quality of teaching and learning is underdone in research and practice and should get greater focus and attention. Gasston-Holmes provided a useful research framework, which also works as a model for building capacity for quality teaching and leading for learning improvement:

1. *Leaders of learning*: View middle leaders as agents of change and leaders of learning and develop trusting relationships between them and teachers (p. 20).
2. *Collaborative learning and knowledge creation*: Importantly there's a '... need for *Leading Teachers to Self-Assess their Professional Growth* framework'. Roles adopted by leaders of learning include: critical friend, supporter, educator and enlightener (p. 20, capitals and italics in original).
3. *Sharing new knowledge and reflection, plus reflection-on-action*: Principals and leaders of learning should work collaboratively, share knowledge, and build a culture of relational trust. There is a need for a shared sense of responsibility and accountability among all school leaders for teacher quality and leadership of learning (p. 20, bold type added by this author for emphasis).

This is a useful research-inspired framework for leading quality learning in schools and it can be used to good effect by all who are involved in innovative learning and teaching-improvement initiatives in schools.

Throughout this book, the author has argued that unusual and uncertain times and conditions require creative, unusual and daring actions and responses. Einstein has frequently been credited with stating, 'The definition of insanity is doing the same thing over and over again, but expecting different results' (His authorship is disputed). The implications of this point of view for educational change in the future is that educational leaders and reformers will need to find new and creative ways and means of encouraging the types of changes that will bring about changed mindsets – i.e. a paradigm shift – about the nature of learning, teaching as a process and a profession, as well as about the architecture of schools and schooling. They need to stop doing things as they have always done them!

Essentially, this is what Finland did as a high achieving country in education when it began to engage in creative and daring action over 30 years ago. Darling-Hammond (2010), in her comprehensive analysis and critique of education systems in a number of countries, noted that starting back in the 1980s, Finland got rid of its '… rigid tracking system that had allocated differential access to knowledge to its young people and eliminated the state-mandated testing system that was used for this purpose' (p. 5). These were replaced by high-quality teachers and '… curriculum and assessments focused on problem solving, creativity, independent learning, and student reflection' (p. 5). These changes moved student achievement in Finland to the top of the international rankings and helped close a once very large achievement gap. All this was achieved without prescribing or restricting the curriculum. Students in Finnish schools are encouraged and supported to engage in active learning in order to '… develop metacognitive skills that help them to frame, tackle, and solve problems; evaluate and improve their own work; and guide their learning processes in productive ways' (Darling-Hammond, 2010, p. 170) – these are also key skills required to navigate successfully through an uncertain and turbulent future. While some may point out that the culture of Finland is quite different from other countries, many of the educational initiatives Finland has taken are compatible with what policymakers and educators say they want in their own education systems.

A key challenge to achieving such goals is that too many education systems and schools don't seem to be capable or willing to break loose from traditional paradigms of education or traditional structures and processes for teaching and learning. To achieve new outcomes, there is a need for a new learner-driven enterprise logic, which would signify a real, perhaps radical paradigm shift in the areas of learning, teaching and leadership, especially in secondary schools. In her work on 'reinventing' a traditional secondary school, the principal, Leoni Degenhardt and her leadership team co-constructed a radical new pedagogy which involved:

> … more than an incremental improvement in teaching and learning; it constitutes a profound change in what is taught, how it is

taught and assessed, and in the relationships between teacher, learner and parent. (Degenhardt & Duignan, 2010, p. 42)

Teachers were expected to be '... teachers of students, not just teachers of subjects' (p. 42). In the summary to their book, titled *Dancing on a Shifting Carpet: Reinventing Traditional Schooling for the 21st Century*, Degenhardt and Duignan summed up their conclusions from this radical educational innovation:

> We have argued in this book that the time for incremental change and tinkering around the edges of schooling has passed, and nothing short of reinventing schooling is required. We believe that we owe it to the children currently in our schools and also to those who will grace the schools of the future. (p. 184)

Dancing on a shifting carpet was how one teacher described her experiences of the whole reinvention process which took place over a seven-year period and still continues. The radical pedagogical reinvention processes involved in this reform initiative extended well beyond the pedagogy itself to embrace a number of educational architectural transformations. The authors explained it thus:

> It was acknowledged by key stakeholders that a "radical new pedagogy" required more flexible learning spaces than traditional school architecture provided. The relationship between form and function meant that "egg-crate" architecture was limiting to both students and teachers. (p. 122)

They reported that new space designs encouraged students and their teachers to:

> [...] interact in more flexible and casual ways, enabling a degree of self-direction and informal interaction [and] students had the opportunity to work in fluid ways as determined by their learning needs: alone, in small groups, in large groups and with technology. (p. 122)

These reinvention processes, which started in 2004 and are still ongoing in 2019, have revolutionised learning, teaching and assessment processes in that school; it substantially improved its performance outcomes and it has enjoyed top percentile rankings year-upon-year in government-administered external examinations in the final year of schooling.

When considering possible future architectural and technological disruptions, like those just highlighted, a question comes to mind: 'How will emerging technological and architectural disruptions impact on the delivery of education in an uncertain, turbulent and rapidly-changing future?', We explore and attempt to provide responses to this question throughout this book, but we also attempt to provide answers to an even more challenging and complex question: When such disruptions occur, in what ways can educational policymakers, planners, leaders and practitioners best respond in order to break down the traditional structures and processes of industry models of education and create new forms – patterns, processes and practices – that will excite, nourish and engage children in a disruptive future?

Gans (2016) provided an interesting leadership framework for considering these two questions. He highlighted a useful distinction between *demand-side disruption* and *supply-side disruption* which helps us better understand the possible sources and dynamics for future changes in education. Demand-side disruptions occur when students, parents and the school's community use advanced technologies that exceed those in their local schools. There is little doubt that this user disruption is already happening in many schools because of a widening gap between the technological savvy and skills of millennials, as well as other younger generations (e.g. Gen Z, Gen Alpha) and many of those currently working within education systems and schools.

Schools leaders, especially teachers, will need to be awake and alert to the changing characteristics, preferences and tastes of new generations who will either be leading, or on the receiving end of, educational pedagogies and technologies in the future. Millennials are currently in leadership positions in our schools and their capabilities, characteristics and leadership strengths are discussed elsewhere in this book. It is predicted that the generation after Millennials, Generation Z will comprise, approximately, one third of the workforce within a decade. They are not just digital natives but digital sophisticates on steroids (Gans, 2016). They have highly developed social acumen, keen global perspectives and tastes, and are extraordinarily mobile – they frequently move their accommodation, jobs and careers. The subsequent group, Generation Alpha, also called iGeneration, are the children of Millennials and are exposed to AI and voice assisted gadgets from the cradle. By the age of eight, just like this author's twin granddaughters, they are more tech-savvy than any previous generation. Industrial models of schools and traditional teachers and pedagogies will not be tolerated by any of these emerging generations. If current educational leaders and educators cannot change their mindsets and ways they may simply be overrun. Watch out, they're coming to your school!

While demand-side disruptions will influence and impact on schools and technologies, it is supply-side disruptions that will fundamentally change the delivery structures, patterns and processes of education offered through our schools. These emerging architectural changes will put increasing pressures on educational policymakers and leaders to reimagine or 'reboot' schools and schooling (Hattie, 2016), especially in the ways in which teachers and other system and school leaders engage with their students and communities. Gans (2016) claimed that supply-side disruption theory '… makes us question whether waiting and then acting can be a cure for this form of disruption, as dealing with this form requires absorbing new architectural knowledge' (p. 79). Gaining knowledge, he says, may be insufficient, instead the challenge will be '… the integration of different ways of doing things into an organisation that already has ingrained processes' (p. 79). Leaders, especially, will need to foresee and prepare for this integration by '… proactively gaining the capabilities for such integration' (p. 79).

When preparing for architectural innovation, educational leaders will need to develop these integration capabilities, which involves continually challenging themselves to better '... understand the linkages in their organisation and evolve them to meet and assimilate innovations that emerge' (p. 98). Moreover, Gans claimed, '... even though it was designed to target supply-side threats, integration also allows [leaders] to develop capabilities to manage all disruptive threats after the fact – both demand- and supply-side' (p. 98). Successful integration requires an end to fixed assumptions and mindsets as well as to silo-mentalities and their accompanying defensive behaviours. Within educational systems and schools, integration, according to Gans, would require an inside-looking-out perspective, akin to Caldwell's view, earlier in this chapter, of schools joining learning networks to transform themselves into dynamic learning hubs to promote the lateral transfer of knowledge. To achieve these ends, educational systems and schools will need to '... absorb resources – particularly talent, skills, and technology – from outside ... in order to anticipate or deal with disruption,' and by achieving integration within their organisations, '... they can also develop experience and capabilities that allow them to integrate these external resources' (p. 105).

Key implications for schools from Gans' conclusions on disruption are that simple adjustments in organisational structures, teaching approaches, learning models, engagement processes, and leadership philosophies and practices will not suffice – bold, courageous and creative leadership will be required. As he pointed out, supply-side architectural disruptions, which include rapidly evolving technological innovations:

> [...] require creating a more integrated, fluid organisation so that there is a reduced focus on component knowledge [e.g., subjects and subject departments] and a recognition and nurturing of new architectural knowledge. (p. 47)

In fact, rapidly transforming technologies and emerging innovations, including those to the physical architecture of schools, are already changing educational systems and institutions and will have considerable consequences for the nature and delivery of education in the future.

Case (2016), Founder of America Online (AOL), presented an important argument for the transformation of American education, based on what he calls 'Third-Wave Technologies and Integrated Networks'; they are similar to Gans' (2017) ideas on architectural changes and transformations. Case argued that similar to what is already happening in Healthcare in America, education is becoming more personal, more individualised and more data-driven. He claimed that, in addition to Healthcare, Third-Wave Forces are changing '... another system that is big, important, complicated, and broken: the American education system' (pp. 46–47). Third-Wave forces, he concluded will '... leverage technology to revolutionise the way we learn' (p. 47). During first- and second-wave technological changes, he suggested, students engaged with technologies, especially computers and hand-held gadgets, using, primarily, '... PowerPoint decks, browsing the web, [and] chatting with pen pals on the other side of the world' (p. 47). None of these technologies, he stated, were designed exclusively for the classroom – they could be used anywhere.

Third-Wave educational technology developments, he claimed, enable teachers and students to connect and network with parents, as well as a host of other educators and selected information sources, like never before. He pointed out that:

> [...] many schools now use virtual dashboards, where teachers post everything from homework assignments and test scores to videos of your child reading a book report in front of the class. Rather than reducing children to numbers, this kind of technology can provide a vehicle for parental involvement that didn't exist before. (p. 47)

Case is heavily involved with schools in America, assisting them to embrace Third-Wave technologies, especially encouraging them to expand their engagement through enhanced connectivity and networking processes. He is promoting and supporting a specific educational company based in Iowa that supports and encourages teachers:

> [...] to share interactive slide decks with their students in real time, while enabling students to indicate to teachers when they are having trouble, so that teachers can adjust their teaching and learning processes. (p. 47)

He also supports the use of new Internet platforms that allow teaching materials to be shared and collectively reviewed.

He reported that a new start-up company, *Teachers-Pay-Teachers*, provided:

> [...] an online marketplace where teachers can buy and sell lesson plans (p. 48) ... giving one teacher involved over US$100,000 in income from sharing her grammar, vocabulary and literature exercises [and] twelve teachers on the site have become millionaires. (p. 48)

He reported that '... companies are also designing technologies to personalise the learning process, [especially] software that adapts based on how a student learns best' (p 48). From his intimate knowledge of emerging adaptive software, he claimed that soon students will have '... the equivalent of a virtual tutor, a textbook replaced by tablet that tracks not only whether a child is learning but how he [she] learns best' (p. 48). Third-Wave technologies will, he says, also:

> [...] change how we measure success in the classroom, [once] teachers and parents can get detailed reports with a wide range of metrics, comparing their students on a regular basis to others in their class or school or state. (pp. 48–49)

The key benefits of such approaches are:

> [...] not to rate students against others, but to personalise each student's learning processes and use their personal results for improvement in their learning, [thereby] ensuring that each child's personalised needs are met. (Case, p. 49)

Case is actually proposing architectural transformations about how education is personalised, delivered and assessed. While he is aware of the powerful forces protecting and supporting the *status quo*, he is convinced that Millennials and future tech-smart generations, like Gen Z and Gen Alpha, will achieve architectural transformations as a matter of course by integrating the best outcomes of First- and Second-Wave changes and combining imaginative and quantum changes in the content, context and community dimensions of education and of schooling. These are exciting predictions for education that are already slowly advancing in many educational systems and schools in a number of countries, as indicated by Schleicher in his OECD Report (2018) on education. Such changes are slow because, as Case (2016) lamented, educational paradigms, including their structures and delivery modes, haven't changed much over a century or more. He challenged us to look closely at just about any public or private school in the USA and we'll see structures and processes that have barely changed since the 19th century. He concluded that too many educators are '... more worried about the risk of trying something new than about the risk of maintaining the status quo' (p. 50).

Too many secondary schools are still characterised by: self-contained classrooms with students rotating through them throughout the day; time slots for 'lessons' that don't differ greatly from the 1960s; subject teachers continuing to dominate classrooms from the front using didactic methods; textbooks transported to and from school by students burdened down by large backpacks; lockers in corridors, still visited by students between lessons, causing *corridor chaos*; little change to the length and structures for learning of the school day; and little change to the length of time students are engaged in learning over each school year. There is, for the most part, no formal learning engagement on weekends and attendance is for, approximately, 200–220 days each year across the different states of Australia – these Australian patterns are recognisable in many other countries.

As well as educational imperatives for change, there are also powerful demographic, social and economic forces that will likely impel schools and schooling to transform their structures and practices. In many Western countries, as well as in some Asian countries (e.g. Japan) populations are getting older and age-care costs are continuing to soar. The increasing voting power of the over-60 age group is, therefore, likely to redirect funding away from primary and secondary education towards care of the aged. The cumulative effects of reducing birth rates will mean that fewer younger workers will join the workforce so the tax base for public services will continue to decline. Simply put, governments will find it increasingly difficult to fund health and education systems, including tertiary education.

Increasingly, politicians and their efficiency gurus will focus more on how effectively resources are currently used in the primary and secondary education sectors and it will be difficult to justify why such very large societal investments are underused. Affordability will become a dominating concern for governments and these concerns will add fuel to the fires for revolutionary changes in education. Current and emerging technologies and new architectural knowledge already provide us with the capabilities to transform the ways in which education is delivered, including the use of exciting connected and networked pedagogies that extend beyond the boundaries of individual schools and persist after graduation, perhaps for a lifetime. The boundaries between school and home will be strengthened, leading to a recalibration of what school time and active-learning-time actually means. The physical architecture of schools will change dramatically (this has been happening for some time) to reflect new and powerful interactive, networking technologies that reduce the need for traditional buildings and the current compartmentalisation in education systems and schools e.g. subjects and departments in secondary schools.

Prince et al. (2018), in a *Knowledge Works Foundation* report, explored the future of learning in the USA and forecast possible changes in education and likely opportunities for educators to respond to the changing educational landscape there. *Knowledge Works Foundation* is a US non-profit organisation that works with state and federal policymakers, schools and school communities to grow a system-wide approach to sustain student-centred practices so that '… every child graduates ready for what's next' (p. 4). In their evidence-driven research report, *Navigating the Future of Learning*: *Forecast 5.0*, Prince et al. (2018) presented a 10-year forecast for educational changes and developments in the USA. A key prediction from their report stated:

> […] people, smart machines and the code that powers them are interacting in new and deeper ways. Over the next decade, exponential advances in digital technologies will require us to redefine our relationships with one another, with our institutions and even with ourselves. Every facet of our lives, including how we teach and learn, will be touched by this new era of partners in code. (p. 3)

Their report includes a very elaborate and comprehensive description and analysis of exciting and creative educational reform initiatives currently underway in the US and provides strong evidence for likely reform trends in the future, especially in the coming 10 years. In *Forecast 5.0*, they point to an unknown future for education but suggested that we can prepare ourselves to help shape this future:

> We can never know how the future will unfold, but we can expand our ideas about what might be possible and necessary for learning. We can also identify where we might want to intervene, harness or adapt to shape a future of learning in which all students can thrive … to help steer society's transition from one era to the next. (p. 4)

As with the OECD Report (2018a) discussed earlier, leaders of educational reform in most countries can draw on KnowledgeWorks' forecasts for useful insights on what may transpire in education in their own countries in the coming decade; they can also use advice from the report to guide leaders and educational practitioners to adapt and thrive in times of disruption and rapid change. Especially important for change leaders are the drivers of change identified and explained by the authors of the report, which are described as '… major societal shifts that will impact education over the next decade. They combine multiple trends, patterns, plans and developments to identify broad patterns of change' (p. 5). Five large-scale drivers are identified and described that are important for all educational leaders and reformers to know and understand:

1. *Automatic choices*: algorithms and artificial intelligence are becoming increasingly embedded in *our* lives. They are automating many of our experiences, services and interactions with one another to achieve efficiency and personalisation and are raising questions related to trust, bias and individual agency.
2. *Civic superpowers*: individuals, nonprofits and volunteer organisations are flexing their civic muscles. They are using participatory media, machine learning and data analytics to fill a growing governance gap, with hopes of reweaving the social fabric and redefining civic engagement.
3. *Accelerating brains*: rapid advances in technology and neuroscience are combining to transform our cognitive abilities in intended and unintended ways. They are shaping how we partner with digital tools, relate with one another and engage with our surroundings.
4. *Toxic narratives*: the narratives and metrics of success and achievement that shape people's aspirations, choices and behaviours are becoming increasingly detrimental to individual and social health and are contributing to growing toxicity in systems and institutions.
5. *Remaking geographies*: migration patterns, small-scale production and efforts to grow place-based and cultural assets are combining to reshape community landscapes in response to economic transition and climate volatility. (Prince et al., 2018, p. 6)

Drawing on these drivers of change, there are a number of implications for educational reform leaders. The *Forecast 5.0* authors claimed that:

> […] as the drivers of change unfold and combine over the next decade, they will present opportunities to imagine new kinds of educational practices, programs, structures and roles that respond to the changing landscape. (p. 17)

They see these opportunities clustering around four future possibilities:

1. *Signature learning ecosystems*, which support learning in place in ways that integrate technology, culture, learner and community identity to enhance and extend opportunities for learning (p. 18).

2. *Human-centred learning*, which involves '… reorienting teaching and learning systems, expectations and experiences to put a holistic view of human development at the centre' (p. 19).
3. *Safeguards for efficacy*, which involve providing vision and stewardship for '… implementing effective data strategies and for embracing emerging technologies for intentional learner support' (p. 20).
4. *Amplified voice*, which involves '… reconfiguring engagement and outcome frameworks and communications channels to bolster individual capacity and to increase community impact' (p. 21).

To assist educational leaders and reformers formulate their reform strategies and reform practices, KnowledgeWorks' *Forecast 5.0*, provided examples of present-day programmes, practices and initiatives that show glimpses of what future education landscapes could look like. They claimed that these signals of change illustrate how some of the future possibilities, just described above, are beginning to play out today (see *Forecast 5.0*, pp. 22–26) and they then go on to discuss possible future responses to education's changing landscape (pp. 27–31). The authors of the report provide positive and heartening advise to all those involved in educational transformation when they claim that there is an opportunity to place human fulfilment and people's mutual well-being at the centre of learning. In the conclusion to their *Forecast 5.0* Report they concluded:

> Digital depth has the potential to create environments that respond to and support core social-emotional skills and cognitive and metacognitive capacities. It offers ways to scale opportunities for learners to develop practices and behaviours, such as empathy, perspective taking, critical thinking, and self-awareness that will support their personal, academic, and professional lives. For education to make full use of digital-depth technologies, careful consideration should be paid to how wearables, augmented reality, and virtual reality are used at the individual, classroom, and system levels. Through careful consideration of the potential these technologies hold for learning and how they might be implemented, education stakeholders can take the lead in shaping their uses, impacting learning in significant ways. (p. 41)

The examples of current practices and future possibilities identified and described in this *Forecast 5.0 Report* provide educational change leaders with rich resources for revisiting, re-forming and re-energising education in their schools (Note, if using these resources, you will need to get permission from *Knowledge-Works* at KnowledgeWorks.org).

In the next chapter, the focus is on reclaiming and re-invigorating the profession of teaching to assist in the effective leadership of change and reform, especially with the use of smart technologies.

Chapter 8

Re-energising Education, Including Teachers' Professional Judgements

Over the past couple of decades, at least, there appears to be a growing movement for change in education and in schools that reflects a more enlightened view of learning, pedagogy, teaching and leadership. In a number of countries and education systems, the emphasis on testing and accountability is slowly being nuanced by an approach that focusses more on students and the quality of their learning, teachers as leaders of curriculum and pedagogy, and principals and leadership teams in schools as leaders of pedagogy. In an important early contribution to this emerging perspective, an OECD Report (2008), titled *Innovating to Learn, Learning to Innovate* seemed to despair of the educational reform movements to that date, and concluded that:

> [...] *reforms have ultimately come up against a wall, or rather a ceiling, beyond which further progress seems impossible, leading increasing numbers of school administrators and educators to wonder whether schools do not need to be reformed but to be reinvented.*
> (p. 22, italics in original)

From our discussions earlier, it seems apparent that while such a reinvention has not yet occurred, there are emerging trends and practices that show great promise for a better future and we should learn from our failed attempts at reform.

One major effect of the apparent failure to reinvent the architecture of education, especially its delivery methods, was foreshadowed by Seldon (2010). He stated that the key consequences of the general failure of state education in England to embrace rich, engaging pedagogies supported by new technologies, as well as the obsession with narrow curriculum and relentless testing and accountability in 'factory schools', included the:

> [...] de-professionalisation of teachers, the dumbing down of teaching, the artificial separating of subjects, the development of superficial content, the destruction of creativity and originality,

Leading Educational Systems and Schools in Times of Disruption and Exponential Change: A Call for Courage, Commitment and Collaboration, 85–94
Copyright © 2020 by Patrick A. Duignan
Published under exclusive license
doi:10.1108/978-1-83909-850-520201009

and the narrowing of the vision for education. (Seldon, 2010, pp. 28–33)

Seldon's conclusions actually pinpointed key areas of education and pedagogy that required attention and transformation.

Adding to Seldon's critical points, Schleicher (2018) urged that:

> [...] schools now need to prepare students for more rapid change than ever before, to learn for jobs that have not yet been created, to tackle societal challenges that we can't yet imagine, and to use technologies that have not yet been invented. (p. 29)

He advised educators, especially teachers, to prepare their students for '... an interconnected world in which [they can] understand and appreciate different perspectives and world views, ... and take responsible action toward sustainability and collective well-being' (p. 29). In today's schools, he stated, the:

> [...] more interdependent the world becomes, the more we need great collaborators and orchestrators [and they] need to become better at helping students learn to develop an awareness of the pluralism of modern life. (p. 31)

Wilson (2018) presented a similar perspective when she noted that if we desire educational transformation, we need to change our educational pedagogies, including structures, processes, time schedules, as well as configurations of space and its use. She suggested that our developmental tasks require:

> [...] deep cultural change – change that recognises the developmental task at hand, that is, that we are embarking on long-term work to transition a system that was designed along the principles of compliance and control, to become much more autonomous and creative. (p. 59)

To achieve these ends, she concluded, educational change leaders must take a long-term view of educational delivery and resulting student outcomes. Politicians should be held to account for allowing short-term political cycles – usually 3–4 years – from dictating that educators and educational change initiatives deliver measurable improvements in the shorter term, often one to three years. Based on her USA-wide research, Wilson concluded that, as nations, we must avoid the destabilising effects of policy reversals when governments (state/federal/system) change, based on policies they have already 'sold' to their electorates Wilson, however, has hope for a brighter future because, in her comprehensive research project, she witnessed teams of teachers, school leaders, students, parents and whole communities collaboratively and creatively attempting to transform educational learning environments and experiences for their students. With an expanding number of such positive initiatives and with their broader application, she believes, they can and will have amplifier and accelerator effects:

> [...] the right answers reside not in change gurus and textbooks, but they are within us. [They reside in] '... our individual and collective will to embrace ambiguity, uncertainty and risk, to hold the vision steady and to work towards it with steadfast commitment and an understanding that it takes time. It takes time, patience, and heart ... It resides in our ability to break free of the double binds of "learned helplessness" and "waiting for permission" that the system perpetuates. (p. 93)

Let's no longer wait for permission to change, she concluded, and demonstrate through our collective actions that we are not helpless or hopeless. We should go forward together with intelligence, conviction and courage. She urged educational leaders to take creative and collaborative action to transform their learning landscapes. Together, she believes, we have the courage to transform education in its many aspects, for ourselves, our children, our grandchildren and for future generations. The time to act is now and we must act as a collective wave! Wilson provided clear indicators as to why we must go forward along this change path:

> I have worked with thousands of adults [on changing education] over two decades. I see the results of an industrial system of education. I see graduates who graduated the system "successfully" yet do not have the skills and knowledge to design and build a life of their own choosing ... I want every child to have the opportunity to build and design a life of their own choosing, regardless of demography ... I know that adults are the key to making this change for our children. I work with burnt out educators, overwhelmed administrators, and anxious parents. The education system has lost its heart. We need to bring back that heart. Why? Because heart is at the core of education. Heart is at the core of change. Heart is where learning and change is possible. (Wilson, p. 105)

As far back as 1973, Joseph Campbell, a prolific, insightful and widely read author, said that the *why* for doing what you do, when shared, '... keeps you focused on your path and is an inspiration for others' (quoted in Wilson, 2018 p. 105). He advised that you have to discover and clear your own path, because:

> If you can see your path laid out in front of you step by step, you know it's not your path. Your own path you make with every step you take. That's why it's your path. (p. 106)

This is a very poignant observation on the need for us, singly and together, to author our own change journey, even if we are uncertain of the steps beforehand.

Together with a clear mind and good heart we can create (not discover) the educational path forward that will maximise opportunities and outcomes for all our students. Already, we are almost two decades into the twenty-first century, and despite all the rhetoric and desire to transform education for our current and future generations, the journey has hardly started and the path ahead is not of our own making. We need to begin to create this path and embrace an exciting educational journey to transform and nourish our education systems, schools, educational leaders, teachers, students and their parents. If we succeed, we will have achieved what so many educators have dreamed about and striven for over the last few decades.

There are many ways in which we can create our educational paths for the future. Schleicher, in his OECD Report (2018), titled, *World Class: How to Build a 21st-century School System,* presented a comprehensive analysis of successful education systems in a number of OECD countries. He compared professionalism in education and medicine and pointed out that in medicine, '... the first thing we do is take the patient's temperature and diagnose what treatment will be most effective.' In education, he stated, there is a tendency:

> [...] to teach all students in the same way, give them the same treatment and, at times, diagnose at the end of the school year the extent to which that treatment was effective. (2018, p. 16)

It is time, he claimed, '... to make education reform, not necessarily less of an art but more of a science' (p. 17). Lifelong learning, he stated, involves '... constantly learning, unlearning and relearning when the contexts change [it requires] continuous processes of reflection, anticipation and action' (p. 29). He posited a challenge for educators and schools to meet the needs of students in fast-changing and uncertain times. Schools he suggested:

> [...] need to prepare students for more rapid change than ever before, to learn for jobs that have not yet been created, to tackle societal challenges that we can't yet imagine, and to use technologies that have not yet been invented.

They, especially, need to:

> [...] prepare students for an interconnected world in which they can understand and appreciate different perspectives and world views, interact successfully and respectfully with others, and take responsible action toward sustainability and collective well-being. (p. 29)

In a highly connected and interdependent world, he recommended that:

> ... we need great collaborators and orchestrators. The well-being of societies depends, increasingly, on people's capacity to take

> collective action ... rewarding collaboration as well as individual academic achievement, enabling students both to think for themselves, and to act for and with others. (p. 31)

New technologies can greatly assist in developing these processes and schools of the future need to:

> [...] use the potential of technologies to liberate learning from past conventions and connect learners in new and powerful ways, with sources of knowledge, with innovative applications and with one another. (p. 34)

Drawing on educational wisdom and outcomes from a number of currently successful school systems (e.g. Finland, Estonia, Alberta and Ontario in Canada, Singapore, Japan), Schleicher encouraged education policymakers, leaders and teachers to study successful countries and make international educational comparisons, '... in the same way that business leaders learn to steer their companies towards success: by taking inspiration from others, and then adapting lessons learned to their own situation' (p. 62). This can be achieved in education, he claimed, through different forms of benchmarking, including:

> [...] analysing observed differences in the quality, equity and efficiency of education between one country and another, and considering how they are related to certain features of those countries' education systems. (p. 62)

Based on his own and Tucker's educational benchmarking research in the USA (Tucker 2017a), Schleicher identified: '... a surprising range of features common to all high-performing education systems':

1. Leaders in high-performing education systems have convinced their citizens that it is worth investing in the future through education, rather than spending for immediate rewards (p. 62).
2. The belief that every student can learn: '... In countries as different as Estonia, Canada, Finland and Japan, parents and teachers are committed to the belief that all students can meet high standards ... these systems have advanced from sorting human talent to developing human talent' (pp. 62–63).
3. Educators address the diversity of student needs with differentiated pedagogical practices. 'They realise that ordinary students can have extraordinary talents and they personalise the education experience so that all students can meet high standards' (p. 63).
4. They educate their teaching staff carefully and provide an environment in which '... teachers work together to frame good practice; they encourage teachers to grow in their careers' (p. 63).
5. They set ambitious goals and are clear about what students should be able to do, and enable teachers to figure out what they need to teach their students.

'They encourage their teachers to be innovative, to improve their own performance and that of their colleagues' (p. 63).

6. They tend to align policies and practices across the entire system [by ensuring] '... policies are coherent over sustained periods of time and ... are consistently implemented' (p. 64).
7. They find, nourish and reward great school leaders, including innovative and courageous principals (pp. 107–108).

Muller (2018) focussed particularly on the importance of teachers and teaching in order to successfully change and renew pedagogical practices. He championed the cause for teachers to re-discover their once highly valued professional judgements in the key areas of teaching and learning. He urged that teachers' professionalism in schools be greatly enhanced and more highly respected, and that the issue of teachers' professional judgement be revisited, revived and re-energised. When comparing levels of professional responsibility between medicine and education, he concluded that professional responsibility and judgement is valued much more in medicine than in education. Patients, for the most part, he claimed, respect the professional judgements of their doctors, even on matters of life and death. Teachers, overall, are not accorded the same respect with regard to their judgements on matters closely related to their students' successes or failures in life, even though many educators have graduate degrees in teaching, as well as other specialty educational areas from prestigious universities.

It appears that most people who have attended school believe that they are entitled to their opinion on all things educational and are willing to challenge educational leaders and teachers on their educational views and practices – i.e. their professional credibility – especially when their own children are involved. When such challenges arise constantly from parents, community and the media, they tend to erode teachers' confidence in themselves collectively, as professionals, and this often leads to negative perspectives on the veracity of their professional judgements when assessing their students. The exponential rise of data-driven assessment and the widespread use of metrics in educational decision-making on what constitutes high standards and valued learning outcomes (Muller, 2018) has also tended to devalue teachers' professional judgements and their right as professional educators to make key decisions on the type of pedagogy, learning outcomes and assessment processes that best suit their students, either as individuals or as collectives.

From a collective view, Harris and Jones (2018) urged teachers to exercise '... professional collaboration with impact' and suggested that there should be '... real choice and freedom for teachers to work together on issues that are directly related to learners and learning' (p. 54). If teachers are encouraged to do this collaborative work, they claimed, '... there is a much better chance of authentic professional engagement and impact' (p. 54). They argued that '... true organisational capacity is built, sustained and enhanced through professional collaboration [and when] authentic professional learning communities [develop] within and between schools, where teachers learn to connect ...' (p. 55). Such collaboration helps generate positive learning cultures and more effective pedagogical skills with enhanced professional insights and capabilities.

Marcella Bremer is an internationally influential author, speaker and change consultant, based in the Netherlands. Bremer's (2018) book, *Developing a Positive Culture Where People and Performance Thrive*, is a veritable encyclopaedia of knowledge on frameworks, methods, techniques and resources for leaders wishing to build positive cultures in their educational systems and schools. She concluded that '… change always starts within ourselves, by seeing it differently and then *doing* something different' (p. 5, italics in original). Referring to the importance of organisational culture in change initiatives, she claimed that a culture of change '… happens when people get together. It entails the shared worldview, values, beliefs and behavioural norms of the organisational members' (p. 13). Change initiatives tend to fail for a variety of reasons but '… the biggest reason is that change doesn't fit the current culture' (p. 26) because the culture often reflects what worked well in the past but, unfortunately. '… it can thwart change efforts because people say: We've always done it like this. It is a collective comfort zone' (p. 29).

A positive culture of change, on the other hand, provides a sense of assurance and belonging, clear collective expectations, as well as the grammar and rules for conversation and engagement. However, organisations with bureaucratic, hierarchical structures, and top-down leadership have their own grammar and rules that may encourage mechanistic mindsets and discourage risk taking, initiative, creativity and innovation. Bremer claimed that a more favourable and productive image of organisations:

> [...] might be a network of leaders and professionals working together on shared goals; this is an organic mindset of organisations. Information flows in all directions [and] the organisation is growing and developing through a myriad of actions and interactions between all organisation members in different roles. (p. 34)

She claimed this '"net-ocracy" is more common than you think' (p. 34). In this organic view, an organisation is seen as '… a network of flowing energy and information with emerging opportunities from countless actions and interactions. It is non-linear and absolute predictions and control are not possible' (p. 55). In leading change and transformation in any educational organisation, Bremer urged leaders to start with mindsets: 'you need to see positive possibilities and have a "growth mindset" that values the process of learning' (2018, p. 132).

Some bureaucratic and hierarchical organisations may need to be redesigned or 'rewired' before change efforts are successful, claimed Gruenert and Whitaker (2015). While many in organisations may see the need for reform, even transformation, these authors claimed that, currently, there is some panic and confusion in many educational organisations because '… the call for accountability has brought an urgency to schools that feels more like panic' (p. 7). The antidote to such panic, they concluded, is to rewire the organisational culture so that:

> [...] it reflects a capacity to imagine a new reality and to understand all the components necessary to achieve and maintain it. Most of

those components are people: imperfect humans with biases, preferences, habits, insecurities, superstitions, families, faiths, priorities, and values that may or may not all be for the best – *because
the culture, whether positive or negative, has told them what "best"
means.* (p. 49, italics in original)

They reminded educational leaders that when they speak of making their systems and schools more collaborative and change-friendly, what they really mean
is that they '… want to change the nature of the relationships, or patterns of relation' (p. 51). In order to rewire their organisation's culture, leaders need to focus
on people's strengths (Rego, Clegg, & Pina e Cunha, 2011), or as Waters puts it,
'… make the strength switch'. Lea Waters (2017) presented a positive vision of
what organisations and our world would look like if we accentuated the positive
more: 'What kind of world would it be if we could fill the earth with people who
know and can operate from their strengths and help others do the same?' (p. 279)

The author of this book worked with and for Dr Waters when she was leader
of a new and progressive Master of Educational Leadership programme at the
Melbourne University Graduate School of Education, which was inspired by
positive psychology. During three years as a Visiting Professor in the programme,
the author of this book learned about the potential of positive psychology to
transform educational cultures in schools, including its impact on leaders, teachers and students. Waters is a researcher, teacher and consultant on positive learning cultures in schools. Working with Professor Martin Seligman, usually credited
with applying positive psychology in educational systems and schools in Australia
and in many areas of the USA, she set a research agenda to determine:

[…] how effective school systems could be for introducing positive
psychology to children so [they] could do better in school, feel better about themselves, and become adults who will shape a society
empowered by positive psychology. (Waters, 2017, p. 4)

In her evidence-based book, *The Strength Switch: How the Science of Strength-
based Parenting Helps Your Child and Your Teen Flourish*, Waters (2017) focussed
on positive parenting but her advice is a goldmine of wisdom for all educators and
educational leaders who wish to initiate and lead positive educational transformation in their systems and schools. Many of her insights and recommendations are
relevant to policymakers, educational leaders and teachers (even students) who
plan to transform their systems and schools. She stated that '… three-decades of
research clearly shows the advantages of taking a strength-based approach for
children and adults alike', including creating:

- Greater levels of happiness and engagement at school;
- Smoother transition from kindergarten to elementary school
  and from elementary to middle-school;
- Higher levels of academic achievement (as found in high school
  and academic students);

- Greater likelihood of being happy with and staying at work; and
- Better work performance. (p. 9)

In her advice to educators, especially teachers, she recommended a number of processes and techniques '… for bypassing the old habits that keep us focused on the negative' (p. 23). She encouraged educational leaders, teachers and parents to make the strength switch, '… a way to quickly short-circuit my negative defaults in real time, real-life situations …' (p. 51). She recommended that educators and parents help grow students' (children's generally) strengths by focussing their efforts on being positive and on believing that by cultivating and sustaining their positive energies, they can greatly improve their performance.

Drawing on the research of Dweck (2016), she described the strength switch as developing a growth mindset and explained:

> My own research with teenagers shows that a teen with a growth mind-set is more receptive to strength-based messages from her parents and more likely to use her strengths, compared to a teen with a fixed mind-set. (Waters, 2017, pp. 112–113)

She described the positive strides being made in education in Australia to promote and support strengths-based education:

> In schools, the strengths movement is growing. The leadership program I developed in partnership with the public education system when I first transferred to the Melbourne Graduate School of Education has trained 100 public school leaders and teachers in strengths. Those leaders and teachers took this learning back to 8,000 teachers and 30,000 students. The ripple effects continue as they move to other schools in the public system and transform those into strength-based schools. (p. 284)

With a colleague, Lela McGregor, Waters developed an interactive online programme for schools and families, called *Positive Detective*, in order to '… help children and teens see strengths in themselves and others' (p. 286). She reported that programmes based on the *Positive Detective* '… are having a ripple effect in many schools and families in the United States, Canada, the United Kingdom, Mexico, Finland, Ghana, Singapore, Hong Kong, Indonesia, Australia, and New Zealand' (p. 286). Waters concluded her book with the following powerful and inspiring message:

> In the long-term, strength-based children grow into strength-based adults who inspire strengths development in their partners, colleagues, patients, clients, and others they meet in life. They infuse strength-based systems into community groups and schools. They raise their children in a strength-based way – reversing the rising

trend of anxiety and depression among our youth – and those children will, in turn, do the same. In time we will reach a tipping point in society where we can access the deep well of collective strengths among us all. I truly look forward to that day. (p. 291)

Some readers may think this last paragraph overly optimistic, 'pie in the sky', but they should note that educating by its nature is a hopeful and optimist endeavour and we should all dare to dream and together find ways of realising our dreams. An exploration of ways and means for realising our educational dreams is presented and discussed in the following chapter.

Chapter 9

Lessons from Successful Educational Transformations Internationally

> Reforming education is not about copying and pasting solutions from other countries; it is about looking seriously and dispassionately at good practice in our own countries and elsewhere to become knowledgeable of what works in which contexts and applying it consciously. (Schleicher in OECD Report, 2018, p. 279)

While educational reports and other research literature on international educational reform are valuable sources of insight and wisdom about what constitutes successful educational transformation across a number of countries, more specific lessons can be drawn from educational transformation projects in specific countries. Ascione (2018), for example, provided a description and analysis of the key findings and conclusions of a competency-based education reform project in the USA in her report, *Show What You Know: A Landscape Analysis of Competency-Based Education.* Her report featured an overview of the current status of competency-based education in the USA and identified the positive forces for and barriers to its success. Educational reform leaders can learn much about what to do and what not to do from this source.

The report is based on interviews with more than 50 expert educators in K-12 schools, higher education, technology and philanthropy institutions, as well as analyses of more than 40 publications and other relevant source materials, including site visits to dozens of schools, and input from numerous education research organisations in the USA. She reported that despite educators' genuine enthusiasm for it, competency-based education seemed slow to spread and scale-up across USA schools due to the existence of sizable barriers and despite the fact that competency-based education has many benefits for students, old educational models block its progress. In this evidence-based report, she concluded that across the US educators are trying to meet students' unique learning needs with competency-based models that let students advance based on skill mastery rather than seat time. She identified key barriers to its success including, outdated

Leading Educational Systems and Schools in Times of Disruption and Exponential Change: A Call for Courage, Commitment and Collaboration, 95–106
Copyright © 2020 by Patrick A. Duignan
Published under exclusive license
doi:10.1108/978-1-83909-850-520201010

education models that sort students based on age, course completion and seat time; these barriers, she claimed, get in the way of educational innovation.

While many schools involved in the competency-based project are measuring student success using competencies, which help students take increasing responsibility for their own learning and develop habits of lifelong learners, there continues to be significant challenges and barriers that impede widespread adoption of competency-based approaches and models – barriers include inadequate support for teachers and students and a lack of sufficient tools and resources in schools. From the findings of recent literature on educational change and innovation discussed throughout this book, it appears that despite the passion and best intentions of many committed educators, and what we know about changing education systems and schools, educational change leaders and other innovators have had limited success in transforming the ways in which education is conceptualised and delivered. Educational leaders need to remind themselves that architectural transformations in educational organisations are not just about the redesign of buildings, learning spaces, and the enhancement of technological connectivity through the use of sophisticated wireless networks and miniaturised gadgets, but is more about connecting, inspiring and transforming the people who are charged with the responsibility of bringing about new conditions, structures and processes for learning, teaching and student engagement. Often reform attempts change structures and processes but the people involved do not change.

As Levine pointed out in the *Foreword* to Wilson's (2018) book, *The Human Side of Changing Education*, '… most education reform or change initiatives fail, not because of the quality of the ideas that underlie them, but because of the people who plan, implement, and institutionalise them' (p. xvi). Wilson argued for greater people-development in educational settings and called for '… not just reform, but transformation' (p. 3). From her extensive research on the subject, she described:

> […] what is possible from a human development perspective when we rethink, reimagine, and redesign a school to unleash potential, spark curiosity, and invite learners [at all levels] to think for themselves and to take ownership of their learning. (p. 3)

She cautioned, however, that while '… the core of change is learning, [ironically] our institutions of learning are slow, some might even say immune, to change' (p. 1). She based her argument on the view that education and school change is, essentially, a developmental task, which:

> […] is centred on the premise that, when we ask schools to change, we are asking human beings to change and this requires special tools and a human-centered approach. We cannot change the heart of the system without enabling the hearts and minds of those who give their all every single day to making schools work. (p. 4)

Nixon and Sinclair (2017) reflected similar sentiments when they cautioned educational reformers to remember that:

> [...] organisations are hard to change, people can, and do ... lead-
> ers must inevitably focus on supporting people to make changes
> ... leaders can't expect their teams to embrace the unknown unless
> [they] also demonstrate their own willingness to be open and adapt
> to what unfolds. (pp. 119–120)

Equally, when we speak of contemporary schools as shape-shifting organisations, we are not, necessarily, speaking of structural and organisational changes,
but more so the mindset and paradigm shifts of people who help enable their
schools to purposefully change their cultures, learning paradigms and pedagogy
in order to transform their teaching and learning delivery spaces, structures and
processes. Innovative individuals or groups may be successful in initiating small-
scale changes in the short term, but they find it extremely challenging to scale
them up to whole-school or whole-system transformation of teaching and learning delivery processes. Cultural change is necessary to achieve such scaled results.
Wilson (2018) explained that it is important to understand that inspiring transformational change in an education system is unlikely to be achieved by individuals
working on their own, no matter how inspirational they are, or even by a single
major initiative or intervention, no matter how planned and persuasive it may be:

> There is no single intervention that will change the system from a
> century-plus-old stagnant bureaucracy to a flexible, individualised
> system that unleashes human potential. There is no single policy, new
> school model, app, charismatic leader, test, or piece of research that
> will precipitate the level of change that we need. It will take many,
> many people working at all levels inside and outside the system if
> we are to see real and sustainable change within this decade. (p. 7)

Wilson is referring to scaled cultural changes without which reform innovations usually perish. She is, however, positive about the future and suggests a
number of important sources that can help leaders identify the '... skills and habits of mind that we need in order to thrive as adults in our volatile, uncertain,
complex and ambiguous (VUCA) world' (p. 9). She discussed and analysed the
findings and conclusions of *The World Economic Forum's*, *The Future of Jobs
Report* (2016), and highlighted the skills needed to thrive in 2020, as: '... complex
problem solving, critical thinking, and creativity – all people skills' (p. 9). She
used a number of important sources to identify key change leadership skills and
combined them with her own extensive research and development on the subject
of change and reform of education and schooling. She concluded that:

> [...] there is widespread agreement that the basic literacy require-
> ments of the industrial model of education are the floor, not the
> ceiling, and we need to set our sights higher for our children. (p. 9)

From these research-based sources, it becomes clearer that educational change
leaders require rich, pedagogically driven transformational advice, including

ideas on mindset and paradigm shifts for educators about the nature of transformational learning and teaching at school and system levels. To date in education, we have had creeping, incremental changes in the architecture of education, focussing, especially, on time and space modifications and limited organisational redesign, but we also need to focus on the transformation of people and pedagogy as a priority. Educational leaders need to encourage the formation of new paradigms and mindsets on the nature of twenty-first century learners, learning, educational architectures, as well as on shifting organisational shapes and structures (see Partnership for 21st Century Learning, 2017).

In Australia, for example, we had a possible stimulus for such transformations in our educational systems and schools, when we created a new National Curriculum that provided:

> [...] schools, teachers, parents, students, and the community with a clear understanding of what students should learn, regardless of where they live or what school system they are in. (*Australian Government, Department of Education and Training*, https://www. education.gov.au/australian-curriculum-0 (accessed 8 October 2018)

Even with selected expert designers, informed advisors, different curriculum frameworks, and creative professional development opportunities for curriculum specialists and teachers at school level, this entire trickle-down-initiative (perhaps drip-down is more accurate) does not seem to meet the requirements of '... a human-centred approach', because, as Wilson reminded us earlier, '... we cannot change the heart of the system without enabling the hearts and minds of those who give their all every single day to making schools work' (2018, p. 4). We need to respond creatively to Wilson's conclusion that transformational change in an educational system is unlikely to be achieved by one person, no matter how inspirational, or even by a major initiative or intervention, such as that of *The National Curriculum* in Australia. The National Curriculum and its supporting experts and developmental documents are, apparently, world class but its greatest weakness is that it focuses its creativity and efforts at the wrong end of the pyramid and expects educational professionals at grass-root levels to be inspired and transformed by speeches, diagrams, and top-down words.

During more than two decades of attempts to reform education systems in many countries, including the USA, UK and Australia, the emphasis has tended to focus on ideas such as, education for all and/or no child left behind. These reforms have focussed, primarily, on the development of standards-based curricula, comprehensive testing regimes, measurable performance outcomes and accountability for educators, especially for teachers. There appears to be strong tensions, even contradictions, in the philosophies and paradigms of such reform; perhaps we will need strong disrupted forces to resolve these tensions. Horn and Staker (2015) recommended that leaders use such disruptive forces to improve their schools. Their book, *Blended: Using Disruptive Innovations to Improve Schools*, provides perceptive analyses and advice for educational policymakers and leaders who wish to transform learning and teaching in their systems and schools. While the book focuses on blending online learning into schools, it introduces, explains and recommends much broader paradigms of teaching and learning that will encourage educators to change contemporary approaches to ones more suited to the growth mindsets of educational leaders, teachers and students in this challenging and disrupted twenty-first century. They concluded that '… an increasing number of students are experiencing online learning while continuing to attend their brick-and-mortar schools – a phenomenon called "blended learning"' (p. 4). To help explain this growing trend, they advised that:

> […] we need to step back and look at the big picture of why the traditional classroom model, even in the best schools, is not up to speed with what students need to succeed in today's world and why we can do better. (p. 5)

They claimed that there is little dispute in educational circles that:

> […] each student learns at a different pace. Some students learn quickly. Others learn more slowly. And each student's pace tends to vary based on the subject or even the concept. (p. 7)

Traditional classrooms, based on factory models, were not set up to cope with such diversity and are, therefore, failing our students. They concluded that '… our world has changed and our hopes for our children have changed but our schools have not' (p. 8). In recent times, many educators have attempted to make appropriate adjustments by emphasising student-centred learning, personalised learning and competency-based learning but Horn and Staker suggested that the concept and practice of blended learning has become an enabler of all three of these approaches. They explained:

> Blended learning is the engine that can power personalised and competency-based learning. Just as technology enables mass customisation in so many sectors to meet the diverse needs of so many people, online learning can allow students to learn anytime, in any place, on any path, and at any pace at scale. At its most basic level, it lets students fast-forward if they have mastered a concept, pause if they need to digest something, or rewind and slow something down if they need to review. It provides a simple way for students to take different paths toward a common destination. (p. 10)

Horn and Staker's book on the characteristics and practices of blended learning focusses, primarily, on ways of implementing it in various contexts, settings, and to scale. Models of blended learning are introduced and explained, supported by 12 examples on video-clips of different approaches. The model most teachers seem to prefer is referred to as the *Rotation Model*, which:

> [...] includes any course or subject in which students rotate – either on a fixed schedule or at the teacher's discretion – among learning modalities, at least one of which is online learning. (pp. 37–38)

This rotation model includes: *station rotation* within a classroom or a set of classrooms; *lab rotation* for online learning; *flipped classroom* approaches which flip the typical classroom processes on their head; and *individual rotation* within which '... students rotate on an individually customised schedule among learning modalities' (p. 45).

Other models of engagement include: Flex Model; A La Carte Model; Enriched Virtual Model, as well as the blending of these different models. Each of the models is comprehensively explained and implementation steps outlined (see pp. 46–52). Horn and Staker emphasised, however, that these blended-learning models are hybrids of the old and new, which '... means they are poised to build on and offer sustaining enhancements to, but not fundamentally re-architect, the factory-style classroom' (p. 77). Earlier in this book, it was noted that despite many attempts by well-intentioned leaders and educators in many systems, schools and countries to reform the architecture of learning and schooling, the outcomes continue to be piecemeal and disjointed. Wilson (2018) supported this view when she stated, '... there is no single model to follow when it comes to redesigning space and the schedule in schools' (p. 54).

Horn and Staker were, however, more optimistic when they stated that:

> [...] disruptive models of blended learning are on a different trajectory from those within the hybrid zone [because] they are carrying online learning on the march upward by helping it improve to intersect with the needs of more and more students and educators who feel enticed by the prospect of new-found opportunities for personalisation, access, and cost control. (pp. 77–78)

They observed, optimistically, that in a number of school systems in the USA: '... models of blended learning are starting to replace the factory model altogether, particularly at the high school level, and to some extent in the middle school' (p. 103). While such optimistic conclusions are heartening for educational reformers, in order to achieve scaled-up transformations of the architecture of learning and teaching, Ashenden (2018) advised that the 'grammar' of schooling has to change, from its '... 30-odd "lessons" per week' each in a "subject", delivered by a teacher, to a group of students of the same age ...' (p. 15) – he claimed it has never worked for a significant number of students. Geoff Masters (2016), CEO at Australian Council for Educational Research (ACER), complemented this view when he stated that traditional teaching and learning scenarios have had:

> [...] great difficulty in exploiting the digital technologies; and is not well suited to the circumstances in which children and young people do and will live, or the kinds of learning they need. (Ashenden, p. 15)

Ashenden believes, however, that a new and different:

> [...] grammar of schooling [is emerging and] it focuses not on the quality of teaching but on the organisation of learning. Specifically, it looks to the reorganisation of schooling around the continuous progress or growth of each student, and to a very different student working day and "learning career." (p. 15)

He is, essentially, referring here to reform of the architecture of schooling.

Horn and Staker (2015) identified, described and discussed a number of possible models of learning and schools they see as enabling positive architectural educational changes, including:

- *Product architecture and interfaces*, which refer to the constituent components and subsystems that contribute to the quality of the end product and how well they combine and integrate – these include interdependent architecture and modular architecture (explained in Horn & Staker, pp. 190–191).
- *Shift in personal computer architecture* to make it easy to use, least likely to crash or be infected with viruses, and is vertically integrated.
- *Shift towards modularity in education* in, for example, course access, course content, schools' modular architectures for computing, and modular design of schools' physical facilities. (see pp. 190–195).
- *Integrated versus modular physical space* where educators, especially teachers '... are choosing to rearrange their furniture and physical space to align with the principles of student agency, flexibility, and choice that are at the core of their new models.' (p. 206)

There are numerous sources of evidence-informed advice for educational leaders and reformers who wish to pursue transformations of the architecture of their schools and learning environments and these innovations can be scaled through technologically enabled networking, discussed earlier in this book. Horn and Staker, however, warned of some of the challenges within educational settings that continue to present leaders of educational architectural transformations with barriers to blended learning:

> In the early stages of blended learning, however, modularity is not always technologically possible. It's tempting to want to make the leap to a modular world immediately, but leaders must take inventory of individual circumstances to identify the right timing. Getting this timing right is a critical part of integrating the school's infrastructure to support the jobs that students and teachers are trying to do. (p. 208)

They also reminded educational leaders that successfully introducing blended learning is a team sport, as '... everyone has a role to play in blended learning' (p. 283). For example, '... teachers can start innovating right away and boost learning by flipping their classrooms and implementing Station Rotation' (p. 283). School leaders '... can support bottom-up approaches for teachers by encouraging and facilitating their efforts to innovate' (p. 283). Parents, they recommended, should also be involved and their collaboration sought and encouraged.

A very important piece of the jigsaw of architectural transformation of the teaching-learning paradigm is the need to re-focus, re-value and re-energise teachers' capabilities and professional judgement, as discussed in Chapter 8. The data that organisations have on performance outcomes would seem to provide them with opportunities to boost reform agendas and performance improvement, but there is an important downside to data-driven improvement processes, including a devaluing of the qualitative judgments of teachers and other professionals. Muller (2018), in *The Tyranny of Metrics*, cautioned about the possible consequences of our contemporary obsession with comprehensive assessment regimes, data use, and metrics generally. He stated that there are:

> [...] unintended negative consequences of trying to substitute standardised measures of performance for personal judgment based on experience. The problem is not measurement, but excessive measurement and inappropriate measurement – not metrics, but metric fixation. (p. 4)

He claimed there is widespread belief in a variety of different types of organisations – e.g. in medicine and healthcare, in K-12 and college or university education, in policing and other public services, in business and finance, and in charitable organisations, that '... gathering metrics of measured performance and then making them available to the public is a way to improve the functioning of our institutions' (p. 4). Based on his extensive research on the usefulness or otherwise of metrics for improving performance in organisations, he argued that '... while they [metrics] are a potentially valuable tool, the virtues of accountability metrics have been oversold, and their costs are often not appreciated' (p. 6). He challenged and rejected many claims made for the importance of metrics in performance improvement, including:

- [...] the aspiration to replace judgment based on experience with standardised measurement [because] judgment is understood as personal, subjective and self-interested (p. 6).
- [...] accountability demands that measurement of performance should be made transparent and public to achieve positive outcomes (p. 4).
- Claims that credibility only comes from evidence-based results, based on hard-data and metrics.

To support his views, Muller presented '... an etiology and diagnosis, but also a prognosis for how metric fixation can be avoided, and its pains alleviated' (p. 6).

His book is an important source of knowledge and insights on ways in which educational leaders can achieve a more productive and rewarding balance between people-based (human character and qualities) and evidence-based (measurement and data) approaches to decision-making (see Fullan on Nuanced Leadership in Chapter 12 of this book). Muller argued that in organisations as in life, there are essential people and performance-qualities that are invaluable yet not subject to standardised measurement – qualities such as mentoring and co-operating with fellow employees. These qualities can be evaluated but that requires personal and professional judgment, not measurement alone.

He argued that, in general, a focus on measured targets, benchmarks, and performance indicators discourages innovation because if the goals are specified in advance, there is little room for initiative or risk-taking. He made a key point often neglected or ignored in assessment processes – measurement is not an alternative to judgment, on the contrary measurement demands judgment because judgment is involved in decisions about whether to measure, what to measure, how to evaluate the significance of what's been measured, whether rewards and penalties will be attached to the results, and to whom the results should be made available. Becoming aware of the characteristic pitfalls of metric fixation is, he claimed, the first step in helping your organisation to recover and to restore professional judgment to its rightful place.

In times of rapid change in education, it is important to be able to make wise choices for the future based on a judicious balance of metrics and professional judgements and, especially about the nature of teaching and learning that will best serve and prepare students for challenging times ahead. In 2018, Schleicher recommended a balance between the use of metrics and a greater reliance on the professional judgements of educators, especially teachers. Muller (2018) pointed out that all high-performing education systems have an accountability system of some sort, usually built around the collection and appraisal of data, even though in his review of different countries and educational systems, he claimed that there is wide diversity in actual accountability processes. He suggested that:

> […] approaches to accountability evolve as school systems themselves evolve – as rules become guidelines and good practice and, ultimately, as good practice becomes culture. Often this progression involves a shift in the balance between "administrative accountability" and "professional accountability." (p. 115)

Administrative accountability, Muller claimed, tends to use data to identify good teachers and good schools and to intervene in underperforming schools (pp. 115–116). On the other hand, professional accountability:

> […] refers to systems in which teachers are accountable not so much to administrative authorities but primarily to their fellow teachers and school principals; professional accountability also includes the kind of personal responsibility that teachers feel towards their peers, their students and their parents. (p. 116)

This form of accountability has to be central if people-inspired educational reform and educational architectural changes are to be fully realised. He gave the example of very successful educational jurisdictions, such as Ontario in Canada, Finland, Japan and New Zealand, placing greater emphasis on more professional forms of work organisation and pursuing more collegial forms of teacher and school-leader accountability (see p. 116).

Schleicher (2018) concluded from his research that the heart of great teaching is not skilful use of technology or pedagogical processes, it is ownership of them and '... successful education systems in the 21st century need to do whatever it takes to develop ownership of professional practice by the teaching profession' (p. 264). When teachers feel a sense of ownership over their classrooms and when students feel a sense of ownership over their learning, '... that is when productive teaching takes place' (p. 264). He also pointed out that the dramatic reduction in the number of low-performing schools in the province of Ontario was not achieved by threatening to close underperforming schools, rather it was driven by the underlying assumption that '... teachers are professionals who are trying to do the right thing' (p. 116). He used Singapore as an example of where administrative and professional accountability are combined:

> The Singapore government sets annual goals, provides support to achieve them, and then assesses whether or not they have been achieved. Data on student performance are included, but so too are a range of other measures, such as teachers' contributions to the school and community, and judgements by a number of senior practitioners. (pp. 116–117)

The pressure for professional accountability in Finland, he stated, is high, and: '... tests are not used to find faults in the system or document underperformance; they help students learn better, teachers teach better, and schools to work more effectively' (pp. 117–118). He also singled out Canada as one of the highest-achieving countries in the 2015 round of PISA tests, ranking third for reading and in the top 10 for mathematics and science. He reported that this puts Canada ahead of Finland for reading and mathematics (see p. 132). In Australia, our best students rate highly on PISA – equal with some of the best performing countries – but, as we say in Australia, '... we have a very long tail in the curve of our results', which means that, for a number of reasons, we have too many underperforming students.

Educators in other countries can learn much from Canada on how to bring about improvements in their results because, as Schleicher reported:

> [...] the stand-out characteristic of Canada's education system is its emphasis on equity and its ability to elicit excellent results from students of different social backgrounds, including students with an immigrant background. (p. 132)

He emphasised that while 'Canada's schools have a high proportion of children from immigrant families, their performance is often not any different from that of non-immigrant children' (p. 132). Canada's approach is to integrate '… content from different cultures into the curriculum, so that students learn early on how to see the world from different perspectives' (p. 132). In addition, Schleicher reported that apart from success in PISA rankings, Canada has an unusually large proportion of tertiary-educated adults and, '… as another indicator of a well-educated society, young people in Canada are more likely to read for pleasure than students almost anywhere else in the world' (pp. 132–133).

Other countries can learn from Canada about the ways in which they are transforming their education systems and schools, especially with regard to educating the children of recent immigrants. As in Australia, immigration into Canada is mostly from Asia – from China, India, the Philippines and Pakistan – but, Schleicher reported that in Canada PISA results show that '… within three years of arrival, the children of new immigrants are scoring as high as their non-immigrant schoolmates' (p. 133). There are a number of reasons for these successes, including that immigrant children, whether from families with high or low levels of education, benefit from Canada's support for new arrivals and efforts to make sure that they are able to integrate:

- There is extra help for language learning and support for children with special needs.
- The education system(s) is able to find the balance between respecting different cultures and helping establish a common Canadian identity. (p. 133)

Despite all we know about successful examples of educational change in the countries just identified, such reforms seem elusive for many other countries and their school systems. The difficulties and challenges of educational reform were identified and discussed in an OECD Report (2018b), *Behavioural Insights for Public Integrity: Harnessing the Human Factor to Counter Corruption* (pp. 203–207). It seems that while our knowledge about what works in education has improved vastly in recent years, as yet no successful and widespread transformation of the architecture and delivery of education has been achieved. We can point to sporadic examples of educational transformation within some countries' school systems and schools but, as of 2019, there is still much to be done in scaling up these successful initiatives. As indicated earlier, there is a wealth of very valuable advice for educational policymakers, bureaucrats and practitioners in Schleicher's comprehensive overview of what works and what hasn't worked in education internationally.

Schleicher (2018), in *What Makes High-Performing School Systems Different* (pp. 61–137), provided detailed, evidence-based advice from a number of successfully reformed educational systems, including about their schools and schooling processes. His report, especially chapter 3, should be consulted by all those who wish to bring about long-term and systematic transformation of their school systems and schools. In chapter 3 (pp. 63–64), a range of features common to all high-performing education systems is presented, discussed and recommended to readers:

- Believing passionately that ordinary students can have extraordinary talents and personalising the education experience so that all students can meet high standards – they have advanced from sorting human talent to developing human talent.
- Addressing student diversity with differentiated pedagogical practices, without compromising on standards.
- Focussing not only on students' academic success but also on their well-being.
- Encouraging teachers to be innovative and to improve their own performance and that of their colleagues.
- Moving from administrative control and accountability to professional forms of work organisation – they create cultures of collaboration with strong networks of innovation.
- Aligning policies and practices across the system and ensuring that policies are coherent over-sustained periods of time and are consistently implemented.

While each of these success factors is analysed and discussed at great length in Chapter 3 of Schleicher's (2018) Report, the discussions and conclusions within this chapter – Chapter 9 – can provide a useful framework for the type of transformations essential for generating architectural reforms of schooling, education and pedagogy in our own educational jurisdictions. Central to any such transformation is an understanding of the type of education that will best serve the needs of our students in tomorrow's world. This is the focus of the next chapter.

Chapter 10

Preparing Today's Students for Tomorrow's World

David Gonski (2018) and an esteemed panel of educational experts drawn from different states, school systems and sectors in Australia, prepared and delivered a report for the Australian government called, *Through Growth to Achievement: Report of the Review to Achieve Educational Excellence in Australian Schools*. The panel concluded that Australian students deserve a first-class school education:

> [...] tailored to individual learning needs, and relevant to a fast-changing world [and they] should be challenged and supported to progress and excel in learning in every year of school, appropriate to each student's starting point and capabilities. (p. viii)

They reported that since 2000 the academic performance in Australia has declined compared to some other OECD countries, which means they '... are falling short of achieving the full learning potential of which they are capable' (p. viii).

The Australian Government established the *Review* in July 2017, chaired by David Gonski AC, and the researchers conducted country-wide consultations with teachers, principals, professional associations, teacher unions, parents and carers, school systems, state and territory governments, researchers, universities, community organisations and business and industry, as well as collecting nearly 300 group submissions/proposals. *The Review* focussed on impactful and practical reforms that could build on existing improvement efforts; critically, the key reforms recommended in the Report featured strongly in the proposals put forward by these groups. The report authors claimed that nationally, '... there is a very strong mandate and desire for change' (p. viii) but they concluded that Australian education has to overcome a number of challenges that require a sustained national response if students and schools are to reach the goal of achieving educational excellence.

These challenges include declines in performance in key areas such as reading, science and mathematics, which have occurred in '... every socio-economic

Leading Educational Systems and Schools in Times of Disruption and Exponential Change: A Call for Courage, Commitment and Collaboration, 107–123
Copyright © 2020 by Patrick A. Duignan
Published under exclusive license
doi:10.1108/978-1-83909-850-520201011

quartile and in all school sectors – Government, Catholic and Independent' (p. viii). A complication identified in the findings is that there is:

> [...] a wide range of educational outcomes in the same classroom or school, with the most advanced students in a year typically five to six years ahead of the least advanced students. (p. ix)

Such disparity in learning outcomes means that, within the current model of school education, '... some students are being left behind while others are not being adequately challenged' (pp. viii–ix). Above all, they suggested that Australia needs to review and change its model for education because, like many countries, '... it still has an industrial model of school education that reflects a 20th century aspiration to deliver mass education to all children' (p. ix).

This model, they said, is not designed '... to differentiate learning or stretch all students to ensure they achieve maximum learning growth every year' (Gonski et al., 2018, p. ix). They also reported that while this problem is widely recognised by teachers and educators, schools' attempts to address the issue are hampered by the methods of curriculum delivery, assessment approaches and work practices, as well as the structural environments in which educators operate. The constraints include '... inflexibility in curriculum delivery, reporting and assessment regimes, and tools focused on periodic judgements of performance, rather than continuous diagnosis of a student's learning needs and progress' (p. ix). The authors of the Report identified a number of priorities and change interventions to enable educators as well as schools and their communities to help all their students reach their full potential. Their first priority was for systems and schools to '... deliver at least one year's growth in learning for every student every year' (p. x). They recommended that forms of:

> [...] personalised learning and teaching – based on each child's learning needs and informed by iterative evaluation of the impact of those strategies – are effective at improving education outcomes for all students. (p. x)

These reforms, they stated:

> [...] depend on creating the conditions that will enable teachers and schools to successfully adopt practices that support tailored teaching for growth, such as collaborative planning, teaching and assessment, and personalised learning for students. (p. x)

Their second priority was to '... equip every child to be a creative, connected and engaged learner with a growth mindset that can help improve a student's educational achievement over time' (p. x). Gonski's panel recommended:

> [...] a nationally coordinated review of the purpose, content and structure of senior secondary education to make sure it is contemporary, and adequately prepares students for post-school

employment, training, higher education and to live and prosper in a rapidly changing world. (p. xi)

Their third priority aimed to cultivate an adaptive, innovative and continuously improving education system, which requires '… continuous improvement across each part of the education system, from curriculum, reporting and assessment models, to workforce development and community and parent and career engagement' (p. xi). Five key findings, selected by this author from a larger number, strongly support the above three priorities (pp. xv–xvi):

> *Finding 4:* Teaching curriculum is based on year- or age-levels, rather than levels of progress that leave some students behind and fails to extend others, limiting the opportunity to maximise learning growth for all students.

> *Finding 7:* There is compelling evidence in Australian schools and internationally to support the view that tailored teaching based on ongoing formative assessment and feedback are the key to enabling students to progress to higher levels of achievement.

> *Finding 9:* To continue to grow student outcomes, we need to attract and retain the best and most effective teachers in the profession – teaching must become a high-status profession of expert educators.

> *Finding 15:* Currently, school leaders are called upon to play a variety of roles, including leaders of learning, but are also business administrators and culture setters with a particular focus on their role as leaders of learning.

> *Finding 17:* To sustain continuous improvement, Australian schools need access to: valid and reliable evidence of effective teaching practice; independent and rigorous evaluations of commercial and other teaching and educational interventions; and the most recent findings on educational innovation and research in classroom-friendly forms (pp. xv–xvi).

The details of the priorities, aims, findings and the recommendations of this report provide educational leaders, teachers and other reformers with a treasure-trove of evidence and advice on what to do and how to do it, citing successful projects aimed at transformations in educational systems and schools in Australia and internationally.

Continuing the theme of priorities and possible interventions necessary to enable educators, schools and their communities to help all students to reach their full potential, the McKinsey Report (Barber, Chijioke, & Mourshed, 2010) examined how the world's most improved school systems keep getting better with the expressed intention of learning how best to redesign and reform education systems and schools to better serve students now and into the future. The researchers and authors of the report, Mourshed, Chijoke and Barber, conducted their research with 200 system leaders, staff and educators across 20 systems in a number of countries. They also engaged with a number of international educational leaders and experts, including Michael Fullan, Saravanan Gopinathan, Peter Hill, and Andreas Schleicher. In the *Foreword* to their report, Fullan – a world expert on whole-of-system reform – reported that the authors focussed on '… the inner workings of successful pathways of reform given different beginning points' (p. 6). They described the purpose of their report as involving '… the experiences of 20 school systems from all parts of the globe that have achieved significant, sustained, and widespread gains, as measured by national and international standards of assessment' (p. 7). They also stated that the report:

> […] attempts to disaggregate the various elements of what makes school systems improve, to parse exactly what one system can learn from another, and how to adjust these elements to the specific, local context. (p. 11)

Their conclusions constitute key evidence and arguments for redesigning and renewing education and schooling and for preparing today's students for tomorrow's world, which is the main focus in this chapter.

A complicating factor, is that practical experience, research and relevant literature support the view that while many educational innovations demonstrate early successes, these are seldom sustained. Ashenden (2015) argued that if we want real educational reforms that last, it is foolhardy to:

> […] persist in the view that if schools are exposed to the right combination of pressures and given the right capacity to respond, they will lift … performance in terms of improved student attainment, as measured by standardised tests. (p. 4)

After analysing a variety of educational reform literature by a number of key Australian academics and reformers, he concluded that while their reform recommendations may show short-term gains they do not last long-term. The McKinsey Report (Barber et al., 2010) also concluded that, over the years, while educational reform initiatives and innovations achieved reasonable success in the short term, they gradually regressed to the starting position over time. For an educational improvement journey to be sustained over the longer term, the authors of the report concluded that the improvements have to be integrated into the very fabric of the system ideology and pedagogy.

The report identified three ways for improving systems and suggested that each of these is '… an interconnected and integral part of the system's pedagogy':

1. Establishing collaborative practices;
2. Developing a mediating layer between the school and the system centre; and

3. Architecting tomorrow's leadership. (p. 72)

They cite Fullan's (2010) work to highlight the power of collaborative practice and the collective capacity of groups to enable ordinary people to accomplish extraordinary things:

> Collective capacity is when groups get better – school cultures, district cultures and government cultures. The big collective capacity and the one that ultimately counts is when they get better conjointly – collective, collaborative capacity, if you like. Collective capacity generates the emotional commitment and the technical expertise that no amount of individual capacity working alone can come close to matching .... (p. 74)

Fullan claimed that the power of collective capacity is that it '... enables ordinary people to accomplish extraordinary things – for two reasons'. First the knowledge on '... effective practice becomes more widely ... accessible on a daily basis', and secondly '... working together generates commitment [which makes] the collective motivational well seem bottomless, [and then] the speed of effective change increases exponentially ...' (Fullan, 2010, p. 74).

The authors of the McKinsey Report (Barber et al., 2010) concluded that leaders new to their positions, experience '... a common and particularly important pattern in igniting school system reforms, occurring in all of the improving systems we have studied' (p. 91). These new leaders, they claim, take:

> [...] advantage of the opportunity afforded by their being new to the role, in following a common "playbook" of practices, and in their longevity, having a much lengthier tenure than is the norm. (p. 91)

The authors cautioned, however, that the improvement journey will be '... gradual and involve modification of perspectives and opinions which we previously held to be true' (p. 110).

An OECD Report (2017) titled, *Schools at the Crossroads of Innovation in Cities and Regions*, provided important evidence on how educational reformers can transform education and schooling to better serve educators and their students into the future; this report served as the background report to the Third Global Education Industry Summit, held on 25–26 September 2017 in Luxembourg. It provided valuable insights on how educators can transform education and schooling to better serve global, local and community needs and aspirations. The report focussed on the recent '... increasing number of arguments and appeals for innovation in our education systems [which tend to] focus on internal components of education systems: teachers, pedagogies, curricula, school organisation, leadership etc.' (p. 3). They concluded, however, that to expect education systems to generate sufficient capacity for innovation internally seems unreasonable.

They pointed out that too few innovations in education '… have looked at the broader context and the external relations of schools as drivers of innovation' (p. 3). They argued that educational leaders and reformers:

> […] need to see schools as networking institutions and part of encompassing ecosystems of learning and innovation. It is only by conceptualising schools as part of broader ecosystems that that they can … understand and foster change and innovation. (p. 3)

Based on their research findings, the authors reported that:

> […] ecological thinking in education has advanced the notion of learning and innovation ecosystems that encompass not only educational institutions and non-formal learning environments, but also broader communities, social organisations, industry and business. (p. 3)

This ecological emphasis and approach to educational reform '… has engendered a renewed interest in locality, the local and regional context in which schools operate' (p. 3). This recognition of the importance of learning and innovation ecosystems coincides with a growing awareness that successful educational innovations occur, predominantly, at the regional and local level, because these levels really influence an innovation '… through the proximity, networking and partnerships which are increasingly important for creating the conditions for innovation to happen' (p. 9). In many cases, they concluded that:

> […] this means rethinking the organisational patterns forming the backbone of most schools today: the separate classrooms, each with its own teacher; the familiar timetable and bureaucratic units; and traditional approaches to teaching and classroom organisation. (pp. 9–10)

The report is referring here to the types of architectural changes needed in education, which are the focus of many of our discussions throughout this book.
They concluded that architectural innovations, including:

> […] opening up schools to their environment, developing real ecosystems of change and innovation, and promoting a more active role for stakeholders and communities seem to be critically important steps in the process of innovation in education. (p. 10)

Successful innovation requires, in addition to creative and smart ideas and technologies, a '… combination of activities and many inter-related actors who generate and use knowledge and information' (p. 25). Effective use of connected technologies can be powerful tools for assisting innovation, [but] '… the mere presence of technology is not by itself enough for innovation. Going digital may only reproduce traditional methods and pedagogies in a different form' (p. 10).

The report identified four key ingredients for building innovative capacity in educational systems and schools: (pp. 112–113, italics added for emphasis by this author):

1. *Teacher education, including rethinking continuous professional development*: we should build the capacity to change and to innovate into teacher education, taking cues from the corporate learning world; the issue is one of performance support, rather than "training"(p. 112).
2. *Design thinking supporting innovation*: educators should adapt ideas from world-class digital designers, because designing for use with digital is a different discipline requiring, for example, an understanding of issues such as user interface/user experience (UI/UX) understanding.
3. *Models of assessment*: digital pedagogies and new teaching practices imply new models of assessment and '… undoubtedly, as students generate massive amounts of valuable data through digital interactions, learner analytics, personalisation and adaptive learning take on a whole new importance' (p. 113).
4. *Student voice*: we can and should learn a lot from how students engage with new technologies and pedagogies. In the digital gaming industry, there is a philosophy of 'player first', giving players an embedded role in product development. Perhaps '… a "student first" approach to developing pedagogies could also be adopted' (p. 113).
5. We can add a fifth ingredient to these four: *teachers' voice*, because teachers need to be partners in implementing the educational ecosystem; they are '… participants, co-authors, co-designers, co-implementers and co-leaders of the process' (this authors italics for emphasis, p. 116).

Tichnor- Wagner and Manise (2019) in the Association for Supervision and Curriculum Development (ASCD) Report, titled *Globally Competent Educational Leadership: A Framework for Leading Schools in a Diverse, Interconnected World*, focussed on a number of the themes already discussed in this book related to leading educational reform in a techno-smart, diverse, unstable and interconnected world. The report examined the challenges and opportunities of leading education in this interconnected world, and the authors presented numerous case studies focusing on future-oriented educational developments in a globalised world. These cases, as well as accounts from numerous school principals on how they are future-proofing their schools, classrooms and learning pedagogies, provide a useful framework and practical guidelines for educational leaders and teachers who wish to encourage and support globally competent teaching, learning and leading in their schools and classrooms. The report is a great source for insights into globalising education in schools and gives advice on ways to connect teaching, learning and leading to successful global developments in education. There are also accounts and practical examples from numerous schools in the USA that have succeeded in transforming themselves into globally inspired educational environments, thereby better preparing their students for a super-interconnected world.

The researchers/authors, Tichnor- Wagner and Manise, identified a number of attributes that comprise global competence, including cognitive, social-emotional, and behavioural ones.

> *Cognitive* attributes include '… critical thinking, problem solv- ing, and an understanding of global conditions, events, cultures, and interconnectedness.' *Social-emotional* attributes include '… empathy, valuing multiple perspectives, awareness of one's iden- tity and culture, appreciation of diversity, openness and adaptabil- ity.' *Behavioral attributes* include '… collaboration, cross-cultural communication, and agency to act on issues of local and global importance.' (p. 3, italics in original)

The authors claimed that globally competent teaching requires students to '… actively construct knowledge through pedagogy that engages learners with authentic audiences addressing real-world concerns' (p. 3). They reported that these students learn content through a global perspective and teachers '… infuse instruction with real-world contexts that resonate with students' lives, interests, experiences, and future goals … students see value and engage in what they are learning' (p. 4). Selected students should also be encouraged and supported to act as tutors of other students, especially those who require personalised attention; student tutors are more likely to use appropriate language to engage more effec- tively with their colleagues. The grammar and architecture of learning in schools must respect and include students' inputs and students supporting each other because it will benefit both the tutor and the learner.

School leaders can play a central role in creating the collaborative school cultures that encourage students to engage with each other, the community and with the wider world. This global engagement is greatly facilitated by access to speedy, interactive and low-cost technologies. Such connected technologies, as well as the emergence of collaborate structures and processes in and between schools, create:

> […] a range of learning opportunities for all staff and students, using data for improvement efforts, and building trust and respect across the organisation [all leading to] student learning and suc- cess. (pp. 4–5)

These leaders can also influence a number of key educational processes within this reform approach, including improving the quality of connected pedagogies for a globalised world. As a result, key improvements will occur, including in '… *cur- riculum, instruction, and assessment; the development of collaborative professional communities; global connections and collaboration; and advocacy and community engagement*' (Tichnor- Wagner & Manise (2019), pp. 8–10, italics in original). According to one of the report's authors, Tichnor-Wagner, educational leaders can '… implement and support curriculum, instruction and assessment that incor- porate and promote the development of each student's global competence' (p. 9).

The authors claimed that teachers can achieve similar results by providing classroom resources that cover the diversity of the students involved, as well as the variety of cultures and countries around the world. They can work with external, connected professional partners who build professional learning communities in their schools by creating '… staff time for leading collaborative, innovative work; providing job-embedded professional development focussed on global competence that allows for teacher innovation, experimentation, differentiation, and leadership…' (p. 9). Teachers and students are encouraged and supported in their collaborative efforts by being provided with '… ample time and space to share their professional global learning experiences and best practices from their classrooms with each other' (p. 9).

These globally inspired and committed school leaders and teachers also help create:

> […] partnerships with schools in other regions and countries; participation in local, national, and international cross-cultural learning exchanges; the forming and maintaining of relationships with local, national, and international colleagues; [and creating] a technology-base that allows for global connections …. (p. 9)

They also encourage the development of advocacy and community engagement skills by '… making the case to parents in newsletters, family nights, and ad-hoc conversations …' (p. 10). School leaders and teachers can engage families in global initiatives by '… creating communication channels for them to share their perspectives, ideas, questions, and concerns, as well as their own global experiences and expertise' (p. 10). The authors of the report are passionate about the need to encourage enhanced globally competent leadership in school systems and schools and they quote a principal of an international school who successfully focussed on the development of globally competent leaders and teachers to justify and support their point of view:

> The mess our world is in right now is because we have people in power who never developed global competence. Our students are our next generation. If we don't like what we're seeing now we need to change some things. We are witnessing a group of people who have had the privilege to opt out of global competence and we are seeing the effects of that. I want to create a space where people can't opt out. You need to be able to embrace it. It's just part of our future living in global society. The idea of America First, we aren't as great as we think we are. We need to understand for being as diverse a nation as we are, we have done our best to keep people segregated. I think it's the responsibility of those of us working in education to change that around. (Dr. Aimee Fearing, Principal, Wellstone International High School, Minneapolis, MN, quoted in ASCD report, p. 70)

Being globally competent includes ways in which we, as educational leaders and teachers, can better prepare our young people for their future working lives (Owen, 2018). Torii and O'Connell (2017) from the Mitchell Institute University of Victoria, Australia, brought together a group of leaders from across Australia to consider ways in which educators can respond to the challenges, including work challenges, that are putting the nation's wellbeing and future prosperity at risk. Their roundtable discussions with education practitioners, government leaders, policy specialists and researchers put forward two ideas about how Australia's education systems can change to accelerate innovation and improve students' transitions to employment:

- Transform senior secondary education and
- Revitalise apprenticeships.

They found that for many twenty-first century school leavers '… the journey from school to the workforce is taking longer and becoming more precarious' (2017, p. 2). They concluded that in Australia:

- Youth unemployment has remained high since the onset of the Global Financial Crisis.
- Fewer young people have full-time work.
- A large proportion of young people engage in unpaid work just to get a foot in the door.
- The traditionally reliable pathways to a permanent job are not providing young people with the same employment outcomes they once did.
- Many young people struggle to find employment in the field they studied and trained for.
- Over a quarter of young people are not fully engaged in education or training at age 24.

These characteristics of school graduates are not peculiar to Australia; they are applicable to a number of the countries already identified in this book. Torii and O'Connell suggested that these changes in young people's pathways into work have clear implications for education and for economic policy in Australia in the future, and they concluded that:

> […] education systems [generally] have not been designed to foster the types of capabilities needed to navigate complex environments and multiple careers [in the future] because the basic model of education has been largely static in the face of changes in the broader economy. (p. 3)

They reported that too many young people are being left behind, and '… this challenge will only intensify into the future' (p. 3). They projected that future generations will navigate a vastly different world of work to that of their predecessors and, as technology is rapidly disrupting how we live and work, many tasks at the core of low skill jobs are being automated or contracted offshore.

Their recommendation was that young people will need different skill-sets to thrive in technology-rich, globalised and highly competitive job markets. They advised that, as educators, we will need '… to adapt our approaches to education to better equip young people with the capabilities that will enable them to thrive in these complex education and employment settings' (p. 3). They concluded that a renewed focus on capabilities must underpin reform in order to '… bridge the academic and vocational divide, providing young people with the resources to navigate the future' (p. 3). While they suggested that '… knowledge is crucial … young people need to understand how to find it, how to interpret it, how to utilise it and how and when to act on it' (quote from Lucas & Claxton, 2009, in Torii & O'Connell, 2017, p. 3).

In September 2019, a *Position Paper* was issued in Australia, titled *Beyond ATAR: A Proposal for Change*. It was researched and written by Megan O'Connell, Sandra Milligan and Tom Bently – internationally recognised educational reformers – and focussed on transforming the transition connections and processes from school to higher education, to life and to work. In the *Foreword* to the paper, Koshland claimed that the report had '… far reaching implications for senior secondary education, post-school recruitment and selection processes, and flow-on effects for middle-school curriculum, career guidance and resource allocation' (p. 2). In their proposals, the authors emphasised the importance of the age 15–19 stage of education – from year 10 to first-year post school – as a '… specific development phase of education in which young people are supported to develop knowledge, skills and capabilities within various domains' (p. 3). They highlighted the need for school educators to help this age cohort of young people develop human-skills capabilities, including creativity and interpersonal skills, to prepare them for '… a lifetime of learning, adaptation and the future economy' (p. 4). They provided strategies and advice for school-level educators to help smooth:

> […] the education to work pathway given that for over half of young people [in Australia] the transition to full-time work takes up to five years, with many young people working a variety of part-time and casual jobs. (p. 4)

According to the authors, these contextual conditions can '… delay young people in developing confidence and optimism about their future, making it more difficult for them to forge foundations for working careers, and family and community life' (p. 5).

They concluded that '… the idea that there is an orderly, step by step progression from school to higher levels of learning and the workplace is a myth …' (p. 5). New analysis from Longitudinal Surveys of Australian Youth (LSAY) separated young people into five transition categories:

- Higher education to work – about 60 per cent of surveyed students made this transition smoothly.
- Early entry to work – about 20 per cent, mainly males, entered work though apprenticeships and traineeships.

- Mix of higher education and vocational education and training (VET) – about 8 per cent, mainly females, took this pathway.
- Mixed and repeatedly disengaged – about 5 per cent of young people transitioned frequently and disengaged from the labour market.
- Mainly working part time – about 4 per cent of young people were likely to leave school early, were less likely to engage in post-school education, and were more engaged in part time work. (p. 5)

This transition from school to higher studies, work and life itself is complex and confusing for many students, and even for secondary school educators. The authors investigated the role of The Australian Tertiary Admission Rank (ATAR) in narrowing the range of student capabilities and life success factors in senior secondary education and concluded that it has increasingly become '... less fit for purpose'. They stated that it causes too many young people to '... abandon their real interests, push aside extra-curricular activities and part-time employment to focus on achieving a score' (p. 7). They concluded that:

> [...] the 70 percent of learners who will neither enter university nor use the ATAR for university entry are subjected to narrow curriculum areas and stressful forms of high stakes assessment for little gain. Assessment by high stakes exams can drive pedagogy focussed around memorising and recalling content. (p. 7)

In their conclusions on the usefulness of ATAR, they stated:

> [...] a single number is a thin representation of the outcome of [secondary] schooling. A single number does not capture the attainments and qualities of any student, and is not a reliable predictor of future academic success for students with scores below 70, or success in life. (p. 8)

They also questioned the role of exams at the end of senior-secondary schooling and concluded that they:

> [...] are not the best tool for assessing complex capabilities in which nuanced responses to specific, practical challenges are desired, or when capabilities such as collaboration, communication, leadership, or enterprise are required. (p. 11)

They urged that all students develop:

> [...] the confidence and capabilities to thrive as citizens and community members [by acquiring the] knowledge, skills, attitudes, values and beliefs they require to navigate a successful transition

from school to employment, further study and to thrive in adult life. (p. 12)

In their first of three proposals, they recommended that:

> [...] the 15-19 stage of education, from Year 10 to the first-year post school, [be] re-cast as a specific developmental phase of education in which young people are supported to develop knowledge, skills and capabilities within various domains. All learners should be supported to navigate this phase and find a line of sight into work or further study that can lead them to a thriving adulthood and builds on their unique interests, capabilities and aspirations. (p. 13)

It seems obvious that many traditional secondary schools and their educators should become familiar with the findings and recommendations of the O'Connell et al. (2019) Position Paper and embrace a number of their recommendations if they wish to better serve their senior-secondary students – indeed all their students – when making the transition from their schools to further education, work and life in general.

Another key challenge for educational leaders and educators, generally, is the nature of professional development and in-service programmes that will better prepare them and their students for a rapidly changing and challenging global world, including contexts where social-media bombard them with opinions and 'news' from numerous perspectives. Tamera Musiowsky-Borneman, a teacher in Singapore, currently the President of the *Emerging Leaders Alumni Affiliate* (ELASCD), has written in-service programmes for teachers on such topics as student-led classrooms and co-teaching within global perspectives. She stated that in today's highly charged social-media climate students are '... bombarded with opinions over facts and speeches of nationalism versus globalism from every perspective – including economically, technologically, scientifically, and educationally' (p. 1). Often, she claimed, students are confused between being a loyal citizen of their own country's interests and global issues and challenges, e.g. climate change; she concluded that:

> [...] we must not think of these concepts as binaries [because] what we do in our local communities impacts the larger community. Our individual and collective actions affect humans and the environment worldwide – positively *and* negatively – more than most of us realise. (p. 1)

She urged that, as educators:

> [...] it is our shared responsibility with parents to help children acquire the skills to listen intently, think critically, filter and curate information, and find ways to participate as globally minded learners.

She advised that:

> [...] teaching and learning are a journey in which all members of the school community should participate in order to develop a strong sense of interconnectedness. Teaching local is not separate from teaching global; it is an interconnected web. (p. 2)

Musiowsky-Borneman (2019) provides practical advice for educators, especially teachers, on how, as a teacher, she navigates '... the crossroads of local and global thinking' (p. 2). She explained:

> While learning about the impact of human interactions on the environment, viewing the video "The Story of Stuff" was a powerful reminder of our global citizenship—so much so that some students watched the video at home with their parents. More recently, I have used the United Nations' Sustainable Development Goals with students and teachers to build interest about their role on our interconnected planet. Reflection tools such as ASCD's Globally Competent Learning Continuum or Whole Child Framework can also support the development of an educator's global mindset.

The key to developing globally competent education, learning and teaching is, according to Torii and O'Connell, to better understand that '... capabilities are a set of skills, behaviours and dispositions which allow an individual to convert ... knowledge into meaningful action in a range of different settings' (quote from Fox, 2016, in Torii & O'Connell, 2017, p. 3). They identified different types of capabilities necessary for a successful future for students, including '... critical thinking, problem solving, creativity, curiosity, interpersonal and communication skills, self-regulation, grit, entrepreneurial skills, teamwork and craftsmanship' (p. 3). An important implication from their data and results is that, currently, there is a disconnect between '... the structure and focus of our education systems and the needs of young people and the economy' and, although progress is being made on embedding the capabilities young people will need into the curriculum, '... there is more to be done to ensure all young people are adequately equipped for the future' (p. 14). The report highlighted a number of must-know understandings for education policymakers, leaders, reformers and practitioners if we are to equip students with the capabilities necessary to successfully navigate through the uncertain and fast-changing times ahead. This must-know knowledge includes:

1. Children starting preschool in 2017 may go on to be employed in jobs we haven't yet imagined. Our education systems are not yet adequately preparing young people for the future, and already the data is showing this strain (p. 4).
2. Our education systems can better meet the needs of young people navigating a complex future but pursuing this kind of systemic change will not be easy.

'It involves a number of fundamental changes to the way we conceptualise and deliver learning opportunities to young people' (p. 15).

3. Of all the priority areas raised in the roundtable discussions which form the basis of the report, prioritising capabilities is the most pressing and the most-ready solution. Strengthening capabilities can help bridge the academic and vocational divide and the authors recommended that governments should '… prioritise testing and reporting of achievement in capabilities alongside core curriculum' (p. 19). Many of these capabilities will be qualitative in nature.

The report provides detailed recommendations for educators and educational leaders at all levels on ways to address these three challenges (See report pages 14, 16, 18, 20). Taken together, these recommendations weave a rich educational tapestry addressing most of the criticisms of current pedagogies and learning approaches, as well as many of the challenges for educators and educational leaders at system and school levels, discussed earlier in this chapter and throughout this book. When discussing the findings of the Gonski Report, it was pointed out that the report authors concluded that if Australia is to have the type of educational architecture already recommended in this book, then its conception, planning and implementation must be a collaborative national initiative, which includes national, state- and system-level inputs, because no one person or group has the helicopter knowledge and resources to plan and undertake these daring and courageous transformations.

A starting point for deep and comprehensive reform could be the creation of a nationally coordinated review of the purpose, content and structure of senior secondary education to ensure it is contemporary and that it adequately prepares students for their post-school and future employment, in order to be successful in a rapidly changing world. If Australia had a much clearer view of the nature of secondary education that will better serve its young people in the future, planning for the earlier years of education, especially in primary schools, would have greater purpose and relevance for students; many other countries are in the same educational space.

This author has worked over a period of time with the Executive Director and leadership team of a Catholic Education System of 142 schools – Brisbane Catholic Education (BCE) – to bring about system and school-level transformation and better prepare them for the disruptions of an uncertain and rapidly changing world. The Executive Director, Pam Betts, has provided valuable insights into ways in which education systems and schools can kick-start transformational processes in their jurisdictions.

Leading a Catholic School System in a Disrupted World: Vision is Our Springboard (By Pam Betts)

In 2017, Brisbane Catholic Education (BCE) made a decision to develop a vision for the years beyond 2020. After a period of consultation and discernment, the new vision was launched in 2019. The vision will guide the system as it moves forward as a 'faith-filled learning community' creating a better future for everyone.

Collectively, we committed to moving forward with positivity and an openness to the possibilities. Instead of 'as usual', we asked 'what if' as we prepare to take the leap and embrace change and creative ways of working.

We are currently collaborating across education providers, with universities and industry sectors to determine how we can serve our students better in an uncertain future. We must, however, anticipate resistance as change can be disturbing, but our vision gives us purpose, resolve and confidence for continuous improvement. If we respond positively and harness the resistance as an opportunity for reflection and accountability, we will be guided to a better future. Our aspirational vision was developed after broad consultation within and outside our organisation and this process served not only to inform its articulation, but to encourage discussion on where we need to be as a system in a fast changing and uncertain future.

Our expressed aspiration is for our schools to be vibrant places where young people come together to learn about themselves, others, and the wonderful beauty and possibilities of the world in which they live; it also includes inspiring students to reach their full potential so they will make the world a better place. Our vision calls on each professional educator in BCE to be creatively responsive to change and disruption, especially to the contemporary demands of literacy and numeracy; calls for more enriching social and emotional intelligence experiences; exposure to cutting-edge, twenty-first century technology skills; and the promotion of creativity and artistry within a culture that nurtures innovation, adaptability and agility. BCE has had structures and practices that served us well in the past, but to realise our vision of being a faith-filled learning community creating a better future for our students, we simply must evolve. Our unified vision and consistent messaging that learning and continuous improvement never stops has enabled us to begin creating our own transformative story.

In planning for the future, we carry a dual responsibility. Firstly, to ensure that the system supports, promotes and assesses student learning and engagement in the present so that students leave school with the skills, knowledge and resilience needed to engage meaningfully in life and work. Secondly, we need to keep a sharp eye to the future of education and the world beyond education. As educational leaders, we have a duty to prepare our learners to be resilient and adaptive to unimaginable change, to be curious and have the courage to seek solutions through collaborative diversity and to try, fail, learn and move forward. Questioning whether our enterprise system is performing to its potential and delivering optimal support to our 142 school communities is confronting and uncomfortable and demands courageous planning and actions, because if we do not repeatedly challenge the status-quo, we will not grow.

Leading with humanity, honesty and a commitment to collaboration will help empower a BCE workforce, which is not only resilient and adaptive to change but is inspired and thrives on growing, achieving and maintaining the positive changes. A key question that our leadership team and our system educators constantly reflect on is: 'Is BCE ready for future disruptions and to be a disruptor itself?' So far, our answer is 'not yet', but we are ready to learn and create a better future in which we are inspired by our Catholic mission, our shared values of excellence, integrity, justice and hope, and our positivism to shape the unknown into a future of our own making (Betts, 2019).

Pam's wisdom and insights on leading system and school transformation in a VUCA world, directly addresses the main focus in this chapter – Chapter 10 – on the challenges of preparing today's students for tomorrow's world. Her system's vision inspires all BCE system and school members to respond creatively to the changes and disruptions impacting upon their work and lives. They are encouraged to take informed and calculated risks to better prepare their students to be curious about and adaptive to constant change, have the courage to seek solutions through collaborative diversity, and, as she stated, '… to try, fail, learn and move forward.'

These positive reform themes will be further investigated in the final two chapters – 11 and 12 – and consideration is also given to how cutting-edge, smart twenty-first century technology skills can assist in supporting, even driving, these reform agendas.

Chapter 11

Navigating the Future of Learning: The Role of Smart Technologies

The OECD Centre for Educational Research and Innovation produced a report in 2016, titled, *Innovating Education and Educating for Innovation: The Power of Digital Technologies and Skills*. This report presented a comprehensive coverage of the potential of smart technologies in education and recommended uses for a variety of such technologies in schools. Several of the issues on technological disruption and pedagogical reform in schools identified in this report address challenges to educational reform discussed throughout this book and key chapters in the report have special relevance for leaders of educational innovations and reform. These chapters include: Chapter 1: 'The innovation imperative in education'; Chapter 3: 'Digital technologies in education', and Chapter 4: 'The potential of technology-supported learning'. A number of dimensions of technologically inspired reform for education are identified and discussed in Chapter 4 of the report, which addresses key contemporary challenges and opportunities for educators who focus on school and classroom-level pedagogical transformation.

The report's conclusions indicated that introducing digital technology into education for technology's sake does not materially improve results because educational reforms need to place '… teaching practice rather than technology in the driving seat' (Report, p. 89). For the most part, they claimed, recent reform attempts characterised by increasing access to a variety of interactive technologies in the classroom, as well as an increasing push for greater accountability, are the 'wrong drivers' of reform (Fullan, 2019a). In several countries, educational reform movements have not '… been accompanied by appropriate strategies to improve pedagogy and teaching practices, [or effective] professional development for teachers [or] the provision of excellent software and courseware' (Fullan, 2011 in OECD Report, 2016, p. 90). The right drivers to achieve educational and pedagogical improvement, even reform, focus on:

> […] the teaching-assessment nexus, social capital to build the profession, pedagogy matching technology, and developing system synergies [as these drivers] work directly on changing the culture

Leading Educational Systems and Schools in Times of Disruption and Exponential Change: A Call for Courage, Commitment and Collaboration, 125–137
Copyright © 2020 by Patrick A. Duignan
Published under exclusive license
doi:10.1108/978-1-83909-850-520201012

of teaching and learning [and] embed both ownership and engagement in reforms for students and teachers. (Fullan in OECD
Report, p. 90)

The report also provided a detailed analytical description of Hewlett Packard's
(HP's) *Catalyst Initiative* as one way to change the educational landscape to
facilitate the successful interdisciplinary implementation of science, technology, engineering and mathematics (STEM) in secondary and tertiary education.
The report identified a number of effective models that emerged from the HP
Initiative – the 5 models most relevant for our discussion here were numbered 6–10
in the report:

1. *Educational gaming* offers '... a promising model to enhance
   student learning in STEM education, not just improving content knowledge, but also motivation, thinking and creativity'
   (Report, pp. 91–92). Educational gaming promotes:

   - *learning by doing*, which enables students to learn about
     complex topics by allowing them to (repeatedly) make mis-
     takes and learn from them;
   - *student learning* by enhancing their subject-specific knowl-
     edge and deep learning skills;
   - greater *student engagement and motivation* in various sub-
     jects and education levels, gaining more skills and capabili-
     ties when they construct games themselves; and
   - *students' thinking skills* through finding new ways around
     challenges and enhancing problem solving;

2. *Online laboratories*: whether remote or virtual, they enhance
   technology-supported teaching and learning by allowing students '... to simulate scientific experiments and, through remote
   access, use real laboratory equipment from a distance through
   the internet' (p. 92). They concluded that online laboratories
   can offer students flexible and lower-cost access, as well as better learning opportunities (p. 94).
3. *Collaboration through technology*: collaboration enhances
   students' '... interaction, engagement, learning and thinking
   skills, in addition to increasing the flexibility and diversity of
   their educational experience' (p. 94). The report advised educators and policymakers to consider technology as '... a way to
   increase collaborative learning – including over long distances
   between different cultures' (p. 96). This global reach can be
   facilitated by '... creating platforms for international collaboration among schools, classes, teachers and students. Collaboration can be supported by tools such as cloud computing, video
   conferencing, or online platforms' (p. 96).

4. *Realtime formative assessment*: smart technologies can significantly facilitate frequent interactive assessment of students' progress and understanding, and aims '... to support student creativity by engaging them in their learning, while instantaneous feedback to their teacher informs subsequent instruction' (p. 98).
5. *Aligning a skills-based curriculum with technology*: while the development of skills-based curricula is increasing in a number of countries, their impact on actual teaching and learning depends on the availability of adequately aligned support systems, including '... facilitative technology, which can measure complex skills, such as reasoning or problem solving, through measures such as essays, blogs or virtual learning environments' (HP *Catalyst Initiative* in Report, p. 100, italics added by this author for emphasis).

The report concluded that the creative use of technology changes classroom practices and that specific *Catalyst* projects '... offer examples of technology-supported education that provide wider ranges of experimentation and learning-by-doing than are possible without technological support' (p. 100). Gaming provides a way for greater experimentation with online laboratories, whether remote or virtual, and it facilitates relatively low-cost flexible access to experiential learning. It can also '... allow increased study time, and offer access that is not restricted to a specific timetable or location' (p. 100). Online and remote technologies, including laboratories, can be used to '... complement the resources available on site and enhance teachers' and students' teaching and learning opportunities' (p. 100).

A key conclusion from the report is that the nature of the pedagogy counts more than the supporting technology, because the real effectiveness of technology in the teaching and learning environment comes from the quality and effectiveness of the pedagogy that it supports. Realtime-technology-assisted formative assessment allows teachers to observe the quality of students' learning and facilitates teachers using this information quickly in their teaching. In order to meet these pedagogic challenges, however, teachers need adequate professional development because:

> [...] a common barrier to adopting new teaching models and resources is lack of formal teacher training, peer learning and more. Teachers also simply need time to integrate new technology-enhanced educational models into their pedagogy. (p. 110)

In addition, the rapid development of sophisticated interactive and connected technologies by Microsoft, IBM and Apple, and of Artificial Intelligence (AI) capabilities by Google, Oxford and the Massachusetts Institute of Technology (MIT), can have a highly positive influence on education and schooling if used creatively. Google claims that *AI* can meaningfully improve people's lives and that the biggest impact will come when everyone can access it. It constitutes an area of computer science that emphasises the creation of intelligent machines that work and react like humans, even simulating human intelligence processes.

Educating in the future will increasingly require educators to prepare students for an AI world (Tucker, 2017a). A joint educational project report by the New South Wales (NSW) Department of Education and Melbourne University, titled, *Future Frontiers: Education for an AI World*, edited by Loble, Greenhaune, and Hayes (2017), presented a collection of research-based essays on possible futures in education and the potential implications for creative technology use in schools. The editors concluded from a collection of essays developed for the project that:

> […] successive revolutions in agriculture, industry and commu-
> nications have created an ecology where human ingenuity and
> autonomy are augmented by artificial intelligence (AI) [and] each
> day, with every new breakthrough in science and technology, it is
> becoming clear that we are racing towards a future with immense
> potential to drive productivity and improve standards of living
> across our community. (p. v)

They cautioned, however, that in order to reach this potential, it is important that education systems and schools are '… adequately resourced and appropriately flexible to ensure that the next generation of students have the requisite skills to thrive in a rapidly changing world' (p. v). In the report, the NSW Government commits itself to '… ensuring that education – from the earliest years through to higher education and beyond – best prepares citizens to navigate an AI-augmented world' (p. v). The Hon. Rob Stokes MP, Minister for Education in NSW, stated in the report that:

> I am proud of how the *Education for a Changing World* initia-
> tive puts New South Wales at the forefront of thinking about the
> implications of AI for education. I warmly thank the leading aca-
> demics and thinkers who have authored these essays. This collec-
> tion challenges us to think deeply about how education responds
> to a fast-changing world and encourages us to pursue greater
> innovation across the education system. (Report, 2017, pp. v–vi)

The pace of AI developments around the world is astounding and in her introduction to the report, Leslie Loble recounted the details of how on the 15 March 2016, a Korean man named Lee Sedol, a grandmaster in the ancient East Asian game of *Go*, and one of the greatest players in history was devastated and in tears because he had just lost 4–1 in a match series against an opponent named *AlphaGo*, an AI programme developed by DeepMind, a Google subsidiary. Noble reported that she was astounded to learn that AI capability had progressed so far and so quickly:

> As I read this, I put it together with other pieces of recent evi-
> dence on the phenomenal accuracy of today's language translation
> programs compared to just a few years ago; Siri, with its sense of
> humour; the sudden arrival of self-driving cars; the maturing of

facial recognition as a corporate product and a tool of government; the intrusion of computers into intellectual professions like law and financial management; and the experiment where two AI programs invented their own language to communicate. It was at that point I realised artificial intelligence isn't coming. It's here. (p. x)

She explained the complexity involved in creating the *AlphaGo* programme:

Its designers had employed "artificial neural networks" – computing systems inspired by the arrangement of neurons in the human brain – that gave it the capacity for unsupervised learning. Nobody programmed *AlphaGo* for victory, nor for its surprising and innovative moves. Instead, the machine played millions of games against itself to develop and refine a strategy. *AlphaGo* had *taught itself* to achieve an intellectual feat that only a few dozen humans on the planet can approach. (pp. ix–x, italics in original)

In the *Future Frontiers* document, Loble et al. (2017) reported that because of the results of this contest, she suddenly, found critical questions about education coming into sharper focus, including, in:

[...] the unimaginable world that today's children will face when they leave school, what will they need to know? What skills and values will they need to lead rich and fulfilling lives? In a world where many of the tasks that make up their parents' jobs will be done by machines, what will our students need to draw on from their school education to thrive? (p. x)

She cautioned, however, that:

[...] if we wait for education to evolve at its usual slow pace in response to change it will be too late. When today's kindergartener is of prime working age and supporting a family, machine intelligence will have penetrated nearly every facet of daily life and corner of the workplace. (p. x)

For students to thrive in such challenging workplaces of the future, she claimed '... they will need to be knowledgeable, curious, dedicated and nuanced learners, equipped with the skills that will enable them to hold their place in the world of machines' (p. xi).

Drawing on Luckin's essay in the *Future Frontiers Report*, Loble suggested that:

[...] everyone needs to understand enough about AI to be able to work with its systems effectively so that AI and human intelligence augment each other and we benefit from a symbiotic relationship between the two. (p. xi)

Students, Luckin claimed, will need to be able to '... critically evaluate information, understand how machines make decisions, identify the choices coded into algorithms and spot the ethical implications of every technological development' (p. xi).

These are daunting predictions for most educational leaders and teachers but like most of the other authors in the *Future Frontiers Report*, Scott sees an important role for AI to assist these educators and he makes the critical point that we '... have to start with education, not hardware' (p. xvi). A key message from many of the authors of various essays in the Report is: 'Don't get seduced by the technology, start with learning' (Report, p. xvi). The good news drawn from the conclusions in the Report is that '... used properly, AI offers a pathway to a goal long sought by the best teachers: learning customised for individual students and around individual subjects' (Report, p. xvii). The evidence from the essays is clear: transformation in pedagogies and their supporting technologies '... can't be technology-led. It can only happen in a culture of dynamic leadership, continuous self-refection, professional assessment, and feedback for and among teachers at the local level' (p. xvii). Loble concluded that there is one crucial theme that emerged across these essays, that is, while reformers have to take the time to get it right, they need to push:

> [...] past the slogans and the false divisions between 'content people' and 'skills people', or between 'test people' and 'project people'. To grab the latest fad will set us back. We need to hold onto what works even as we seek reform. (p. xvii)

In Chapter 2 of the report, Tucker summarised the key lessons from the contributors, by stating that in the future:

> [...] many more students will need strong cognitive skills, much deeper knowledge and much more sophisticated skills in general, if they are going to be partners to increasingly intelligent agents and not be put out of work by them in the near to intermediate term. (Report, p. 34)

He claimed that education in the future will be decisive in determining the future of humanity and suggested that '... answering the question of what it means to be human has never been more urgent' (p. 34). He urged educators and educational leaders to transform schooling in ways that will prepare students for a world that is constantly and rapidly changing and assist them better understand and appreciate the emerging nature of work that is being influenced, even transformed, before their eyes by intelligent technology. He cautioned that:

> [...] if we fail at this task, it may only be a matter of time before the machines and a very small technological elite are deciding these issues, and we are not likely to be happy with their decisions. (p. 35)

In 2017, the Department of Education NSW commissioned Marc Tucker to write a major paper on educating students for a challenging future for their

Occasional Paper Series, *Education: Future Frontiers, Educating for a Digital Future: The Challenge*. Marc is the President of the National Centre of Education and the Economy, Washington, DC, and a Visiting Distinguished Fellow at the Harvard Graduate School of Education. In the commissioned paper, he provided an incisive analysis of the relationships between humans and intelligent machines now and into the future. He, especially, addressed the possibility of new sophisticated technologies robbing humans of their jobs:

> It is not a law of nature that the introduction of new technologies will put a lot of people out of work in the short term, but will then create just as many new jobs that are even better in the long term. What is distinctive about these technologies is that they incorporate the very thing that makes us so different from any other thing animate or inanimate on earth: high intelligence. It is now becoming clear that intelligent agents already exceed human capacity in some domains of intelligent behaviour. The only question is whether they have the potential to exceed humans in all domains of human intelligence, and, if they do, how long it will take to get there. (p. 10)

Tucker advised that we must deliberately reshape, even redesign, our education systems and schools so that:

> [...] many more students will [develop] strong cognitive skills, much deeper knowledge and much more sophisticated skills, if they are going to be partners to increasingly intelligent agents and not put out of work by them in the near to intermediate term. (p. 12)

They will need to develop strengths:

> [...] where the intelligent agents are, at least for the time being, relatively weak – in areas like creativity, imagination, and the whole range of social, emotional and communication skills that will be the necessary complements to intelligent agents. (p. 12)

He concluded his essay by recommending that we provide for a greatly enhanced development of '... students' communication, social and emotional skills and, more broadly, their character ...' (p. 12). Above all, they will increasingly be challenged about '... what it means to be human and what we value about being human' (p. 12). Scott, in Chapter 5 of *Future Frontiers Report* by Loble et al., acknowledged that while we cannot predict the future and the skill requirements of employees of the future:

> [...] we do know the type of learners that we want to develop through schooling – students who are critical and reflective, open to a lifetime of learning and re-learning, who are comfortable with change and have empathy and a global outlook. (p. 98)

Tucker (2017b) published a second commissioned discussion paper, *Education, Future Frontiers – The Implications of AI, Automation and 21st Century Skills*, for the NSW Department of Education. In it he addressed the possible impact on education of developments in automation and AI. In the introduction, he stated:

> There's been much written about the profound impact that technological advances will have on the way we live and work. Developments in automation and new frontiers in artificial intelligence (AI) are predicted to fundamentally alter the nature of society and work by 2040. The kindergarten students who entered the school gate for the first time in 2017 will be graduating by 2030. These students and the 8 million young people [in NSW, Australia] estimated to finish school over the next two decades will be the workers of 2040. While it is difficult to imagine the world and the way we will work in 2040, it is this world for which these students must be prepared. (p. 2)

Tucker's discussion paper predicted that, given the dynamic effects of changes in the future, schools will need to equip young people with '… enduring capabilities and skills to harness the opportunities of technological change' (p. 2). Many examples of the emerging impact of AI and advanced automation across industries are presented in this discussion paper; these examples paint a picture of a future based on innovations that are already happening. A number of them are briefly discussed here because they provide us with strong indicators of some of the exciting technological developments and trends that are currently emerging. (p. 4):

- IBM Watson – an open, multi-cloud platform that lets you automate the AI lifecycle – made headlines when it diagnosed a rare form of cancer faster and more accurately than doctors.
- The LA Times generated attention when it published a story about an earthquake in the USA, written entirely by algorithm.
- Peer-to-peer models in insurance and financial lending are using bots and machine learning to generate quotes and approve requests without the need for human brokers.
- Contract law, legal research and accounting are already experiencing increased automation of what were considered high-skilled tasks.
- Advances in cognitive computing, which combines natural language processing and machine learning, will enable people to ask their smart computer to undertake specific tasks that are not pre-programmed and which, currently, involve significant human labour to analyse data, synthesise research and model outcomes.
- Automated pharmacy systems have been launched in two US hospital medical centres, where robots dispense individual medications.
- Domino delivered its first pizza by drone in 2016. Developments in drones and self-driving vehicles are expected to fundamentally alter transport logistics.
- AI-based platforms, including games and simulations, are being used as recruitment tools and for training, including in military settings.

The profound changes ahead in the nature of work and in its supporting intelligent technologies require approaches to education that will enhance the capabilities and proficiency of all students in order to cope, never mind thrive, in this exciting new world. Tucker's *Education, Future Frontiers* (2017b) discussion paper recognised the challenges involved in responding creatively to such technological changes by highlighting the fact that it is difficult to predict exactly the skills workers will require in two decades time.

Nevertheless, there is an emerging view that young people, in addition to strong literacy, numeracy, content knowledge, and technical skills, will require '... both cognitive and non-cognitive skills – in particular problem solving, critical thinking, digital literacy, collaboration and communication' (p. 10). He suggested that the demands in the future for highly specialist skills will require schools '... to be talent incubators, and even talent factories. It is not enough to identify talent in our schools anymore; we have to create it' [Dylan Wiliam, Institute of Education, University of London, quoted on page 10 of Tucker's (2017b) *Discussion Paper*]. Despite criticisms by many educational commentators that reform of education is too slow, too piecemeal and lacking in cutting-edge research, there are emerging signs indicating that a new era in education is unfolding.

Prince et al. (2018) developed a 10-year forecast for *KnowledgeWorks* on education, titled, *Navigating the Future of Learning: Forecast 5.0: A New Era Unfolding. KnowledgeWorks* has a vision to change the education culture in the USA to better prepare each student for future success through personalised learning. The authors of *Forecast 5.0* concluded that numerous expected changes have the potential to influence education over the course of the next decade, both positively and negatively. They are confident that educators can respond to these expectations in creative ways by regarding these changes as opportunities, not just challenges (See also Vehar, 2015 for the best ways of leading innovations). Parents and educators, they claimed, need to take the lead in ways that '... will support the healthy development of young people, enable effective lifelong learning and contribute to community vitality over the coming decade and beyond ...' (p. 17). In parallel, educational institutions and educators will need to embrace the following opportunities with both hands (from *Forecast 5.0*):

- *Design for equity*: new educational practices, programmes, structures and roles will be required to help dismantle inequitable systems that marginalise some students and communities based on race, gender, income or ability (p. 28).
- *Prioritise human development*: educators will need to provide increasing opportunities for student-centred approaches and stakeholders will need to keep learners' fundamental human needs at the centre of their decisions (p. 28).
- *Distinguish between efficiency and transformation*: educators operate in an environment where increased efficiency is often touted as system transformation; while increased efficiency will be an important aim, it should not be confused with transformation (p. 29).

- *Develop new terms and conditions for technology use*: educators will need to create new ethical frameworks for new technology tools in order to provide better privacy protection, including unbiased data systems, transparent algorithms, and equitable access to high-quality technology solutions that enable students to take ownership of their learning (p. 30).
- *Identify your organisation's role in social generation*: educators are ideally placed to understand and respond to their community's needs and aspirations, while schools can contribute positively to social cohesion and community well-being (Forecast 5.0, p. 3, italics by this author for emphasis).

The authors of *Forecast 5.0* concluded that upcoming changes and opportunities offer a chance for education institutions, community organisations, students and families to:

> [...] put human fulfillment and people's mutual well-being at the centre of learning. Redefining human agency ... will enable critical education institutions ... to navigate the uncertainties on the horizon in intentional ways, leading the way toward a bright future for everyone. (p. 31)

Anderson et al. (2017) produced a futures-oriented research-based report, titled, *The Paradigm Shifters: Entrepreneurial Learning in Schools*, for the Mitchell Institute, University of Victoria, Australia. It was a robust, collaborative research project involving credentialed researchers, expert advisors and educational specialists. Partners in the research and the report included the New South Wales (NSW) Secondary Principals' Council (NSWSPC); the Victorian Association of State Secondary Principals (VASSP); and the Mitchell Institute, Victoria University – which aims to improve the connection between evidence and policy reform – promoting the principle that high-quality education, from the early years through to early adulthood, is fundamental to individual wellbeing and to a prosperous society. This collaboration sprang from the work and advocacy of international scholar, Professor Yong Zhao (Foundation and Distinguished Professor in the School of Education, University of Kansas). Twenty-one government secondary schools joined the initiative which ran from May 2016 to May 2017. They committed to creating the conditions, or to extend what they already had in place, '... to develop young people who are more entrepreneurial-minded', by applying three principles in their local contexts:

1. Develop more personalised education experiences, so each person can pursue passions and talents to excel in unique ways.
2. Engage in creative and entrepreneurial product-oriented learning experiences that can, in authentic ways, benefit local and global communities.
3. Cultivate and prototype new approaches, processes and or products in teaching and learning. (p. 10)

These principles, Yong Zhao argued, can bring about a paradigm shift in schooling, which is better suited for times when students are '… creators and co-creators of their futures [and] active partners in the initiative' (Zhao reported in Anderson et al., 2017, p. 10). Students were, therefore, given the opportunity to be in the '… driving seat, pursuing their strengths and passions, identifying and solving problems worth solving or of value to others …' (p. 10). The schools contributed funding towards their participation in the initiative and accessed support and mentoring from their membership of a state-based network, which included a network coordinator and opportunities to participate '… in regular professional learning workshops attended by students, teachers and often school leaders' (p. 10). The research sought to identify and understand the conditions that help, limit or prevent the development of entrepreneurial-minded young people.

In all, 19 of the 21 schools in the initiative accepted the invitation to participate in the research – 10 in NSW and 9 in Victoria. There were four different groups of research participants: students, teachers, school leaders, and network coordinators who were both former principals. The students and teachers interviewed were '… those best-placed to comment, as they were in their school's core group or "action team", with the teacher member(s) also responsible for coordinating the school's involvement' (p. 11). Data were collected using three methods: interviews; two short questionnaires (one for teachers and one for students); and a documentary analysis of 'artefacts'. The data provided insights into:

> […] the different ways in which schools' starting points, contexts and strategic priorities influenced their decisions on why and how to participate in this initiative as part of a learning network, as well as their interpretation and implementation of the three guiding principles. (p. 11)

In their research-based and futures-oriented report, *The Paradigm Shifters*, Anderson et al. (2017) suggested a number of key characteristics of entrepreneurial learning for the consideration of educational and pedagogical reformers. Key conclusions were:

1. *Entrepreneurial learning* requires ways of grouping skills and capabilities to position secondary students for success. It aims to cultivate mindsets and capabilities needed to identify and respond to new opportunities and problems, through creating artefacts for authentic audiences, real-world learning and iterative experimentation (Lackéus, 2015, in Report, p. 9).
2. *The demand for graduates with capabilities* such as creativity, critical thinking and advanced problem solving, collaboration and communication skills, is unprecedented and continuing to grow (*Foundation for Young Australians* 2016; *World Economic Forum* 2016; OECD 2016, referenced in Report, p. 9).
3. *Australian schooling needs a paradigm shift* because globalisation and technology are transforming the world; mastery of knowledge and test-taking skills are no longer enough to succeed (Zhao, reported in Anderson et al., 2017, p. 9).
4. *Entrepreneurial education, student engagement and related programmes*, suggest schools could consider a range of ways to pursue and embed entrepreneurial learning, and to enhance student participation and engagement. (p. 13).

These four suggestions apply not only to entrepreneurial learning but to many of the educational innovations at the school and pedagogical challenges discussed in this book. OECD Secretary-General, Angel Gurría, in an OECD (2019b) report, *OECD Employment Outlook: The Future of Work*, offered positive and encouraging words to educational leaders and reformers on how they can transform education at government and system levels:

> The key message of this *OECD Employment Outlook* is that the future of work is in our hands and will largely depend on the policy decisions countries make. It will be the nature of such policies, our ability to harness the potential of the unprecedented digital and technological change while coping with the challenges it poses, which will determine whether we succeed or fail. (From the *Foreword* to the report by Angel Gurría, OECD Secretary-General)

It would appear that the future of work and the education required to deliver this future is in our hands. Let's start on this exciting journey of learning! We need to collaborate intelligently and professionally so that we can create a future of our own making. A number of conclusions from this chapter can inform us to professionally navigate this learning journey:

- Introducing digital technology into education for technology's sake does not materially improve results because educational reformers need to place pedagogy rather than technology in the driving seat.
- Educators should remind themselves that the nature of the pedagogy counts more than the supporting technology because the real effectiveness of technology in teaching and learning environments comes from the quality and effectiveness of the pedagogy that it supports. A lesson from relevant research is, 'don't get seduced by the technology, start with learning'.
- The transformation in pedagogies and their supporting technologies can only happen in a culture of dynamic leadership, continuous self-refection, professional assessment and feedback for and among leaders and teachers at the local level.
- Students and teachers will need to be better prepared for the onslaught of AI because the pace of AI developments around the world is accelerating.
- In the future many more students will need strong cognitive skills, much deeper knowledge and more sophisticated skills in general, if they are going to be partners to increasingly intelligent agents, and not be put out of work by them.
- In order to meet future pedagogic challenges, teachers will need enabling professional development because a common barrier to adopting new teaching models and technological resources is lack of relevant teacher training, peer learning and targeted professional learning experiences.
- While we cannot predict the future and the skill requirements of employees of the future, we do know the type of learners that we want to develop through

schooling – students who are critical and reflective, open to a lifetime of learning and re-learning, are comfortable with change, and have empathy and a global outlook.

- To meet future educational challenges, there is a need to bring about a paradigm shift in schooling, which is better suited for times when students are creators and co-creators of their futures and active partners in reform initiatives.

Chapter 12

Transforming Education and Schooling: Where to from Here?

This final chapter is organised around three key themes: the nature of schools and schooling in a future of rapid change and uncertainty; preferred forms of learning and teaching, including the need to reclaim and re-energise teachers' professional judgement; and forms of leadership best suited to dynamic and rapidly changing educational landscapes.

What Types of Schools and Schooling are Best in an Uncertain Future?

The terms school and schooling generally imply that students go through a set of fixed steps and processes to prepare them for success in life. It currently implies that all young people need to be 'schooled' in a 'school' by following a prescribed curriculum, with only minimal changes periodically: this curriculum is often created by educators and bureaucrats based on their experiences of what was successful in the past. Many of the arguments on educational leadership, schools and schooling, pedagogy and learning, discussed earlier in this book, indicated the need for the transformation of education and schooling as we now know it, as well as changes to the current architecture of schools. A new narrative is required on what constitutes school and schooling for a fast-changing and uncertain future, not the least of which is a transformation of educational mindsets from fixed to growth forms (Caldwell, 2018). Possible answers to the question about the nature of schools and schooling for an uncertain future are presented and discussed throughout this chapter, especially in the sections on revisiting and re-energising teachers' professional judgement; preferred forms of pedagogy, learning and teaching; and the nature of leadership for an uncertain future.

An important contribution to successful quality education in the future is that the professional judgement of teachers be revisited and elevated to reflect their standing as professionals (Hunter, 2017). In his monograph on valuing expertise to develop worthwhile outcomes in Australian schools, Hattie (2019) singled out three key emphases for the transformation of education and schooling. First,

Leading Educational Systems and Schools in Times of Disruption and Exponential Change:
A Call for Courage, Commitment and Collaboration, 139–157
Copyright © 2020 by Patrick A. Duignan
Published under exclusive license
doi:10.1108/978-1-83909-850-520201013

he claimed that educational success includes a basket of educational goods not just one or two and critiqued the almost exclusive focus in Australian education on NAPLAN – an Australian national testing regime – as well as international OECD sponsored tests, PISA & TIMS, which represent '... a well-trodden but narrow path to educational excellence' (p. 5). He recommended that educators include a 'basket of goods' with which they '... couch their success and pursue excellence' (p. 5). While academic achievement scores should still be included in measures of educational success factors, he suggested that '... instead, the basket could be broadened to include indices of success and human development such as health, equal opportunity, safety and security, good governance, innovation, and quality living' (p. 5).

He pointed to some further desirable and valued goods in his basket, including:

> [...] communication, self-respect, respect for others, collaboration, a hunger for learning, and reduced inequalities [which] are but a small sample of the large range of possible outcomes for which indices can be built and striven towards. (p. 9)

Second, Hattie singled out the expertise of educators as '... the major underlying factor to success for students' (p. 9). He claimed that:

> [...] expert teachers 'see' classrooms differently. They are more likely to see classrooms as they 'ought to be', more likely to note atypicalness earlier, and are more critical of their teaching. (p. 10)

He included how teachers think, what they value, and their passion to optimise their impact on student learning as key characteristics of successful teachers and teaching and concluded by stating that his key message is that '... we need to esteem, debate, research, privilege, and scale up this expertise' (p. 10).

Third, Hattie advised that the Gonski 2.0 reform recommendations (discussed earlier in this book) '... if well implemented, could make substantive differences to performance in Australian schools' (p. 14). These include a move in the narrative of education, as expressed in the title of the Gonski 2.0 report – *Through Growth to Achievement* – which recommends:

> [...] the development of learning progressions and a related formative assessment tool; developing a research and evidence base; enhancing a structured career path; and attention to Year 11 and 12 curricula offerings. (p. 14)

Hattie concluded his 2019 monograph with insightful comments based on his analysis of the Gonski 2.0 report, including the need to:

> [...] provide an ideal base to focus on policies about expertise, and ensure systems provide resources and directions that allow the expertise of teachers and school leaders to dominate the successful

implementation in classrooms, such that the policies can positively impact on the learning lives of students. (p. 15)

In his monograph, *Shifting Away from Distractions to Improve Australia's Schools*, Hattie (2016) identified what really matters in schools when he described the positive and revolutionary highlights of *The Revolution* School, as featured in an Australian Broadcasting Corporation Television (ABC TV, 2016) documentary:

> *You can see and hear the passion, the dedication, the commitment, the expertise, the never-give-up, the transformations, and the joy of being a teacher. You see the raging hormones of the students as they develop into wonderful young adults and you can see that teachers have much to be credited with during this transformation.* (2016, p. 12, italics in original)

Based on their research about teachers leading educational improvements in Ontario, Canada, Campbell, Lieberman, and Yashkina (2015) reported that teachers had the capacity and willingness to provide leadership of educational reform because:

> [...] teachers can be the developers of their own and their peers' leadership rather than only the recipients of externally provided or directed leadership development. Second, teachers can be the leaders of professional knowledge and practices for educational improvement within and beyond their schools. Third, teachers can lead through collaboration and networks rather than only through formal hierarchies. (p. 91)

In the conclusions to their research, they stated that educational leaders in schools need to put in place three innovations to enable teachers to contribute to school and system improvement:

> First, provide enabling conditions and expectations to support teachers to be developers of their own and their peers' leadership. Importantly, teachers learn leadership by doing leadership. Second, the purpose of this leadership can be for teachers to (co)lead the development and implementation of professional knowledge and practices rather than teacher leadership being only about formal school organisational roles .... Third, in contrast to formal leadership through governance hierarchies, teacher leaders can productively support wider sharing and the spread of improvement practices through professional collaboration, communicating and networking in-person, in-print and online. [They say that such a leadership culture results in] teachers de-privatising their practices, collaborating, co-learning and leading, and contributing to improvements in classrooms, schools, and systems. (pp. 103–104)

There is evidence from a range of research literature that quality teachers and their teaching are important influences on the quality of learning and learning outcomes in schools. Robinson and Aronica (2016) provided strong arguments for revolutionising schools and schooling by enhancing teacher creativity for an uncertain future. Hattie (2009), in his research, *Synthesis of over 800 Meta-analyses Relating to Student Achievement*, reported that quality teachers and quality teaching have the single largest influence on student achievement and outcomes. He concluded that through direct instruction – not to be confused with didactic teaching – teachers can have a very strong impact, as measured by effect size, on learning outcomes generally and student achievement more specifically. While his findings have been reinforced by a number of educational researchers since 2009, educators continue to ask about the forms of learning that will best serve students to meet the challenges and opportunities of an uncertain and rapidly changing future. The answers to this question will have major implications for teachers and their teaching methods in the future.

Forms of Learning and Teaching Required for a Fast-Changing and Uncertain Future

Before considering preferred teaching and learning approaches, we first look at the implications from recent work by Shekshnia, Kravchenko, and Wiliams (2018) who asked the question: How will educators of future CEOs prepare them for their uncertain and challenging world? They conducted research interviews with a selection of top international CEOs from the G20 nations, that is, the world's 20 biggest economies. They included educators of aspiring CEOs to determine if their curricula, subject matter and methodologies added value to the education of CEOs. As well, they included school teachers and stated:

> we'd even like high-school teachers to read this book, as they're in a position to encourage and nurture the skills that will eventually take some of their current students to the top of great companies two or three decades from now. Come to think of it, why not kindergarten teachers too? After all, many future CEOs haven't started 'big school' yet. (p. vii)

They highlighted the central importance of quality leadership in schools. Increasingly, they said, '... there is an emphasis on 'authentic leadership', which means finding the leadership style that suits you, rather than following someone else's recipe for success' (p. 8). They concluded that there are three personality traits that experts believe to be essential for any CEO's success: curiosity, ambition and passion. They explained that curiosity is a non-negotiable characteristic for success in leadership and '... it can be enhanced by experimenting, travelling widely and speaking with strangers' (p. 11). They concluded that the nature of their school education experiences can also be a powerful contributor to preparing prospective candidates for the leadership of large organisations in the future.

They advised that to help prepare their students for a future of leadership possibilities and for being successful CEOs, educators at school level should help them develop their '... systematic thinking, emotional acumen and desire to learn, [and by] encouraging experimentation and facilitating collaboration with other people ...' (p. 135). Parents and teachers should, they claimed:

> [...] encourage [students] to have a dream, to explore the world, to develop passions, to learn from people and experiences, to interact with other kids and adults and – above all – to understand them-selves. (p. 135)

Teachers from kindergarten through high school must, they recommended:

> [...] foster curiosity, enthusiasm and collaboration [and] have grand ambitions for themselves, as well as to formulate big ideas that will inspire others to follow. Give them opportunities to decide, to experiment and to make mistakes. Then help them learn from their mistakes. (p. 135)

They concluded that the ideal candidate for a leadership position in future organisations will be a person with high CAP [curiosity, ambition, passion], 'consummate social skills, an eye for the whole as well as the parts, the ability to learn from any situation, boundless enthusiasm [for job and life], compassion, empathy, physical fitness and self-discipline' (p. 158). Many educators have emphasised for years the need for students' educational experiences to better prepare them to acquire similar skills, but it would appear that schools still have a way to go – perhaps the research of Shekshnia et al. provides the insight and impetus for educators to push the 'refresh' button.

The recent research work of McTighe and Willis (2019) focussed on learning and brain functioning to develop new insights into the nature of teaching and learning for the future. They reported that:

> The past two decades of brain research have provided insights that have profoundly extended our understanding of how to maximise the brain's development of the neural networks related to executive functions. These functions are exactly what students need for success in this era of surging amounts of information and rapidly transitioning technology. The school years are critical times in children's development of their sense of themselves and their relationships to the world. (p. 25)

In a detailed analysis of brain functioning and its contribution to learning, they provided valuable advice to teachers and other educators on methods to stimulate their students' neural networks in order to enhance their learning and the construction of their skill-sets to succeed in complex, challenging and changing environments:

> The executive-function command system evolving in the prefrontal cortexes of students' brains need experience and guidance to build the skill set required for setting and achieving long-term goals. Teachers have the opportunity and important responsibility to guide their students' construction of the skills needed to successfully, and ultimately independently, identify goals, evaluate appropriate actions, plan goal achievement, delay immediate gratification, and use and revise strategies to realise their goals and aspirations. (pp. 25–26)

They also identified the challenges for educators who assist their students transfer knowledge from their school environment to the world of work and advised that '… the ability to effectively transfer knowledge and skill involves the capacity to take what we know and use it creatively, flexibly … in different settings or with different problems' (p. 27). They argued that:

> […] the way learning is organised and sequenced can influence students' engagement and the ultimate success of learning. The typical sequence of conventional lessons [they concluded] involves a linear, topic-by-topic or skill-by-skill progression. (p. 130)

This logic of learning does not, they claimed, '… automatically align with how the brain best learns – especially if the goals are to develop understanding and transfer abilities' (p. 130). They recommended, as an alternative, performance-based learning, which is designed '… to solve complex problems, explore real issues and reach decisions, analyse real [or simulated] cases, or produce a genuine product or performance' (p. 131). They are highlighting, not alone the cognitive functioning of the brain but also personal and socio-emotional development, which are essential for a nuanced and self-fulfilling life experiences.

Ashenden (2018) supported this viewpoint on learning and education when he stressed that cognitive or academic outcomes are insufficient to prepare students for the present never mind the future when he claimed:

> non-cognitive outcomes, the values and attitudes that students take from schools are just as important as cognitive outcomes. The actual experience of school matters as much as outcomes of whatever kind …. Schools are about the ties that bind, or fail to, as well as each individual's learning and experience. Schools matter more to the social order than they do to the economy. (p. 9)

For real reform of the evaluation of educational outcomes, especially students' achievement, he recommended a:

> […] set of indicators that more fully reflect what parents (and students) want from schools, what teachers do and try to do, and the

complicated, multi-purpose, difficult-to-steer reality of schools, that would all help turn ... passive resistance to reform into active support. (p. 9)

Hopkins (2017), however, is not confident that past and current attempts at educational reform are capable of delivering the desired transformation of education required to adequately prepare students for their challenging futures. He provided a very comprehensive analysis of the past, present and future of school improvement and system reform in a number of key countries that embraced the so-called, Global Educational Reform Movement (GERM) over the last two or three decades. He claimed that:

[...] the ubiquity of the 'Myths', 'Wrong Drivers' and 'GERM' approaches to school reform have placed a ceiling on student performance in those jurisdictions that follow the paucity of that orthodoxy. (p. 12)

He used the examples from Australia, England and Wales as systems that have ceilings on their students' performance, while Finland, Ontario, Singapore and Hong Kong have achieved much higher levels of student performance. Hopkins (2017) identified a number of key drivers that need to be collaboratively planned and implemented if the promises of recent reform movements are to be realised (pp. 19–21):

1. *Authentic system leadership* where system and school leaders collaborate and systematically support each other '... in an actively interdependent, mutually beneficial relationship' (p. 19). In these ways, they build capacity and collaboration within the system:
2. *Personalised learning* involves '... putting students at the heart of the education process so as to tailor teaching to individual need, interest and aptitude in order to fulfil every young person's potential ...' (p. 19). A successful system of personalised learning, he claimed, will ensure students become independent, e-literate, fulfilled and lifelong learners.
3. *Professional teaching*: it is recognised in relevant literature that the quality of teachers and their teaching has the largest impact on student learning and learning outcomes (e.g., Hattie, 2009). Professional teachers consistently expand their repertoire of pedagogic strategies to personalise learning for all their students.
4. *Intelligent accountability* is necessary to balance external forms of accountability through testing with internal forms of accountability by teachers. These include teacher assessment strategies, value-added measures of performance and professional discussions of the strengths and areas for improvement using the professional judgement of teachers.

5. *Networking and collaboration* helps because '... networks support improvement and innovation by enabling schools to collaborate on building curriculum diversity, extending services and professional support to develop a vision of education that is shared and owned well beyond the individual school gates' (p. 20 – italics used by this author for emphasis).

In 2019, Hopkins recommended that personalised learning should become a key plank for educational and school reform. He pointed out that personalised learning:

[...] has recently been capturing the imagination of teachers, parents and young people around the world. It is an idea that has its roots in the best practices of the teaching profession, and it has the potential to make every young person's learning experience stretching, creative, fun and successful. (p. 18)

He claimed that we see this approach most '... in the concern of the committed, conscientious teacher to match what is taught, and how it is taught, to the individual learner as a person' (p. 18). He urged teachers to '... touch hearts as well as minds, nourish a hunger for learning and help equip the learner with a proficiency and confidence to pursue understanding for themselves' (p. 18). The idea is not new, he stated, because great teachers have always done it but it now needs to be scaled to system and country levels.

He claimed that re-imagining the education system around the personalised learning needs and talents of young people should be the basis for every school becoming a great school. He provided a useful summary for educational leaders and reformers of the intentions and focus of personalised learning (p. 18):

- *As an educational aspiration*, personalised learning reflects a system-wide commitment to moral purpose, high excellence and high equity, and to every school being or becoming great.
- *As an educational strategy*, personalised learning relates to and builds on learners' experiences, knowledge and cognitive development; 'it develops their confidence and competence and leads towards autonomy, emancipation and self-actualisation'.
- *As an approach to teaching and learning*, personalised learning focusses on individual potential, develops the individual's learning skills – particularly in ICT – and enhances creativity and social skills.
- *As a curriculum orientation*, personalised learning offers an approach to subject teaching that balances societal aspirations and personal relevance, and it unifies the curriculum offerings across sectors and age groupings.

He provided a detailed model for personalised learning (see p. 20), which is a valuable resource and guide for educational leaders and practitioners wishing to initiate and implement such a learning approach within their own or across schools. He also offered recommendations on growing personalised learning to scale (see pp. 21–22).

In the USA, Jenkins, Olsen, Pace, and Sullivan (2019) in a *KnowledgeWorks* report on personalised learning, placed a premium on assisting school systems and schools to successfully implement such learning programmes, and they believe that meeting students where they are and providing comprehensive supports to help accelerate their content and skill mastery, holds the promise to close opportunity gaps by race, income, geography and learning differences. They urged educational communities to lead improvement conversations about possible learning models that will best serve their students and explore how to incorporate technology into their learning platforms and classrooms. They reminded educators that at the centre of strong and effective teaching and learning is the relationship between a student and a teacher and, they claimed, technology can't replace that. Jenkins et al. (2019) designed and developed a *State Policy Framework for Personalised Learning: Designing Education Systems Where Every Student Succeeds*:

> [...] to assist states and stakeholders define and navigate pathways from the exploratory phase of system design, where a limited number of districts engage in personalised learning practices, to state-wide transformation. (p. 3)

This policy framework for personalised learning constitutes a blueprint for introducing personalised learning into systems and schools and provides useful pathways for educational leaders and teachers who plan to embrace a personalised approach to learning within and across their classrooms. They cautioned, however, that:

> [...] the path to state-wide transformation is not linear [so their framework] is designed to help states build awareness of what it will take to support personalised learning state-wide and to consider important decision points with key stakeholders. (p. 3)

While there is strong support in recent relevant literature for personalising learning for all students, there is also an awareness of its challenges and some educators recommend that it be embraced within a broader framework or platform, which they refer to as blended learning. This framework and its applications within classrooms and schools was discussed in detail in Chapter 9. Reform leaders, however, need to be aware that there are some subtle negative forces, often invisible to them, that may thwart their proposed changes. Hattie (2016) claimed that:

> [...] a major enemy of reform is complacency, ... blaming the postcodes, deploring the parents, fixing the students not the system, and arguing for more resources to continue what is not working ... complacency is our enemy; more of the same, our crime. Giving our students more of what we had when we went to school may prepare them better for our world but not for their world. (p. 21)

The type of leadership exercised in the change process may also be a limiting force.

Throughout this book, it is argued that we need to hit the refresh button on educational pedagogy, as well as on the architecture of schooling, schools and learning practices, in order to prepare students for a future full of surprises and uncertainty. Evidence was presented that traditional leadership for learning no longer adequately serves our students' needs. It is pointed out, repeatedly, that if we don't change from traditional paradigms of education, leadership, teaching and learning, we will be faced with a future for which our students are ill-prepared. The message is that educational leaders, at all levels, must become more inspiring and transforming, leading to greater human fulfilment for all who work and study within their school communities.

What Forms of Leadership Will Work Best in an Uncertain Future?

A much-repeated mantra in recent educational reform and transformation literature by a number of educational change and leadership researchers and writers is that, given the poor record of reformers in recent decades, primarily because the industrial model of schooling still prevails, we urgently need a *new narrative* for educational reform and transformation (italics to indicate this author's emphasis). A problem is that the proposed narrative is not new, it has been around for many years, at least, since the time of Professor Thomas Greenfield in the early 1970s; even earlier if we go back to the work of Mary Parker Follett in 1924. She emphasised a humanistic and socially just viewpoint on management structures and conflict resolution within organisations. The narrative has been influential in some educational leadership circles since Greenfield's rejection of the 'theory movement' – a positivist and behaviourist framework in educational administration – in the early 1970s. He was in favour of seeing and defining educational organisations as, primarily, comprising the actions, perceptions and values of the members; organisations, he argued, are created by their people who, in turn, create their organisation's culture.

The author of this book published a paper in 2014, focussing on the history and development of the humanistic and cultural dimensions of organisational and educational leadership thought, research, theory and practice throughout the twentieth century (Duignan, 2014, "Authenticity in educational leadership: History, ideal, reality", in the *Journal of Educational Administration*; it was awarded the *International Paper of the Year 2015* by Emerald Publishing, UK) The author concluded that while a 'theory-movement' approach has dominated the literature on educational administration and leadership for almost five decades, there has also been an enduring co-emphasis on leaders as human beings living and working within complex human organisations. There also has been a focus on the qualitative dimensions of organisational life and the importance of ethics, morals, values and organisational culture. In the legacy paper referred to above, Duignan (2014) stated:

Throughout this paper, I have argued the need for authentically professional leadership in our schools; a leadership infused with integrity, moral purpose and ethics. Like principals, teachers are influential leaders but cannot achieve their goals on their own; they must embrace a deep professional commitment to work collegially. It is only when this focus becomes a collective professional, ethical and moral imperative that the teaching and learning landscape is likely to change. What is needed is 'a renewed sense of vocation for educators and a collective and passionate commitment to creating learning environments and cultures [in schools] that will help transform the lives of learners and their learning.' Authentic leaders help create the type of organisational cultures that value professional collaboration and collective responsibility in order to achieve high quality outcomes.

As far back as 1977, Robert Greenleaf argued for a human-centred approach to leadership; he urged educational leaders to be 'servant leaders' who are there, first and foremost, to serve and nurture others. Christopher Hodgkinson in his *The Philosophy of Leadership* (1983) and *Educational Leadership: The Moral Art* (1991) contributed to thinking about educational leadership as an ethical, moral and authentic enterprise. In his book, Hodgkinson's (1983) key arguments were taken up by a number of educational leadership theorists, including Gronn (1982), Duignan and Macpherson (1992) and Duignan and Bhindi (1997). In 1993, Terry published a seminal work called *Authentic Leadership: Courage in Action.* Professor Jerry Starratt (1993, 2004, 2011) of Boston College and Strike (2007) had a large influence internationally on the theory and practice of ethical leadership. In recent years, the research of Avolio and Gardner (2005), Cameron (2003, 2008, 2013), Duignan, (2006, 2012, 2014) and Walumbwa et al. (2008) have extended the boundaries of our understanding of how authentic leaders can create organisational cultures that enhance the well-being of all key stakeholders as well as the performance outcomes for individuals, groups and organisations. A number of researchers and authors have emphasised balanced leadership (Boris-Schacter & Langer, 2006) or nuanced leadership approaches (Fullan, 2019b), valuing both quantitative and quality performance outcomes, while highlighting the human and cultural dimensions of organisational life.

In his meta-analysis research reported in *Visible Learning*, Hattie (2009) concluded that excellence in teaching is the most powerful influence on student achievement, and Leithwood, Lewis, Anderson, and Wahlstrom (2004) found that leadership is second only to quality teachers and quality teaching in influencing student achievement. It is important to remember that the research on which meta-analyses studies are based tend to focus on a narrow range of measures of student learning, primarily on student achievement based on test scores in literacy, numeracy, science and/or reading. Such tests tend to undervalue the qualitative dimensions of human behaviour and performance and often fail to appreciate that many of the most significant influences of leaders on student learning may not be linear or measurable (Duignan, 2012).

For over two decades, Richard DuFour has been recognised as an international voice for creating and leading professional learning communities in schools. He has consistently claimed that the thrust of *No Child Left Behind* and *Race to the Top* national policies in the USA was harmful to educators, students and schools, because they were frequently labelled 'failing' if they didn't measure up on national standardised tests each year (from an interview by Thiers (2016), with DuFour). In the interview, DuFour advised principals: 'don't put your school improvement eggs in the evaluation basket. Put them in the collaborative team and PLC [Professional Learning Community] basket' (p. 15). School leaders, he claimed, can assist teachers form professional, purposeful, supportive and collaborative cultures by inspiring them with the conviction that:

> [...] no one person has enough energy, influence, or expertise to do this on his or her own. You have to have a guiding coalition of leaders working hand in hand with the principal, shaping practices, and then look for ways to keep expanding leadership outward. (p. 15)

He recommended that there is a need to rethink and redesign schooling and school leadership to be more inclusive and collaborative not just because the principalship is inadequate or no longer appropriate but, if we want to build world-class communities of learning, it can only be done in inclusive and collaborative ways.

Educational leaders can learn important lessons from the business world if they wish to reform their school cultures, structures and practices. Satya Nadella (2017), the current CEO of Microsoft, in his book, *Hit Refresh: The Quest to Discover Microsoft's Soul and Imagine a Better Future for Everyone*, shared his leadership philosophy, beliefs and preferred practices for leading in an uncertain future. He suggested that at appropriate times in the lifecycle of an organisation, like Microsoft, there is a need for key leaders, supported by the CEO, to hit the refresh button to preserve and nurture the culture and soul of the organisation so as to re-imagine a better future for everyone. Bill Gates, founder and former CEO of Microsoft, wrote the *Foreword* to Nadella's book, in which he stated: 'When Satya took over as CEO of Microsoft ... he immediately put his mark on the company' (p. ix). As the title of his book, *Hit Refresh*, '... implies, he didn't completely break with the past – when you hit refresh on your browser, some of what's on the page stays the same' (p. x). Satya Nadella, himself, discussed the challenges and opportunities of leading in a fast-changing and high-tech world, which, he claimed, is greatly influenced by cloud-computing:

> The cloud business taught me a series of lessons .... Perhaps the most important is this: a leader must see the external opportunities and the internal capability and culture – and all of the connections among them – and respond to them before they become obvious parts of the conventional wisdom. It's an art form, not a science. And a leader will not always get it right. But the batting

average for how well a leader does this is going to define his or her longevity in business. (Nadella, 2017, p. 62)

Educational leaders, too, live and work within a connected-cloud world and Nadella's approach to leading in complex, technology-rich environments is instructive for them. He asked the question: 'What is the computer platform of the future?' He pointed out that while windows was the PC platform of choice for decades, leaders now have to imagine a new era, because the cloud with its '... multisensory and multi-devise experiences will enable new computers and new computing that is sensitive to human presence and responsive to individual preferences' (p. 110). He advised that we are currently entering an era with:

> [...] the ultimate computing experience, blending mixed reality, artificial intelligence, and quantum computing and he asked: Which of these will dominate the computing world of 2050 – or will some new breakthrough emerge that is currently unimagined? (pp. 110–111)

If the future appears somewhat uncertain for Microsoft's CEO, no wonder educators and educational leaders are struggling with how this multisensory and multidevice future will affect them, both positively and negatively. We require more courageous conversations among educational policymakers and educational leaders, including teachers, about possible ways a multisensory and multidevice future will impact their lives and leadership.

Whitby (2019), CEO of a Catholic Education System in Australia and an expert on technology-driven reform in education, advised that educational leaders need to develop new models of thinking if they are to thrive in a rapidly advancing cloud world. He stated that 'technology has democratised our access to information, knowledge and the capacity for lifelong learning in ways never seen before.' Thus, old models of delivering schooling and ways in which leaders strategically plan have been found wanting. The industrial toolkits (e.g. processes, structures and mindsets) that have been relied upon in the past to manage the linear and predictable are no longer relevant in a non-linear and unpredictable world. Whitby recommended that contemporary educational organisations need to be on a journey from improvement to transformation or they:

> [...] risk becoming irrelevant, and schools require a paradigm shift from the industrial model – prescriptive, one-size-fits-all, delivers to the masses, reinforces routines – to a new mode, which has to be adaptive, personalised, and delivers learning to diverse learners. (p. 10)

He recommended that school personnel '... swim with the digital tide, not against it, to ensure the best outcomes for each child whatever his or her needs' (p. 10).

Fullan (2019b) raised similar leadership challenges and queried why some educational leaders succeed when others fail their students in a rapidly changing and technology-rich world. He concluded that the exclusive emphasis by educational policymakers and most educational leaders in recent decades on student achievement – measured primarily by tests in literacy and numeracy – to the minimisation and even exclusion of other valued outcomes of schooling, for example, student well-being and connectedness to each other and the world they live in, seems to have had detrimental effects on many schools. He advised that:

> [...] instead of making student achievement the be-all and end-all; instead of adopting a Procrustean approach to shoehorn everything (e.g. social-emotional learning) in the service of academic performance [we need to] *change the moral imperative itself to what is good for us as individuals and society.* (p. 8, italics in original)

Fullan (2019b), a long-term advocate of the need for education to be inspired by a moral imperative, usually expressed in academic achievement and performance terms as, 'raise the bar and close the gap', currently accepts the need to redefine or refresh this imperative to achieve greater nuanced and balanced outcomes:

> Let's redefine the moral imperative as 'high expectations for all students in both academic performance *and* in *connectedness* in life' (defined as having connections to one's situation and life). Thus, academic achievement and connectedness would be equally valued; both would be on the same high pedestal, both would be pursued in concert (indeed, synergistically); and both would be measurable and measured; success would be defined as high performance on *both* dimensions. Being good at schooling and being good at life would be integrated [seamless], starting with early learning. (p. 8, italics in original)

Despite the fact that academic performance measures of success have been vigorously and consistently articulated for over three decades, he concluded that currently student achievement, as measured in a number of countries, has actually been '... losing ground (for some 30 years now) with current strategies, not because teachers or even the education system is at fault, but rather because *the world has changed*' (p. 8, italics in original). Realising that the world has changed is a key to understanding why so many educational initiatives and innovations in leadership and pedagogy have fallen on barren ground; a clear message to educational policymakers and reform leaders is that doing the same things over and over again in a changing world is doomed to failure and will continue to fail.

Using narrow educational measures of performance – often only literacy and numeracy – as proxies for students' success in education and life is questionable at the very least. As a result, it appears that students are increasingly finding their school experiences less relevant for them in their fast-revolving lives; research indicates that a large proportion of secondary students report that they are not actively engaged in their learning, are not enjoying their school experiences, and that their educational experiences are not preparing them well enough for the world they now inhabit, never mind in an uncertain future. Fullan summarised the contemporary negative results of learning for many students:

> In sum, an increasing percentage of students show lower and lower wellbeing scores, and connections with others are not strong ... the increased stress on academic achievement as the sole goal worth striving for simply can't work – it is neither relevant enough nor compelling enough to warrant the effort, [and] the achievement gap is doomed to keep on failing. (p. 9)

We need more educational reformers like Fullan who are willing to let go of educational beliefs, theories and paradigms that no longer work as the world inexorably continues to change (see Facchinetti, 2013). For over three decades, Fullan believed that the moral imperative for schools should be 'raising the bar and closing the achievement gap for students' but he has now decided, based on his recent research and observations on numerous educational systems and schools across a number of countries, that the moral imperative for education and schooling has to change; he is now open to mindset change as all effective reformers have to be. He is clearly telling educators to stop '... privileging student academic achievement' as the holy grail of educating and achieve a more effective balance with student '... connectedness [and] being good at life' (p. 9). He claimed that his new definition of moral imperative requires a new vision, new policies, revived measures of success and different leadership. While he pointed out that these changes do not reduce the importance of academic achievement, '... they place it in the context where more students will be successful in both academic excellence and excellence as citizens' (p. 10).

Based on Fullan (2019a) more balanced or 'nuanced' (Fullan's term) view of education and educational leadership – his book title is *Nuance: Why Some Leaders Succeed and Others Fail* – he recommended that educational leaders need to become more nuanced and have a greater '... curiosity about what is possible, openness to other people, sensitivity to context, and loyalty to a better future' (p. 12). Such leaders, he claimed:

> [...] connect people to their own and each other's humanity. They don't lead; they teach. They change people's emotions not just their minds ... they are humble in the face of challenges, determined for the group to be successful, and proud to celebrate success ... Above all, they are courageously and relentlessly committed to changing the system for the betterment of humanity. (Fullan, *Nuance,* 2019a, p. 12)

In a number of the arguments presented throughout this book, there has been a plea for educational leaders at all levels to re-position or re-boot their leadership priorities, approaches and practices by generating a healthy balance between an emphasis on performance outcomes, including students' performance on tests, and greater attention to the human-side of leadership, that is culture, relationships, ethical, moral and authentic practices. Fullan's new nuanced stance on educational leadership is welcomed because a key dimension of nuance is to be able to see and appreciate '... the big picture – the *system* – while at the same time being able to understand the details of their connections and hidden patterns operating within the system itself' (p. 3). To be successful in complex organisations, Fullan stated, leaders need to:

> [...] see below the surface, grasp hidden patterns, find new pathways to alter and shape better outcomes, and have a burning desire [a passion] to make things better for the vast majority of people. (p. 3)

He developed a three-dimension framework for leadership, which he refers to as the **JAC** model – *Jointly determined change, adaptability,* and *culture-based accountability* (p. 13, italics in original). He described and illustrated the characteristics and impact of each of these three leadership dimensions, using examples from his research on successful change from a variety of educational systems and schools in different countries. He explained them as:

> **J** – *joint determination* means that the vast majority of people, teachers in schools for example, '... want to make a difference. *They care!* Nuance leaders unlock, mobilise, and create collective care. Nuance leaders prove that the seemingly impossible can be done.' (p. 42) This emphasis is one that is argued throughout this book, that is, the importance of educators collectively taking responsibility for the quality of life and work in their systems and schools;
>
> **A** – *Adaptability* refers to the dynamic balancing required from leaders in a fast-changing organisational life; it includes '... learning and leading in equal measure and the ability of leaders to change their minds when a strategy isn't working ...' (p. 43) Much has already been written in this book about the necessity for educational leaders, including teachers, to transform their thinking and practices and make a growth paradigm shift by being courageous in the face of complex challenges;
>
> **C** – *Culture-based accountability* reflects the need for '... individual and collective responsibility that become embedded into the values, behaviour, and actions of people in the situation; they come to embrace a focus on continuous improvement as something that they have to do and prove to themselves and to

others' (p. 75). In recent decades, accountability in education tended to be regarded simply as reaching standards measured by students' performance on tests. Fullan also wisely emphasised the collective, human-dimension of accountability that aims at continuous improvement within an organisational setting. This focus on the need for the development of collective cultures of responsibility for the quality of life, work and educational outcomes in schools has been highlighted earlier in this book.

Fullan's JAC model provides educational leaders and reformers with a comprehensive overview of preferred leadership pathways in times of cloud-computing and it responds to Nadella's view that leaders now have to imagine a new era, because the cloud with its '… multisensory and multi-devise experiences will enable new computers and new computing that is sensitive to human presence and responsive to individual preferences' (p. 110, quoted previously). One thing seems clear, culture, human presence, individual preferences, relationships and the human-side of leadership – ethical, moral and authentic practices – will need to continue to be central in schools and schooling, even in an iCloud world.

Fullan concluded his book on Nuance Leaders with good news for all educational leaders:

> The good news is that nuance can be learned. All of the leaders we examined in this book got stronger and stronger over time through what they experienced and learned. They became stronger characters and more courageous as a result of what they learned. Formation comes hand-in-hand with action as nuance leaders go deeper and deeper consolidating their learnings and processing their doubts … If you integrate the three key themes of nuance [i.e., JAC model], you end up being a better leader without realising how and when it happened. (p. 124)

Fullan's new moral imperative for educational leaders also gives careful consideration to the positive impact of ethical, moral and authentic principles and behaviours in organisations, as key benchmarks for leaders and leadership. These include, as discussed in a number of sections in this book: a moral compass as a guideline for action; the capacity to acquire and use moral knowledge and judgement in action; the development of ethical reasoning skills; overcoming the negative possibilities and the impact of personal and interpersonal ethical and moral blind spots (Moberg, 2006), including the need for reflection on moral self and authentic relationships, as well as other closely connected cultural and organisational concepts. Bye (2017), in her extensive research on Millennials, claimed that while they are well prepared for and suited to a fast-moving, uncertain and a disrupted world, they have also cultivated a character-driven and courageous core for their lives and their leadership. They tend to operate from both high character and high courage, and they have a willingness to take responsible risks and communicate authentically with their teams; a balance of character and courage is foundational to their confidence and 'it's beyond mental toughness' (p. 140). It appears Millennials will naturally be nuanced in their leadership and their work.

Gail Kelly – former CEO of one of Australia's largest international banks, Westpac (discussed earlier in Chapter 4) – complemented Fullan's idea of nuanced leadership when she advocated that highly successful leaders emphasise both performance outcomes and the quality of people's relationships in life and work. She stated that as a leader, she accepted the responsibility to help her colleagues find meaning and fulfilment in their work. She urged leaders to be authentic, transparent, to keep listening and to be open to learning. Leading with courage is her catchword, and she encouraged all leaders to '... persevere when the pressure is on, to stand firm under fire from the naysayers, and to persist in what you believe is right' (Kelly, 2017, pp. 91–92).

The findings from positive psychology research on leadership (e.g. Cameron, 2013; Seligman, 2011) have a nuanced-orientation about leaders and leadership in that they encourage and facilitate organisational members and leaders to maximise their interpersonal relationships, while still optimising organisational performance:

> *Positive leadership refers* to implementation of multiple positive practices that help individuals and organisations achieve their highest potential, flourish at work, experience elevating energy, and achieve levels of effectiveness that are difficult to attain otherwise. The practices included in this book [Cameron's book] have proven to be effective in producing extraordinarily results. (Cameron, 2013, p. 149, italics in original)

Much of the relevant literature discussed in this book, appears to indicate educators, educational leaders, and educational reformers are increasingly aware of their need to encourage and facilitate organisational members to value the human dimensions of organisational life while optimising their organisation's performance. As discussed in Chapters 2 and 5, Wilson (2018) hopes for a brighter future for education and recommended a human-development approach, which requires educational reformers to rethink, re-imagine, and redesign their schools so as to unleash potential, spark curiosity and invite learners take ownership of their learning.

Throughout the literature on educational change and reform reviewed in this book there is a perceptible emphasis on the need for leaders to focus more on the people involved in the change processes than on the change itself. An emphasis on people, especially on character, authenticity, relationships and interrelationships, instead of on systems, strategies, plans, data, and logically ordered change processes, are identified and recommended by Wilson as keys to effective, long-term reform in organisations. As reported earlier, she recommended that as leaders of change we all must be part '... of a rising army of hundreds of thousands of people doing something about it – with humility, with heart, and with faith' (p. 107, quoted earlier). Personally, I want to be part of this army and I hope that the discussions and conclusions in this book will encourage you, too, to join and become a positive force for the transformation of our educational systems and schools as well as for the life opportunities of current and future students.

References

Agle, B. (2006). Does CEO charisma matter? An empirical analysis of the relationships among organisational performance, environmental uncertainty and top management team perceptions of CEO charisma. *Academy of Management Journal, 49*(1), 161–174.

Anderson, M., Hinz, B., & Matus, H. (2017). *The paradigm shifters: Entrepreneurial learning in schools*. Research Report No. 04/2017. Mitchell Institute, Melbourne, Australia. Retrieved from www.mitchellinstitute.org.au/reports/the-paradigm-shifters-entrepreneurial-learning-in-schools/. Accessed on November 3, 2019.

Arney, K. (2016). *Herding Hemingway's cats: Understanding how our genes work*. London: Bloomsbury Publishing.

Ascione, L. (2018). Show what you know: A landscape analysis of competency-based education. Report commissioned by XQ Institute USA: https://xqsuperschool.org.

Ashenden, D. (2015). *Reform, reformers and segregationist logic of Australian schooling*. Seminar Series Paper No. 250. Centre for Strategic Education, Melbourne, Australia.

Ashenden, D. (2018). *Australia's school reform strategy has failed: What now?* Melbourne, Australia: Centre for Strategic Education (CSE).

Australian Broadcasting Corporation Television (ABC TV). (2016). The revolution school. Retrieved from http://www.cjz.com.au/programs/revolution-school/. Accessed on November 3, 2019.

Avolio, B. J., & Gardner, W. (2005). Authentic leadership development: Getting to the root of positive forms of leadership. *The Leadership Quarterly, 16*(3), 315–338.

Avolio, B. J., Gardner, W. L., Wernsing, T., & Peterson, S. (2008). Authentic leadership: Development and validation of a theory-based measure. *Journal of Management, 3*, 89–126.

Barber, M. (2011, January). *How school systems improve*. Presentation at Harvard University. Retrieved from www.youtube.com/watch?v=vTvk95OkErM. Accessed on November 3, 2019.

Barber, M. Chijioke, C., & Mourshed, M. (2010). *How the world's most improved school systems keep getting better education*. New York, NY: McKinsey & Company.

Bentley, T. (2008). *Open learning: A systems-driven model of innovation for education. OECD Report 2008, Innovating to learn, learning to innovate*. Paris, France: OECD Centre for Educational Research and Innovation.

Betts, P. (2019). Leading a Catholic school system in a disrupted world: Vision is our springboard. Statement prepared by Pam Betts for Chapter 10 in this book on educational system and school transformation.

Bezzina, M., & Tuana, N. (2011). *From awareness to action: Some thoughts on engaging moral leadership*. Strathfield, Australia: ACU National.

Bodell, L. (2017). *Why simple wins: Escape the complexity trap and get to work that matters*. Brookline, MA: Bibliomotion, Inc.

Boris-Schacter, S., & Langer, S. (2006). *Balanced leadership: How effective principals manage their work*. New York, NY: Teachers College Press.

Branson, C. M., & Gross, S. J. (2014). *Handbook of ethical educational leadership*. New York, NY: Routledge.

Bremer, M. (2018). *Developing a positive culture where people and performance thrive*. Melbourne, FL: Motivational Press.

Bridges, W. (2009). *Managing transitions: Making the most of change* (3rd ed.). London: Nicholas Brearley.

Brock, P. (2011). *Towards schooling in the 21st century: 'Back to the basics' or 'forward to fundamentals?* (*Vol. 49*, pp. 3–25). Sydney, Australia: The Australian Council for Educational Leaders (ACEL).

Bye, D. (2017). *Millennials matter: Proven strategies for building your Next-Gen leaders*. Racine, WI: BroadStreet Publishing.

Cain, S. (2012). *Quiet: The power of introverts in a world that can't stop talking*. London: Penguin.

Caldwell, B. J. (2006). *Re-imagining educational leadership*. Camberwell, Australia: ACER Press.

Caldwell, B. J. (2018). It's time for a new narrative on leading learning communities in Australia. *Australian Educational Leader, 40*(4), 8–11.

Caldwell, B. J. (2019). Visionary leadership in the search for certainty. *Australian Educational Leader, Leading with Vision and Voice, 41*(3), 12–15.

Cameron, K. S. (2003). Ethics, virtuousness, and constant change. In N. M. Tichy & A. McGill (Eds.), *The ethical challenge*. San Francisco, CA: Jossey Bass.

Cameron, K. S. (2008). *Positive leadership: Strategies for extraordinary performance*. San Francisco, CA: Berrett-Koehler.

Cameron, K. S. (2013). *Practicing positive leadership: Tools and techniques that create extraordinary results*. San Francisco, CA: Berrett-Koehler.

Cameron, K. S., Bright, D., & Caza, A. (2004). Exploring the relationships between organisational virtuousness and performance. *American Behavioral Scientist, 47*, 766–790.

Campbell, C., Lieberman, A., & Yashkina, A. (2015). Teachers leading educational improvements: Developing teachers' leadership, improving practices, and collaborating to share knowledge. *Leading & Managing, 21*(2), 90–105.

Cantwell, J. (2015). *Leadership in action: Lessons for the real world from a real leader*. Melbourne, Australia: Melbourne University Press.

Case, S. (2016). *The third wave: An entrepreneur's vision of the future*. New York, NY: Simon & Schuster.

Collins, J. C. (2001). *Good to great: Why some companies make the leap and others don't*. New York, NY: Harper Collins.

Cooperrider, D., & Whitney, D. (2005). *Appreciative inquiry: A positive revolution in change*. San Francisco, CA: Beret-Koehler.

Darling-Hammond, L. (2010). *The flat world and education: How America's commitment to equity will determine our future*. New York, NY: Teachers College Press.

Davies, B. (2006). *Leading the strategically focused school: Success and sustainability*. London: Paul Chapman Publishing.

Degenhardt, L., & Duignan, P. (2010). *Dancing on a shifting carpet: Reinventing traditional schooling for the 21st century*. Melbourne, Australia: ACER Press.

Dinham, S. (2009). *How to get your school moving and improving*. Camberwell, Australia: ACER Press.

Duignan, P. (2006). *Ethical leadership: Key challenges and ethical tensions*. Melbourne, Australia: Cambridge University Press.

Duignan, P. (2012). *Educational leadership: Together creating ethical learning environments*. Melbourne, Australia: Cambridge University Press.

Duignan, P. (2014). Authenticity in educational leadership: History, ideal, reality. *Journal of Educational Administration, 52*(2), 152–172.

Duignan, P., & Bhindi, N. (1997). Authenticity in leadership: An emerging perspective. *Journal of Educational Administration, 35*(3 & 4), 195–209.

Duignan, P., & Cannon, H. (2011). *The power of many: Building sustainable collective leadership in schools*. Melbourne, Australia: ACER Press.

Duignan, P., & Macpherson, R. J. S. (1992). *Educative leadership: A practical theory for new administrators and managers.* London: Falmer Press.

Dweck, C. S. (2016). *Mindset: The new psychology of success.* New York, NY: Ballantine.

Espinoza, C., & Uklega, M. (2016). *Managing the millennials: Discover the core competencies for managing today's workforce* (2nd ed.). Hoboken, NJ: Wiley.

Ethisphere Institute. (2017). *Ethisphere. Q 2.* Scottsdale, AZ: Ethisphere Institute. Retrieved from www.ethisphere.com

Ethisphere Institute. (2018). *Ethisphere* (Fall ed.). Scottsdale, AZ: Ethisphere Institute. Retrieved from www.ethisphere.com

Facchinetti, A. (2013). Balancing NAPLAN results with teacher judgement. *Australian Educational Leader, 35*(1), 5–6.

Follett, M. P. (1924). *Creative experience.* New York, NY: Longmans, Green and Company.

Frydenberg, J. (2019, August 29). *Sir Zelman Cowen oration: The age of disruption.* Melbourne, Australia: Victoria University.

Fullan, M. (1999). *Change forces: The sequel.* London: Routledge Falmer.

Fullan, M. (2008). *The six secrets of change: What the best leaders do to help their organisations survive and thrive* (bold in original). San Francisco, CA: Jossey-Bass.

Fullan, M. (2010). *All systems go: The change imperative for whole-system reform.* Thousand Oaks, CA: Corwin.

Fullan, M. (2011). *The moral imperative realized.* Thousand Oaks, CA: Corwin.

Fullan, M. (2013). *Motion leadership in action: More skinny on becoming change savvy.* Thousand Oaks, CA: Corwin.

Fullan, M. (2019a). *Nuance: Why some leaders succeed and others fail.* Thousand Oaks, CA: Corwin.

Fullan, M. (2019b). The nuance of academic achievement. *Australian Educational Leader: Leading Student Learning, 41*(1), 8–10.

Fullan, M., Hill, P., & Crévolla, C. (2006). *Breakthrough.* Thousand Oaks, CA: Corwin.

Gans, J. (2016). *The disruption dilemma.* Cambridge, MA: The MIT Press.

Gasston-Holmes, B. (2019). The connection between leadership and learning: A middle leader's experience navigating the waters. *Leading & Managing, 25*(1), 15–28.

George, B. (2003). *Authentic leadership: Rediscovering the secrets to creating lasting value.* San Francisco, CA: Jossey-Bass.

George, B. (2015). *Discover your true north: Becoming an authentic leader.* New York, NY: John Wiley & Sons.

Global Integrity Summit. (2015, October 13–14). *Integrity 20.* Brisbane, Australia: Griffith University.

Goffee, R., & Jones, G. (2015). *Why should anyone be led by you? What it takes to be an authentic leader.* Boston, MA: Harvard Business Review Press.

Goffee, R., & Jones, G. (2016). *Why should anyone work here? What it takes to create an authentic organisation.* Boston, MA: Harvard Business Review Press.

Gonski, D., Arcus, T., Boston, K., & Review Team Members. (2018). *Through growth to achievement: Report of the review to achieve educational excellence in Australian schools.* Canberra, Australia: Australian Government © Commonwealth of Australia 2018.

Greenfield, T. B. (1974). Organisation theory as ideology. In *International inter-visitation conference,* Bristol, England.

Greenleaf, R. K. (1977). *Servant leadership: A journey into the nature of legitimate power and greatness.* New York, NY: Paulist Press.

Gronn, P. (1982). Neo-Taylorism in educational administration. *Educational Administration Quarterly, 20*(1), 115–129.

Gross, S. J., & Shapiro, J. P. (2005). *Our new era requires a new DEEL: Towards democratic ethical educational leadership.* Philadelphia, PA: Temple University.

Gruenert, S., & Whitaker, T. (2015). *School culture rewired: How to define, assess, and transform it.* Alexandria, VA: ASCD.

Gurvich, J. (2018). Principals' perceptions of regional networks. *Leading & Managing, 24*(1), 47–58.

Hargreaves, A. (2009, September). *The fourth way of educational reform* (Vol. *45*). Sydney, Australia: The Australian Council of Educational Leaders.

Hargreaves, A., & Fink, D. (2006). *Sustainable leadership.* San Francisco, CA: Jossey-Bass.

Hargreaves, A., & Shirley, D. (2009). *The fourth way: The inspiring future for educational change.* Joint publication by Ontario's Principals' Council and National Staff Development Council. Newbury Park, CA: Corwin.

Harris, A. (2006). Opening up the 'black box' of leadership practice: Taking a distributed leadership perspective. *International Studies in Educational Administration, 34*(2), 37–45.

Harris, A. (2009). *Distributed leadership: Evidence, issues and future developments* (*Vol. 44*, pp. 3–17). Sydney, Australia: The Australian Council for Educational Leaders.

Harris, A., & Jones, M. (2018). Beyond four walls. Professional learning communities within and between schools. *Australian Educational Leader, 40*(4), 54–55.

Hattie, J. (2009). *Visible learning: A synthesis of over 800 meta-analyses relating to achievement.* London: Routledge.

Hattie, J. (2016). *Shifting away from distractions to improve Australia's schools: Time for a reboot* (*Vol. 54*, pp. 3–22). Sydney, Australia: The Australian Council for Educational Leaders.

Hattie, J. (2019). *Implementing scaling up, and valuing expertise to develop worthwhile outcomes in schools* (*Vol. 58*, pp. 3–17). Sydney, Australia: The Australian Council for Educational Leaders.

Hayne, K. M. (2019). *The Royal Commission into misconduct in the banking, superannuation and financial services industry* (A Report). Canberra, Australia: Government of Australia.

Hewlett Foundation. (2013). Deeper learning competencies. Retrieved from htpps://www.hewlett.org/wp-content/uploads/2016/08/Deeper_learning_defined_April_2013

Hodgkinson, C. (1983). *The philosophy of leadership.* Oxford: Basil Blackwell.

Hodgkinson, C. (1991). *Educational leadership: The moral art.* Albany, NY: University of New York Press.

Hopkins, D. (2017). *The William Walker oration: The past, present and future of school improvement and system reform* (*Vol. 56*, pp. 3–21). Sydney, Australia: The Australian Council for Educational Leaders.

Hopkins, D. (2019). Leadership of personalised learning. *Australian Educational Leader: Leading Student Learning, 41*(1), 18–23.

Horn, M. B., & Staker, H. (2015). *Blended: Using disruptive innovation to improve schools.* San Francisco, CA: Jossey-Bass.

Hunter, N. (2017). A statement of commitment to the values and practice of the Australian teaching profession: An idea whose time has come. *Australian Educational Leader, 39*(2), 10–14.

Jenkins, S., Olson, A., Pace, L., & Sullivan, T. (2019). *State policy framework for personalised learning: Designing education systems where every student succeeds.* Cincinnati, OH: KnowledgeWorks.

Johansen, B. (2012). *Leaders make the future* (2nd ed.). San Francisco, CA: Berrett-Koehler.

Johansen, B. (2017). *The new leadership literacies: Thriving in a future of extreme disruption and distributed everything.* Oakland, CA: Berrett-Koehler.

Kahneman, D. (2011). *Thinking, fast and slow.* New York, NY: Farrar, Strauss and Giroux.

Kelly, G. (2017). *Live, lead, learn: My stories of life and leadership.* Melbourne, Australia: Penguin, Random House Australia.

Keltner, D. (2016). *The power paradox: How we gain and lose influence*. London: Penguin, Random House UK.

Leithwood, K., Lewis, K., Anderson, S., & Wahlstrom, K. (2004). *How leadership influences student learning: Review of research*. St. Paul, MN: University of Minnesota, Center for Applied Research and Educational Improvement (CAREI).

Levin, J. A., & Datnow, A. (2012). The principal role in data-driven decision making: Using case-study data to develop multi-mediator models of educational reform. *School Effectiveness and School Improvement, 23*(2), 179–201.

Loble, L., Greenhaune, T., & Hayes, J. (2017). *Future frontiers: Education for an AI world*. Melbourne, Australia: NSW Department of Education, Melbourne University, Melbourne University Press.

Mackenzie, G. (1996). *Orbiting the giant hairball: A corporate fool's guide to surviving with grace*. Melbourne, Australia: Penguin Books Australia.

Masters, G. N. (2016). *Five challenges in Australian school education*. Melbourne, Australia: ACER Press.

Maxwell, J. C. (2005). *The 360-degree leader: Developing your influence from anywhere in the organization*. Nashville, TN: Thomas Nelson.

McTighe, J., & Willis, J. (2019). *Upgrade your teaching: Understanding by design meets neuroscience*. Alexandria, VA: ASCD.

Mintzberg, H. (2005). *Managers not MBAs: A hard look at the soft practice of managing and management development*. Oakland, CA: Berrett-Koehler.

Moberg, D. J. (2006). Ethics blind spots in organisations: How systemic errors in person perception undermine moral agency. *Organisation Studies, 27*(3), 413–428. Retrieved from http://oss.sage pub.com/feedback. Accessed on November 7, 2011.

Morrell, M., & Capparell, S. (2001). *Shackleton's way: Leadership lessons from the great Antarctic explorer*. New York, NY: Viking Penguin.

Morris, M., & Garrett, J. (2010). Strengths: Your leading edge. In P. A. Linley, S. Harrington, & N. Garcea (Eds.), *Oxford library of psychology. Oxford handbook of positive psychology and work* (pp. 95–105). New York, NY: Oxford University Press.

Morrison, K. (2002). *School leadership and complexity theory*. London: Routledge Falmer.

Muller, J. Z. (2018). *The tyranny of metrics*. Princeton, NJ: Princeton University Press.

Musiowsky-Borneman, T. (2019). 5 ways to build students' global competency. *ASCD express – ideas from the field – teach local, reach global, 15*(1). (Archived: For photocopy, electronic and online access, and republication requests go to the Copyright Clearance Center and enter the periodical title within the "Get Permission" search field).

Nadella, S. (2017). *Hit refresh: The quest to discover Microsoft's soul and imagine a better future for everyone*. London: Harper Collins.

Nixon, C., & Sinclair, A. (2017). *Women leading*. Carlton, Australia: Melbourne University Press.

Normore, A. H., & Brooks, J. S. (Eds.). (2017). *The dark side of leadership: Identifying and overcoming unethical practices in organisations*. Bingley: Emerald Publishing.

O'Connell, M., Milligan, S., & Bentley, T. (2019). *Beyond ATAR: A proposal for change*. Melbourne, Australia: Koshland Innovation Fund.

OECD Report. (2008). *Innovating to learn, learning to innovate*. Paris, France: OECD Centre for Educational Research and Innovation. Retrieved from www.oecd.org/publishing/corrigenda. Accessed on June 28, 2019.

OECD Report. (2016). *Innovating education and educating for innovation: The power of digital technologies and skills*. Paris, France: OECD Publishing. Retrieved from https://www.voced.edu.au

OECD Report. (2017). *Schools at the crossroads of innovation in cities and regions*. Paris, France: OECD Publishing. Retrieved from http://dx.doi.org/10.1787/9789264282766-en

OECD Report. (2018a). *World class: How to build a 21st-century school system*. Paris, France: OECD Publishing. Retrieved from https://www.oecd-library.org

OECD. (2018b). *Behavioural insights for public integrity: Harnessing the human factor to counter corruption*. Paris, France: OECD Publishing, Public Governance Reviews Publishing. Retrieved from https://dx.doi.org/10.1787/9789264297067-en

OECD Report. (2019a). *Trends shaping education 2019*. Paris, France: OECD Centre for Educational Research and Innovation. Retrieved from http://www.oecd.org/education/ceri/trends-shaping-education.htm

OECD Report. (2019b). *OECD employment outlook 2019: The future of work – Highlights*. Paris, France: OECD Centre for Educational Research and Innovation. Retrieved from https://www.oecd.org/employment/outlook/

Owen, J. (2018). *The new work reality*. Melbourne, Australia: The Foundation for Young Australians.

Parks, S. D. (2005). *Leadership can be taught: A bold approach for a complex world*. Boston, MA: Harvard Business School Press.

Partnership for 21st Century Learning. (2017). Framework for 21st century learning. Retrieved from http://www.p21.org/our-work/p21-framework

Perkins, D. N. T. (2000). *Leading at the edge: Leadership lessons from the limits of human endurance – The extraordinary saga of Shackleton's Antarctic expedition*. New York, NY: Amacom.

Peterson, J. B. (1999). *Maps of meaning: The architecture of belief*. New York, NY: Routledge.

Peterson, C. (2006). *Positive psychology: A primer*. New York, NY: Oxford University Press.

Peterson, J. B. (2018). *12 rules for life: An antidote to chaos*. London: Penguin, Random House.

Pompper, D. (2018). *Corporate social responsibility, sustainability, and ethical public relations*. Bingley: Emerald Publishing.

Prince, K., Swanson, J., & King, K. (2018). *Navigating the future of learning: Forecast 5.0: A new era unfolding*. Cincinnati, OH: KnowledgeWorks USA.

Quick, L., & Platt, D. (2015). *Disrupted: Strategy for exponential change*. Melbourne, Australia: Resilient Futures Media. Retrieved from www.resilientfutures.com

Rego, A., Clegg, S., & Pina e Cunha, M. (2011). *The positive power of character strengths and virtues for global leaders*. In G. Spreitzer & K. Cameron (Eds.), *The Oxford handbook of positive organisational scholarship*. New York, NY: Oxford Library Press.

Robinson, V. (2008). Forging the links between distributed leadership and educational outcomes. *Journal of Educational Administration, 46*(2), 241–256.

Robinson, K. (2011). *Out of our minds: Learning to be creative* (Rev., updated ed.). Chichester: Capstone Publishing.

Robinson, K., & Aronica, L. (2016). *Creative schools: Revolutionizing education from the ground up*. London: Penguin Books.

Rost, J. C. (1991). *Leadership for the 21st century*. London: Praeger.

Salicru, S. (2017). Leadership results: How to create adaptive leaders and high-performing organisations for an uncertain world. Milton, Australia: John Wiley.

Sarros, J. C., Cooper, B. K., Hartican, A. M., & Barker, C. J. (2006). *The character of leadership: What works for Australian leaders – Making it work for you*. Milton, Australia: John Wiley.

Schleicher, A. (2018). *World class: How to build a 21st-century school system. Strong performers and successful reformers in education*. Paris, France: OECD Publishing. Retrieved from http://dx.doi.org/10.1787/4789264300002-en

Schwab, K. (2017, January). *The Fourth Industrial Revolution* [Video]. World Economic Forum, Davos-Klosters, Switzerland. Retrieved from https://www.weforum.org›videos›the-fourth-industrial-revolution-by-Klaus Schwab.

Seba, T. (2014). *Clean disruption of energy and transportation: How Silicon Valley will make oil, nuclear, natural gas, coal, electric utilities and conventional cars obsolete by 2030.* Silicon Valley, CA: Clean Planet Ventures.

Seldon, A. (2010). *An end to factory schools: An education manifesto 2010–2020.* London: Centre for Policy Studies.

Seldon, A., & Abidoye, O. (2018). *The fourth education revolution: Will artificial intelligence liberate or infantilise humanity?* Buckingham: The University of Buckingham Press.

Seligman, M. E. (2003). *Authentic happiness: Using the new positive psychology to realize your potential for lasting fulfilment.* London: Nicolas Brealey.

Seligman, M. E. (2011). *Flourish: A new understanding of happiness and well-being – And how to achieve them.* New York, NY: Simon and Schuster.

Selznick, P. (1992). *The moral commonwealth: Social theory and the promise of community.* Los Angeles, CA: University of California Press.

Senge, P. (1992). *The fifth discipline: The art and practice of the learning organisation.* New York, NY: Random House.

Shapiro, G. (2013). *Ninja innovation: The ten killer strategies of the world's most successful businesses.* New York, NY: Harper Collins.

Sharratt, L., & Fullan, M. (2009). *Realization: The change imperative for deepening district-wide reform.* Thousand Oaks, CA: Corwin.

Shekshnia, S., Kravchenko, K., & Wiliams, E. (2018). *CEO school: Insights from 20 global business leaders.* Milton Keynes: Palgrave Macmillan.

Spillane, J. P. (2006). Distributed leadership. San Francisco, CA: Jossey Bass.

Stangis, D., & Smith, K. V. (2017). *The executive guide to 21st century corporate citizenship: How your company can win the battle for reputation and impact.* Bingley: Emerald Publishing.

Starratt, R. J. (1993). *The drama of leadership.* London: Falmer Press.

Starratt, R. J. (2011). *Refocusing school leadership: Foregrounding human development throughout the work of the school.* London: Taylor & Francis.

Starratt, R. J. (2004). *Ethical leadership.* San Francisco, CA: Jossey-Bass.

Stein, G. (2018). *And now what? A guide to leadership and taking charge in your new role.* Bingley: Emerald Publishing.

Strike, K. A. (2007). *Ethical leadership in schools: Creating community in an environment of accountability.* Thousand Oaks, CA: Corwin Press.

Sukhdev, P. (2012). *Corporation 2020: Transforming business for tomorrow's world.* London: Island Press.

Surowiecki, J. (2005). *The wisdom of crowds.* London: Abacus, Little, Brown Book Group.

Susskind, R., & Susskind, D. (2015). *The future of the professions: How technology will transform the work of human experts.* Oxford: Oxford University Press.

Taleb, N. N. (2010). *The black swan: The impact of the highly improbable* (2nd ed.). New York, NY: Random House.

Taleb, N. N. (2018). *Skin in the game: Hidden asymmetries in daily life.* London: Penguin Random House.

Terry, R. W. (1993). *Authentic leadership: Courage in action.* San Francisco, CA: Jossey Bass.

Tett, G. (2015). *The silo effect: Why every organisation needs to disrupt itself to survive.* London: Abacus, Little, Brown Book Group.

The World Economic Forum. (2016, January). *The future of jobs: Employment, skills and workforce strategy for the Fourth Industrial Revolution.* Geneva, Switzerland: The World Economic Forum. Retrieved from reports.weforum.org › future-of-jobs-2016

Thiers, N. (2016). Educators deserve better: A conversation with Richard DuFour. *Educational Leadership, 73*(8), 10–16.

Tichnor-Wagner, A., & Manise, J. (2019). *Globally competent educational leadership: A framework for leading schools in a diverse, interconnected world.* Alexandria, VA: Association for Supervision and Curriculum Development (ASCD).

Torii, K., & O'Connell, M. (2017). *Preparing young people for the future of work: Policy roundtable report*. Policy Paper No. 01/2017. Mitchell Institute, Melbourne, Australia. Retrieved from www.mitchellinstitute.org.au

Tucker, M. (2017a). *Education: Future frontiers, educating for a digital future: The challenge*. Occasional Papers Series. Sydney, Australia: New South Wales Department of Education.

Tucker, M. (2017b). *Education: Future frontiers – The implications of AI, automation and 21st century skills needs*. Discussion paper. The National Initiative and Performance Directorate, New South Wales Department of Education. Retrieved from nationalinitiatives@det.nsw.edu.au

Vance, A. (2015). *Elon Musk: How the billionaire CEO of Spacex and Tesla is shaping our future*. London: Penguin Random House.

Vehar, J (2015). *The 5 biggest keys to leading innovation*. La Jolla, CA: Centre for Creative Leadership. Retrieved from https://www.ccl.org/blog/5-biggest-keys-leading-innovation

Wagner, T. (2014). *The global achievement gap: Why even our best schools don't teach the new survival skills our children need – And what we can do without it*. New York, NY: Basic Books.

Walker, A. (2011). *School leadership as collective activity (Vol. 48)*. Sydney, Australia: The Australian Council for Educational Leaders.

Walumbwa, F. O., Avolio, B. J., Gardner, W. L., Wernsing, T. S., & Peterson, S. J. (2008). Authentic leadership: Development and validation of a theory-based measure. *Journal of Management, 34*(1), 89–126.

Waters, L. (2017). *The strength switch: How the new science of strength-based parenting helps your child and teen to flourish*. Sydney, Australia: Penguin, Random House.

Weber, K. (Ed.). (2010). *Waiting for Superman: How we can save America's failing public schools*. New York, NY: Public Affairs.

Whitby, G. (2019). Leading in a digital environment. *Australian Educational Leader, 41*(2), 8–11.

Wilson, J. M. (2018). *The human side of changing education: How to lead change with clarity, conviction, and courage*. Thousand Oaks, CA: Corwin.

Wiseman, L. (2017). *Multipliers: How the best leaders make everyone smarter*. New York, NY: Harper Collins.

Wooten, L., & Cameron, K. (2010). Enablers of positive strategy: Positively deviant leadership. In A. Linley, S. Harrington, & N. Garcea (Eds.), *Oxford handbook of positive psychology at work*. New York, NY: Oxford University Press.

Index